THE SOCIAL AWAKENING IN LONDON

By ROBERT A. WOODS,

HEAD OF ANDOVER HOUSE, BOSTON, AND SOMETIME RESIDENT AT TOYNBEE HALL

THE EAST END—THE GROWTH OF KNOWLEDGE OF THE POOR—CHURCH WORK—
THE SALVATION ARMY—CHARITY ORGANIZATIONS—THE SOCIAL MOVEMENT
AT THE UNIVERSITIES—EDWARD DENISON—ARNOLD TOYNBEE—SAMUEL A.
BARNETT—TOYNBEE HALL—OXFORD HOUSE—THE UNIVERSITY SETTLEMENTS
—THE PEOPLE'S PALACE—THE KYRLE SOCIETY—SOCIALISTIC ORGANIZATION
—JOHN BURNS—THE NEW TRADE-UNIONISM—THE FABIAN SOCIETY—THE
LONDON GOVERNMENT—MR. CHARLES BOOTH.

THERE is a place in London—as Leadenhall Street, coming past the site of the East India House, runs into Aldgate— where in a few steps one parts company with the decreasing number of merchants and clerks, and is swept into the strange current of East-End humanity. One feels a sudden chill, as when passing out of a warm breeze into another with a touch of coming winter in it. Aldgate is still, almost as distinctly as when the wall stood, the limit in that direction of the old City of London; while the movement of life from the East End turns sharply to the north there, going up through Houndsditch, the region of old clothes, trafficked in through brokers and exchanges after the manner of other lines of commerce.

From this point several miles eastward, from the water several miles northward, live a million people, whose existence is very largely taken up with a close struggle against poverty. A hundred thousand East Londoners rise each morning with little or no assurance as to where their daily bread may come from. Another great

Auctioning Fish in the " Bitter Cry " District of London.

region, equal in size and population to the East End, and on a par
with it as to social conditions, stretches off to the south from the
river Thames.   So much of London may fairly be said to be given
over to poverty.   But this is not to say that poverty is absent elsewhere.   It is never far away in London.   The Seven Dials, like the
Five Points in New York, has lost its old identity ; but such regions
as Drury Lane still remain, and St. Luke's, and even the quarter
which stands in contrast to the nation's historic glory at West-
minster.

But the East End will still continue to be thought of in a special
way as the nether London.   It has a clearly marked life of its own.

South-London life is characterized by a pathetic monotony. East London has its gloom lit up by many picturesque features. A walk down the broad High Street on a Saturday evening, among the dockers, with their slouched caps and flannel neckcloths, the factory girls in their plumage hired by the week, and the many curious types of people—gazing into the glaring shop windows; inspecting and variously testing the wares of the booths set up by the road-side, which have gone far on the way of all earthly treasures, moth-eaten, rusted, if not indeed stolen; listening to the noisy fakirs; or joining in the sports of the improvised fair—gives one a strong sense of the romantic side of existence in the East End.

It is this quality, in addition to the extremity of its need, that has done so much toward making East London, for the world at large, the classic ground of poverty. The new efforts for the elevation of East Londoners, of which nearly everyone has by this time heard the rumor, are confirming the claim to an undesirable pre-eminence. Toynbee Hall and the People's Palace are now entered in Baedeker, and one wonders whether the majority of their visitors are not made up from the one hundred and fifty thousand Americans who in the early weeks of summer populate the great hotels and the lodging-houses of Bloomsbury. It is a good thing if it is so. In America they are kept from a full sympathy with their poorer brethren not only by the barrier of different social position, but by the more impassable barrier of alien race. In London the faces of the poor have the familiar Anglo-Saxon lineaments. One of the unsuspected reasons for that home feeling which all intelligent Americans experience in London is that there they are able to see themselves in tatters. It is this fact especially which causes the average American to return from even a carriage ride in the East End with some new care for the men and women who have to pass their lives in a great city's closely crowded quarters.

The little tract, "The Bitter Cry of Outcast London," which in 1883 precipitated the agitation as to the condition of the poor, took its facts very largely from South London, from a region where the

London Congregational Union has one of its outposts. Collier's Rents, as it is called, seems like an eddy in the vast current of London life. It has drawn in those who could hardly float with the tide. It is at a distance from any main avenue of travel. Long Lane is its thoroughfare and avenue of trade in stale provisions; and its side openings are noisome alleys and dark, winding passage-ways. A night journey through Collier's Rents, under the guidance of a missionary, gives one enough to see to assure him that the picture of existence given in the tract is in no way overdrawn. One also has the feeling that English people, in their concern brought on by the knowledge of such a state of things, have not estimated too greatly the shame of it, and, in the higher sense, its danger.

Rev. Samuel A. Barnett, Vicar of St. Jude's, Whitechapel, and Warden of Toynbee Hall.

The social awakening began in an agitation. All classes were moved by it. The state of the London poor was felt to be to English civilization something like an imputation of failure. It touched British pride, and, by the very greatness of the difficulty, stirred that wonderful reserve energy which distinguishes the British race. Each of the various elements in the life of London felt the summons. And so the social awakening has many phases. It includes one of the most significant labor movements in the whole history of labor since the Egyptians lost their Israelitish slaves. There is a social movement from the universities; there is a social movement in art; a strong social movement in politics; and a social movement, having much of the impulse of original Christianity, in the Church. These all, according to English nature, go their several ways. They know little about each other. They do not hold joint conventions, nor organize bulky federations — each sacrificing much of what makes it worth while, in order to unite with the rest. Each is rather inclined to minimize the influence of the others. And yet they

Making Tambourine Frames at the Salvation Army Factory, Hanbury Street.

are having a united influence which is bound in a large degree to make over the life of London, making it prolific in resources for the educational and moral advancement of the people, and for comprehensive economic and political administration.

The East End of London as a field for work among the poor was in undisputed possession of the Church, at least from the time of the Franciscans, who had a mission station just inside the wall, down to the present generation. If its work has but slightly met the problem of London poverty, it has at least held its ground until in

these last days there has begun to be a feeling that other elements
in society also owe a debt to the two great cities of the poor which
are included within the limits of the metropolis. The Church, in
all its branches, is meanwhile learning to magnify its office to the
people. It finds that those whose life is almost filled with the
struggle for physical existence, who know as yet hardly anything
about the human side of life, are in no way the fit objects of a merely
religious ministry. They must be sought where they are. They
must be helped toward a healthier and happier state of being, before they can be sensitive to appeals to the finer nature. And so
churches in the poorer parts of London are fast coming to fill the
highly Christian use of centres for every influence toward the better
life. So far as he has light and power, a clergyman in East or
South London is, in a very deep sense, eyes to the blind and feet to
the impotent. In another point of view, he often shows much of
that new kind of statesmanship which aims to organize a body of
people, larger or smaller, for the enjoyment of all that anywhere
makes life more fully worth the living.

The churches of the Establishment in London enter upon their
social work with the double advantage of the parish system, by which
each church has a definite responsibility for a certain district ; and
of the long tradition which makes it natural for a church to have a
number of workers with a variety of occupation. But otherwise
they are not more forward than the Nonconformist chapels and mission societies, in entering upon the new duties which new occasions
have brought.

Everywhere the work of charity—which has always been a conspicuous part of the activity of Christian churches—is being done
with increasing wisdom and effectiveness. The sick among the
poor are ministered to by regular visitors, and in many cases by
trained nurses assigned to special districts. Social clubs for men,
for women, and for young people relieve the hardness and monotony of existence from day to day, and counteract the fascination
of evil. Some churches invite trade-unions to meet in their parish

Prayer-meeting at a Salvation Army Factory.

rooms, and thus save them from accepting the hospitality of the public-house. The matter of recreation is being taken up in a way that our Puritan churches in America can as yet but dimly appreciate. Of two very ritualistic churches, one has occasional dancing

in its parish house, which seems none the less enjoyable on account
of the young cassocked ascetics who stand solemnly by; and the
other, in a criminal quarter, has a large boys' club, with new applicants constantly begging to be admitted, whose main feature is
prize sparring contests. At St. Jude's Church, in Whitechapel, of
which the Rev. Samuel A. Barnett, founder of Toynbee Hall, is the
vicar, there is every year a picture exhibition lasting for three
weeks, including Sundays, which was visited the last time by seventy thousand people. This same church has a unique musical
service called "The Worship Hour," on Sunday evening, at which
the seats are nearly all taken by an audience including even some
of those hapless castaways of humanity, such as are seldom seen in
church, even in East London. From this kind of service, and the
frequent organ recitals, and oratorios given in churches, to the
brass-band concert which forms part of the exercises at the Rev.
Hugh Price Hughe's great Wesleyan West-London Mission, and
even to the timbrels of the Salvation lasses, music is found to be
one of the essential means of grace.

It goes almost without saying that the churches in London are
still far from meeting the critical facts of life under the extremes of
poverty and degradation. The Salvation Army, with all its gro-
tesqueness, stands for a sympathetic and thorough-going attempt to
meet these facts, before which the churches are standing powerless.
The Army acknowledges the failure of merely evangelistic methods. And now first for London, afterward wherever its soldiers go,
the enthusiasm of this unique and wonderful organization is to run
in the channels of social activity. Ever since 1884 the slum sisters
have been freely going in and out like sweet angels among the
haunts of the lost. For as long a time, the prison-gate brigades
have been setting discharged convicts on the way to manhood
again. But the large scheme of the book "In Darkest England,"
of which an encouraging yearly report has just been published, is
intended to be a comprehensive mission of helpfulness to all the
elements of people in the lower social grades.

ST. JUDE'S CHURCH AT "WORSHIP HOUR," 8.30 P.M.

The food and shelter depots, which have displaced the meeting-halls in several instances, take care of those who are without other resort, at a charge of fourpence for supper, lodging, and breakfast. Thence the men are introduced into the Army's factories and work-shops, where they are put to wood-chopping, mat-making, carpen-

General Booth, Commander-in-Chief of the Salvation Army.
(From a photograph by Elliott & Fry, London.)

tering, and other industries. The women are employed at sewing and laundry-work, and in the match factory. There are homes specially provided for the wards of the slum corps and of the prison-gate brigades, where they are given work suitable to their skill and strength. The general city colony has already found its outlet in a large rural community, which is to be a training place for farm work and shop work ; for the different tasks which the living of life imposes, and for some of the consolations which it affords. Aside from the united force which the discipline of the Army gives it for undertaking such a movement, its followers, more than any other type of person in these days, are moved by a passion for the outcast and distressed. In the presence of so rare a feeling of humanity, the technical objections that have been urged against the scheme have seemed rather empty. One cannot but believe that there is a suggestion in this scheme of other better schemes which shall lead us toward that devoutly to be wished consummation, the abolition of poverty, of which, even so judicious an authority as Professor Marshall bids us not to despair.

The effort to reduce to the semblance of a system the almost infinitely various and numerous charities of London has been continued through the past twenty years with really encouraging success. Every district in the metropolis has, in addition to its public relieving office, a head-quarters for the administration of voluntary charity. The district secretaries are coming to be persons of special skill and training. Each local committee is composed of representatives of the charitable agencies at work in its district. In the East End the members of committees are largely men and women who live in other parts of the metropolis, but take up a sort of partial citizenship in one or another poor district. The influence of charity organization in banishing beggary and whatever would confirm the poor in pauperism has been very marked. It is almost a part of popular ethics now in London to refrain from giving without due investigation. And many have arrived at the higher stage where they can see the importance and the human interest of learning for themselves how the poor live, and of helping them as their deepest needs require.

Charity organization is taking a wider scope as it progresses. It is making its framework available for those better forms of charity which have to do with prevention. It has given a clue to various associations for befriending children and young people. Among these is the Country Holiday Fund, which, every summer, sends twenty thousand slum children singing through the underground tunnels on their way to the sunny fields. The Charity Organization Society also lends facilities to a most useful society which is taking in charge the question of the sanitary conditions of tenement-houses. Indeed, the newer tendencies of organized charity begin to impart to this kind of work a kind of attraction such as one has not been able to feel before. The leaders are now going forward in the attempt to make each district committee include representatives of every agency working in any way for the bettering of the local community—churches, schools, parish officials, relief societies, working-men's provident organizations, trade-unions, co-operative stores. With the combination of these forces the aim is to have each committee take in hand the whole social situation in its own district, endeavoring to bring the people to a true understanding of this situation, and to a willingness each to do his share toward making existence in that district wholesome and enjoyable.

With this comprehensive system, centred in one metropolitan council, it becomes possible for the Charity Organization Society to wield a considerable influence upon matters that affect the conditions of life in London. There is only one regret about it all. It is that the methods of the Society lack, to a degree, the element of sympathy. So much of its work has all along had to do with curbing harmful sentiment, that it is likely to be suspicious of sentiment in any form. A man holding a high position in the Society, who acknowledged the difficulty, is responsible for the statement—which I hope it may not seem unchivalrous to repeat—that the women members of the committees were oftener unsympathetic with their "cases" than the men. The explanation of this anomaly seems to be that when the finer feelings are put under restraint, as must be in the administration of charity, women come more completely than men under the letter of rigid precepts.

The special signs of the social awakening among the more favored classes are to be found not so much in the development of

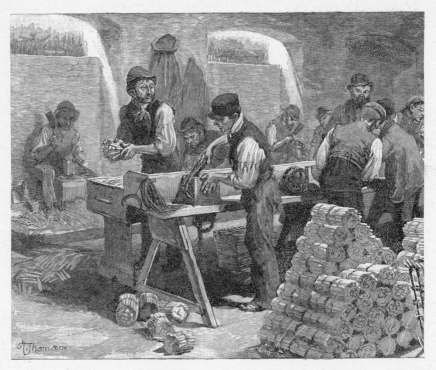

Making up Bundles of Firewood at the Salvation Army Factory, Hanbury Street.

previously existing agencies as in the making of new experiments. These at first are necessarily on a small scale, and affect only their own particular localities. But already the success of some of these experiments has suggested that it is practicable to repeat them in the different working-class districts of the metropolis. As a result, there are now taking their place in the life of London new kinds of profession, new forms of institution, new lines of education, new phases of literature. How much it means for the future that the idea of social duty and an interest in social activity are beginning so largely to give character to thought and work at the universities!

The social movement originating at the universities has had a quality of the moral picturesque from which neither cynicism nor fashionable cultivation has been able to take away the charm. The appeal to the imagination which it has made has exercised a most potent influence in removing the impression that work among the poor was dulness and weariness, and that utterly. The power to make social service truly interesting, one might almost say, has been the determining factor in the present great changes that are going on in England. It was this power that constituted the great distinction of John Ruskin. Every department of social activity in England has been stirred by his message. The men who founded the first university settlement are in a special sense his followers.

But the settlements stand for certain principles that are quite out of the scope of the criticism that is always waged against the sentimental side of such a movement. They stand distinctly for the fact, not before accepted, but now growing more and more clear, that social work demands the close, continued care of men and women of the best gifts and training. They show that if society would start afresh the glow of life in its far-out members, it must bring there the same fulness and variety of resource that is needed to keep life glowing at the centre. They are also the beginning of a better understanding of the truth which is confessed, but not believed, that where one member suffers all the members suffer with it. In a just view of the case, the massing together of the well-to-do over against the poor, neither group knowing how the other lives, involves as great evil to the one side as to the other.

In 1867 Edward Denison, a young Oxford man, born to that inclination toward public duty which characterizes the high-class Englishman, conceived the purpose of endeavoring to meet some of the problems of poverty by taking up his abode in the midst of the poor. He went into the parish where John Richard Green, as vicar, was heroically at work. Denison died in a few years, and in 1875 Arnold Toynbee, a young tutor at Oxford, first took up his residence in Whitechapel during the long vacation. Several summers were spent in visiting as a friend among the people and joining with working-men in the management of their clubs. But failing health compelled him to relinquish his social work, and in 1883 he, too, came to an early death.

It was just when Toynbee's friends at Oxford were planning, in devotion to his memory, to take up some of the work which he had left unfinished, that the feeling of anxiety caused by "The Bitter Cry" was at its height in London. And Mr. Barnett, who had been

The Work of the Country Holiday Fund.
(Underground train filled with little gamins singing "Annie Rooney.")

working for ten years in Whitechapel, came to Oxford and met this little circle in a college room. He told them that it would be of little use merely to secure a room in East London where University Extension lectures might be given, as they were thinking of doing. He said that every message to the poor would be vain if it did not come expressed in the life of brother-men. With this, he proposed his plan for a settlement of university men, where a group should reside together, and make their home a living centre of all elevating

A smoking Conference.

A. Thomson.

influences. There was that touch of inspiration about the plan which is able to bring into form and substance a somewhat vague and transcendental idea. A small settlement was at once begun in temporary quarters. The co-operation of Cambridge was soon secured. In a little more than a year a suitable building was completed, and the work of Toynbee Hall began.

In the Quadrangle
Toynbee Hall.

Toynbee Hall is essentially a transplant of university life in Whitechapel. The quadrangle, the gables, the diamond-paned windows, the large general rooms, especially the dining-room with its brilliant frieze of college shields, all make the place seem not so distant from the dreamy walks by the Isis or the Cam. But these

things are not so much for the sake of the university men as of their
neighbors, that they may breathe a little of the charmed atmosphere. For this purpose Toynbee Hall becomes a hospitable home.
All that it includes of earnestness, learning, skill, and whatever
may rise out of a spirit of friendliness, is meant to be put at the
service of the people of the East End. Everyone that is in any
way in relation with what goes on at the Hall is now and then the
guest of the residents at some informal gathering. Particular provision is even made that the residents may ask their new-made
friends to break bread with them.

The fifteen or twenty men constantly at the Hall, together with
a considerable body of associate workers, by the skilled direction
of Mr. Barnett, have been able to accomplish some valuable results
for the improvement of politics and social life in Whitechapel.
There is a public library in Whitechapel to-day—beside the Toynbee Hall library—voted for by the local constituency as a result of
political canvassing from Toynbee Hall. The great improvement in
facilities for housing the people, in the administration of charity,
and in the respect for law and order shows striking results of the
work of the warden and residents. As for the increase of the
healthful pleasures of life which has been brought about in that
joyless region, it is alone enough to justify the faith of the found-
ers. The lines for a people's university are being broadly and
soundly laid. A long list of courses of study is carried through, to
the advantage of thirteen hundred students, male and female. The
facilities for study are gradually being improved, and there are
now two houses adjacent to Toynbee Hall where forty young men,
members of the classes, live a kind of college life. In addition to
all the classes, each week during the winter there is a concert, two
popular lectures, and a smoking conference. At the smoking conference specimens appear of nearly every sort of East Londoner—
all brought together by that general instinct for debate, which is
only a turn of the old unconquerable spirit of the Briton.

The second settlement—the Oxford House in Bethnal Green—

took a more distinctly religious basis.   In addition to carrying on
many efforts similar to those at Toynbee Hall, the Oxford House men
enter actively into the work of the neighboring churches, preach
out-of-doors, and have Sunday services and addresses in their own

hall.   The University Club, which is carried on under its auspices,
is the most successful working-men's club of its kind in London.   It
has about fifteen hundred members, and includes a great variety of
features.   It is kept from being lost in its extensiveness by having
the constant support and direction of Mr. P. R. Buchanan, a City
merchant, who lives in Bethnal Green with his family for the sake

Drawing Room
Toynbee Hall

of entering into an intimate, helpful relation with working people. The club building has thus far been the head-quarters of the larger activities of the Oxford House, and the residents have occupied a disused parish-school building. But they expect by midsummer to enter the new Oxford House, which will be well suited to all the needs of the settlement.

In various parts of London there are college missions, some of which were carried on before the university settlements were established. Altogether they number more than twenty. In most cases a mission is merely kept going by funds from the college or pre-

paratory school for which it is named, the missioner being a graduate; but now the missions are more and more coming to have
groups of residents. For the rest of the settlements, there are:
the Women's University Settlement in Southwark, which has suggested the Mayfield House in Bethnal Green, St. Jude's House in
Whitechapel, and a new women's settlement in Canning Town; the
Mansfield House, begun by Oxford Congregationalists in Canning
Town, and Browning Hall, begun by Cambridge Congregationalists
in Walworth; a Wesleyan settlement in Bermondsey; and Mrs.
Humphry Ward's University Hall, at a little distance from the
British Museum. Some educated young Jews have recently pro-
posed taking quarters in the midst of their brethren of Rag Fair and
Petticoat Lane. And no man can see where the end will be.

The novel philanthropy which has attracted the greatest attention is that of the People's Palace, which is the result, in the first
instance, of the turn given by Mr. Walter Besant's "All Sorts and
Conditions of Men" to a bequest that had already been made for
establishing an institute for working people in East London. The
People's Palace is essentially an institution. At Toynbee Hall they
resent the term. The People's Palace is now not much different
from a great technical school, where boys and girls may receive instruction in nearly all lines of art and skill. It has ample facilities
for recreation—a gymnasium and swimming-bath, one of the most
beautiful halls in London for concerts and other entertainments, a
large winter garden, and a well-supplied library and reading-room.
The People's Palace, under the care of Sir Edmund Currie, was conducted so that it seemed to be filling out the dream with which it
began. But too much was attempted at once. It became involved
in financial difficulties, and necessity constrained its managers to
seek the powerful aid of the Drapers' Company, one of the old City
guilds which exercise a perfunctory charity as a tribute for being
permitted to continue a rather luxurious existence. The management of the Palace is now directed from the office of the Drapers'
Company, and shows that lack of appreciative sense which one

might expect under the circumstances. The circulars have "Drapers' Company's Institute" in large letters, and "The People's
Palace" in small.

Yet one ought not to make too much of the partial failure of this
noble scheme. The People's Palace, as it is, brings a great enlarge-
ment to life in the East End. And there is still sufficient reason for
believing that the idea, as it was at first held, is a practicable one.

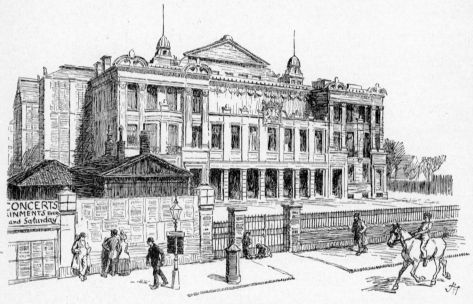

The People's Palace.

It is indeed determined upon that the plan shall be undertaken in
London on a very extensive scale. The Regent Street Polytechnic,
through the generosity and devotion of Mr. Quintin Hogg, has
achieved a settled success at the points where the People's Palace
has, up to the present, failed. And there is now in hand a plan by
which a part of the vast accumulated resources of the old City
parishes is to be given for the purpose of establishing a polytechnic
in every considerable district of the metropolis, putting each one,
to a large extent, under the responsible control of people living in

DRAMATIC ENTERTAINMENT AT THE BORO' OF HACKNEY WORKINGMEN'S CLUB

the district, or in some way connected with its interests. It is not too much to hope that, gradually, through failures and successes, all the more gloomy regions of London shall be lit up with veritable Palaces of Delight.

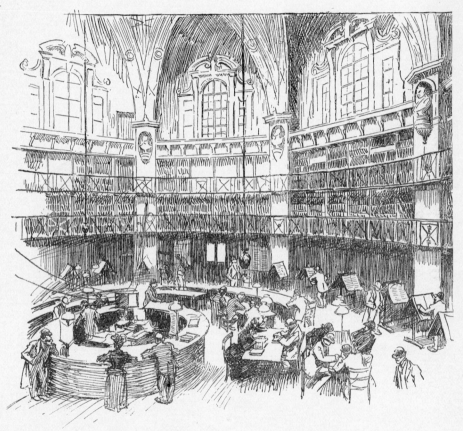

The Library of the People's Palace. (From a photograph.)

The university settlements and the polytechnics in their work draw deeply upon the æsthetic impulse for ways of cheering and elevating the poor. But quite apart from them is the unique movement which begins distinctly from the artist's point of view. Ruskin is its prophet. It has two quite different, though not mutually exclusive, phases.   On the one hand is the effort, which has a strong element behind it in the artistic circles of London, toward social reconstruction as a necessity if the mass of the people are ever to be saved from the degradation that comes from surroundings of wretchedness.   Among its supporters are William Morris, revolutionary socialist; Walter Crane, moderate socialist; and Burne-Jones, socialistic radical.   On the other hand is the simpler and more immediate programme for " bringing beauty home to the people."   The Kyrle Society makes this its special object.   The members of the Society busy themselves with adorning working-men's clubs, girls' homes, and mission halls.   Some beautiful mural paintings have recently been executed in such places.   There is a musical section which gives concerts and oratorios in working-class districts; a branch for the distribution of good literature ; a branch which works actively for securing and beautifying public parks and open spaces, and seeing that they are managed for the enjoyment of the people.   The Kyrle Society is under the special direction of Miss Octavia Hill, who has carried on such a courageous warfare against the evils of London poverty for almost a generation.   It includes in its membership many leading artists and patrons of art.

By far the most stirring social developments in London, during the last five years, have been in connection with strikes and socialistic agitation among the working-men.   There is an intenseness and reality about these facts there, even to the minds of people in the upper classes, which can be but dimly understood by those not living in the scene.   In London, more than in any other great city in the world at the present moment, the near interests of the majority of the people are slowly rising into a solitary prominence.   And the main tide of the influence toward democracy comes not by the way of charity of any kind, but directly out of the working class itself.   Close alongside the working-class movement, and often mingling with it, is the increasing tendency among men and women, not of the labor ranks, who, with different social creeds, are committing

themselves definitely to the cause of the fourth estate in its demand
for justice.   Many of these persons have themselves felt the bitter-
ness of poverty ; others have been moved by a more distant sympathy.   But it is certain that the radical social attitude of a large

Charles Booth, Author of "Labor and Life of the People."
(From a photograph by Elliott & Fry, London.)

body of educated men and women in London comes not merely
from what others have suffered.   They belong to what is called the
" literary proletariat."   With the ever greater crowding of the professions in the metropolis, especially as women are increasingly
entering into the competition of one form or another of intellectual

work, there is a constantly growing number of persons of trained mind and delicate sensibilities who find themselves hard pressed in the struggle.   Even after success in it, the keen remembrance of its pangs lingers.   Events have already shown in London, and are bound to show still more clearly, the profound significance of this personal sense of social wrong which is creeping in among those who have the power that knowledge, skill, and influence give them to attack what they find to be false in social conditions.

London has been behindhand in the matter of movements of importance among the artisans.   It is among the strong, self-reliant North-country men that the old trade-unions and the co-operative stores have made their great attainments.   The working-men of London are of a less sturdy race, though that is in part because the industries of the metropolis call for skilled labor in a smaller proportion than do those of the northern towns.   In general, the northern towns have the factories; London, the warehouses and the docks.

In 1886, under the lead of the Socialists, who were then more violent and less powerful than they now are, the agitations of the unemployed began.   The unemployed represent the two or three most helpless grades of poverty.   Some of them belong to the idle and vicious, but a large proportion of them are willing to work according to their power.   At any rate, it appeared clearly enough that they represent a serious problem.   Trafalgar Square, at one of the main centres of traffic, was made a forum for the expression of their demand for the means of subsistence.   These meetings took so threatening a turn that several efforts were made by the police to disperse them.   They continued intermittently during three years.   In addition to the Trafalgar Square demonstrations, there were parades to district poor-houses; church parades in which Lazarus came to the portal that Dives, going in to worship, might see him; and even some riotous marches in which the windows of clubs in Pall Mall and of shops in Piccadilly were made havoc of. By the summer of 1889 these agitations had died away.   But the

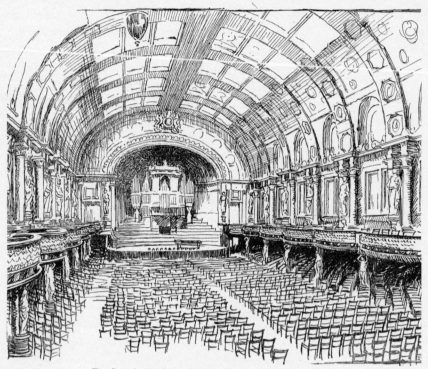

The Queen's Hall in the People's Palace. (From a photograph.)

temporary lull merely gave time for shifting the scene of action to
the principal seat of the difficulty at the docks.

The long miles of docks down along the north bank of the river,
beginning at the Tower, which are so great a source of England's
wealth, contribute to East London life little more than a grudging
partial support to the vast body of casuals and hangers-on whom
they bring there. They are the last miserable hope of the unfortunate and shiftless of every calling. A certain number of men are
regularly employed. After that, however, it is open to every man
to come with the rest in the morning, and join with them at the
dock-gates in fighting like wild beasts to see which ones of the number shall get in to secure a day's work—every man's hand against
his brother, with bread and starvation for a wager. The dock-

owners had been taking advantage of this situation by paying a miserable pittance by the hour, sometimes even dismissing men in the middle of the day, so as to get the full use of men's fresh force.

Things became so unendurable that some of the stronger spirits among the dockers decided to ask John Burns, who is a skilled mechanic, to come and see if there was not some help for them. Burns had just been leading a successful strike of gas-workers; and, before that, had been one of the speakers at Trafalgar Square. In the face of seeming impossibility, the men being wholly undisciplined and completely dependent upon their employment for the bare necessaries of life, John Burns determined to call out the thousands of dock-workers of London. It was an act of surpassing courage. It was not mere reckless daring. He saw that the market was rising, so that the dock-owners could with difficulty hold out against the demands of commerce. He knew from recent strikes, especially from one in which the woes of the match-girls had been brought to light, that public sentiment was turning strongly toward the support of down-trodden toilers. And he believed that the working-men of England would uphold him with their hard-earned shillings. These things all acted in his favor. Large quantities of relief-supplies were sent in by the people of London every day. More than a quarter of a million dollars were contributed to support the strike. English trade-unions gave ninety thousand, and twice that sum came by telegraph from Australia. The rest of the work was accomplished through Burns's marvellous power to hold great masses of men with his voice—there were over one hundred thousand men on strike at once—and through the statesmanlike inner direction of the strike by his friend and fellow-craftsman, Tom Mann. After six weeks of daily speaking, systematic distribution of food and strike-pay, proposing and rejecting of overtures, and withal no little apprehension on the part of good citizens of some violent disturbance—the great strike was won, and a beginning made of the organization of the great army of the unskilled, which has grown steadily from that time to this. In less than three

JOHN BURNS ADDRESSING THE DOCKERS ON TOWER HILL.

years the Dockers' Union, and two other unions of the unskilled, have come to include upward of three hundred thousand men in the United Kingdom. Under the general name of the New Trade-Unionism, with Burns and Mann for leaders, they have won continual victories, extended aid to weaker unions, pushed their policy to the front in the Trade-Union Congress, and gained a political power which will give them at least John Burns for a representative in the next House of Commons. If John Burns and Tom Mann should both be elected Members of Parliament, there would be among the nation's legislators no men of truer hearts and more temperate lives, and few of greater native ability than these heroes of the masses.

Organized Socialism, out of which the movement of the laborers sprang, has, as a result of this success through peaceful methods, become steadily more moderate. One hears, even in Hyde Park, where, on Sunday afternoon, advocates of every cause hold noisy rivalry, less of fiery harangue and more about uniting for the sake of keeping up wages and of putting representatives into the County Council and into Parliament. William Morris's Socialist League, which still represents the poet's impatience of all mechanical methods, and clings to his fantastic revolutionary hope, has been growing weaker and weaker, until it has now dwindled almost down to the single group which has a meeting in a hall back of Morris's house, in Hammersmith, on Sunday evening, and sups in common afterward.

The rising tide of Socialism in London, so far as it goes in the channels of organization, lies in the progress of the Fabian Society. This unique association of Socialists is now in the seventh year of its existence. It has about two hundred members, most of whom are cultured people. Mr. Grant Allen, a year or two ago, deserted the banner of Mr. Spencer, and became a Fabian. Mr. Walter Crane is on the list of lecturers. The Rev. Stopford Brooke gives his adhesion, and occasionally takes up his strong poetic prophecy at Bedford Chapel, with denunciation of the present state of things, and aspiration toward all that can lead to a better.

John Burns.
(From a photograph by the London Stereoscopic Company.)

Pursuing the policy of masterly delay which the old Roman advocated, the Fabian Society has exerted a marked influence in London through its fortnightly meetings, its tracts, and the volume of essays by its leading members. These essays, which have had a very large sale, were first given as lectures at the Society's meetings, and may be regarded as the best published exposition of Socialism from the point of view of enlightened Socialists. The Society is gradually coming to be a political power in the metropolis. This is partly because some of its leaders have become acknowledged specialists as to questions of advanced municipal administration; but it is more largely because of a series of campaigns in the working-men's clubs. There are two hundred of these in London, on a wholly independent basis. Outside of the entertainments which are provided, the members of the clubs seem to be most attracted by political and industrial discussion. At least once a week in all the larger clubs some person is present to lecture. The men smoke their pipes, drink beer out of huge pewter mugs, and listen. The Fabian Society has detailed a group of its ablest speakers for this special service, and the result has been, through influences direct and indirect, that the working-men of London—who but a few years ago all supported Mr. Brad-laugh and his unsatisfying political radicalism—are now well-nigh unanimous in favor of the programme of immediate social legis-lation which the Fabian Society is proposing.

The variety of social work in London is, it is true, almost end-less, and each department has but little relation with the others; yet it would be far from the truth to represent the general social situation as being a mere confused mass of expedients, of turnings hither and thither. In fact every year shows in metropolitan life a marked increase in the aggregate result of philanthropic and indus-trial movements. It is certainly a new and remarkable exhibition of the English power of achievement that, notwithstanding the vastness of the problem, and its intangibleness, and the plausible claims of superficial reform, the steady impulse from the beginning, on nearly every side, should have been toward attacking the prob-lem at its centre, and toward devis-ing broader plans of remedy as rap-idly as the working out of any act-ual results could suggest them.

The governing bodies of London are showing themselves ready to undertake large social schemes based upon previous approved ex-periments. The County Council, by its fair way of treating men working under it, has established a "moral minimum" for wages, and a "moral maximum" for hours. It has greatly developed the "lungs" of London—the parks, open spaces, and playing fields. In the way of

Tom Mann.

new kinds of municipal administration the Council has in charge a very large building enterprise in Bethnal Green, for model tenement-houses which shall accommodate several thousands of people ; and it has recently voted to assume control of one of the leading tramway lines. The School Board requires all of its contractors to comply with trade-union conditions as to wages and the length of the working day, and provides dinners for ill-fed children at the schools.

The extensive investments of private capital, for the sake of improving the housing of the working-people, have resulted in completely wiping out many unsanitary and criminal quarters. In nearly every part of London one now sees great model tenement-houses, constructed after the most recent patterns, and sometimes with much architectural beauty. The buildings give a return of four or five per cent. on the capital. The coffee-houses of London, besides being one of the best of temperance measures, have proved advantageous business investments. Even the newest form of people's café, the Tee-to-tums, are conducted so that expenses are covered. These unique institutions are the creation of Mr. P. R. Buchanan. They combine the features of a coffee-house, supplying a variety of good food and non-alcoholic drinks, with those of a club, having numerous facilities for improvement and recreation. The patrons of each Tee-to-tum are organized by skilled social workers, who direct their amusements. Mr. Buchanan well illustrates the new type of man now coming forward in England, who, with intelligence, means, and energy, shall devote himself and his possessions to working out plans for widening the circuit of life for the toiling majority of his countrymen. Of this same fine public spirit is Mr. Charles Booth, a wealthy merchant, who at the time when feeling was highest went alone to the East End and took lodgings for the sake of making a careful study of the whole situation. Enlisting the aid of some able young students of economics, and engaging a regular staff of clerks, he began his great work, in which he is putting together a most painstaking, unbiassed, and lucid account of the labor and life of the people of London. Six volumes, of which Mr. Booth, with undue modesty, stands merely as the editor, have

A lecture at The Fabian Society, Essex Hall.
A question from the rear.

already appeared, giving a close description of the homes of the
poor in different degrees of poverty, and of the condition of work
at the different trades. With these volumes are colored maps in-
dicating the character as to poverty and wealth of every street in
London. The remainder of the work will treat of all the trade-
unions and organizations for self-help among working people, and

of the efforts toward social improvement in the way of charity and philanthropy.

With the publication of these volumes the social problem of London begins to be understood and realized in its length and breadth. "The Bitter Cry," the agitations of the unemployed, and the great strike, served to arouse the sense of social responsibility. The efforts of many sorts and conditions of people, with diverse points of view and concerned about different social evils, have gradually been showing the methods for success under specific conditions. And now comes this quiet, patient man, having worked along through the years of turmoil and novelty, trusting implicitly to the truth which the facts might express, and presents the whole of the metropolis as an intelligible object of social study, and makes it easy to see how in each neighborhood, according to its needs, there may be free course for whatever agencies have been found to be of value in any other.

The first stage of the social awakening is over—that of scattered experiments and of general investigation. The next, and even more significant stage, the stage of expansion, is already entered upon. There is sufficient reason to expect that the County Council will not stop in its undertaking of social administration in the interest of the people, until it has assumed the complete ownership and direction of the gas and water supply and of the tramway lines. The replacing of large insanitary tracts of buildings with model tenement-houses will have to be continued in several other places after the work in Bethnal Green is completed. There is coming to be a marked increase of efficiency in the local parish boards, which are charged with executing the laws for sanitation and poor-relief. The co-ordination of all more obvious charities, and their comprehensive working in each district, will go on until there shall be as well organized checks against pauperism as there now are against crime.

With the field in general thus laid out, there is already full promise that each considerable section of the metropolis will have at

least one public institution for the recreation and higher education
of the people. The churches and the university settlements may be
looked to for the gradual development of all less formal and more
personal influences toward making life healthier, happier, nobler.
Meanwhile the long, slow struggle of the working-men, rising into
dramatic interest in its fitful outbursts, is destined to bring them
to a position of independence, and in so strong and pure a democracy as the County of London, ultimately, as they become worthy
of power, into a position of control.

LIFE IN NEW YORK TENEMENT-HOUSES AS SEEN BY A CITY MISSIONARY

By WILLIAM T. ELSING,

MINISTER OF THE DE WITT MEMORIAL NON-SECTARIAN CHURCH IN RIVINGTON STREET, NEW YORK

THE EAST SIDE—TENEMENT LIFE—CONTRASTS IN THE TENEMENTS—DIRT AND
CLEANLINESS—CLASSES OF HOMES IN THE TENEMENTS—RENTS—CHANGES IN
THE TENEMENT POPULATION—STATISTICS OF A TYPICAL BLOCK—NATIONALI-
TIES—INFLUENCES OF THE PUBLIC SCHOOLS—THE FRESH-AIR EXCURSIONS—
THE COLLEGE SETTLEMENTS—STORIES OF THE POOR—THE CHARITY ORGANI-
ZATIONS—THE CHURCH—SUGGESTIONS TOWARD IMPROVING "DARKEST NEW
YORK."

FOR nearly nine years I have spent much of my time in the
homes of the working people, on the East Side, in the lower
part of New York City. I have been with the people in their
days of joy and hours of sorrow. I have been present at their
marriage, baptismal, and funeral services. I have visited the sick
and dying in cold, dark cellars in midwinter, and sat by the bedside of sufferers in midsummer in the low attic room, where the
heat was so intense and the perspiration flowed so abundantly that
it reminded me of a Turkish bath. I have been a frequent guest
in the homes of the humble. I have become the confidant of many
in days of trouble and anxiety.

I shall in this paper tell simply what I have heard, seen, and
know. I shall endeavor to avoid giving a one-sided statement. I
have noticed that nearly all those who work among the poor of our
great cities fall into the natural habit of drawing too dark a picture
of the real state of things. The outside world has always been

more inclined to listen to weird, startling, and thrilling statements than to the more ordinary and commonplace facts. If I were to crowd into the space of one short chapter all the remarkable things which I have heard and seen during the past nine years, I might give an absolutely truthful account and produce a sensation, and yet, after all, I should give a most misleading idea of the actual condition of the homes and the people with whom I have been so intimately associated. We must not crowd all the sad and gloomy experiences of a lifetime into a history which can be read in an hour.

What I have said applies especially to the homes of the people in the tenement-houses. An ordinary tenement-house contains five stories and a basement, four families usually occupying a floor. The halls in nearly all the houses are more or less dark, even during the brightest part of the day. In the winter, just before the gas is lighted, dungeon darkness reigns. When groping my way in the passages I usually imitate the steam craft in a thick fog and give a danger-signal when I hear someone else approaching ; but even when all is silent I proceed with caution, for more than once I have stumbled against a baby who was quietly sitting in the dark hall or on the stairs. In the old-style halls there is no way of getting light and air, except from the skylight in the roof, or from the glass transoms in the doors of the apartments. In the newer houses a scanty supply of air comes directly from the air-shafts at the side of the hall. The new houses are not much better lighted than the old ones. The air-shafts are too narrow to convey much light to the lower floors. In the older houses the sink is frequently found in the hall, where the four tenants living on the same floor get their water. These sinks in the dark halls are a source of great inconvenience. A person is liable to stumble against them, and they are frequently filthy and a menace to health. In the new tenements the sink is never placed in the hall. In addition to the owner and agent, in connection with every large tenement-house, there is a housekeeper. The housekeepers are usually strong and thrifty housewives who take care of the halls and stairs, light the gas, sweep the sidewalks, and show the rooms to new applicants, and frequently receive the rent until the agent or landlord calls for it. Sometimes the housekeeper deals directly with the landlord, who

The Home of a Thousand People.

comes once or twice a month to look at his property and collect the rent. The housekeeper is frequently a widow, who gets free rent in exchange for her work, and by means of sewing or washing is able to provide food and clothing for her children. It pays the landlord to have one tenant rent free in order to have a clean house. If the house is small the housekeeper usually receives her rent at a reduced rate in exchange for her services. There is never any difficulty in getting a good housekeeper. The landlord or agent sees to it that the housekeeper does her duty and the housekeeper watches the tenants. If they soil the stairs and halls, she reminds them of the fact in no uncertain way. If a careless tenant gives unnecessary labor to the housekeeper that tenant will soon be compelled to seek other quarters. The result is that the stairs and halls in all the large tenement-houses are remarkably clean. I have visited a great number of them, and can confidently say that I have never seen the halls of a large tenement-house in as neglected and dirty a condition as the corridors of the New York Post-Office. But the moment you enter the rooms of the occupants you often step from cleanliness into filth. The influence of the housekeeper and the sight of the clean halls and stairs is to some the first lesson in cleanliness, and is not without its beneficial effects. There is a slow but constant improvement in this direction, and every year strangers from many lands are getting gradually acquainted with the use, value, and virtue of clean water.

The housekeeper is frequently wanting in the older and smaller houses, which were formerly occupied by one family, but now serve as homes for three or four. Every tenant is here expected to perform a portion of the housekeeper's duty without remuneration. These houses are sometimes extremely dirty, and the death-rate is higher than in the larger and better kept tenements.

Let us leave the hall and enter some of the homes in the larger houses. To many persons, living in a tenement-house is synonymous with living in the slums, yet nothing is further from the truth. It would be an easy matter for me to take a stranger into a dozen or more homes so poor, dirty, and wretched that he would not forget the sight for days, and he would be thoroughly convinced that a home cannot exist in a tenement-house ; but I could take that same person to an equal number of homes in the same section of the city, and sometimes in the same house, which would

The Bright Side of Life in a Tenement-house.

turn him into a joyful optimist, and forever satisfy him that the
state of things is not by any means as bad as it might be.　To the

The Dark Side—under the Same Roof.

casual observer the tenement-houses in many portions of New York present a remarkable degree of uniformity. The great brick buildings with their net-work of iron fire-escapes in front, their numerous clothes-lines running from every window in the rear, the well-worn stairs, the dark halls, the numerous odors, pleasant and otherwise, coming from a score of different kitchens presided over by housewives of various nationalities—these are all similar ; but from the moment you enter the rooms you will find every variety of homes, many of them poor, neglected, wretched, and dirty ; others clean, thrifty, and attractive ; indeed, as great a variety as exists in the interior of homes in an ordinary town. There are homes where the floor is bare and dirty, the furniture broken and scanty, the table greasy, the bedlinen yellow, the air foul and heavy, the children pale, frowsy, and sticky, so that you squirm when the baby wants to kiss you ; but there is also another and brighter side. There are at the same time thousands of cheerful, happy homes in the tenement-houses. The floor is frequently as clean and white as soap, water, and German muscle is able to make it. The tablecloth and bedlinen, although of coarse material, are snowy white. The stove has the brightness of a mirror, the cheap lace-curtains are the perfection of cleanliness, and the simple furniture shines with a recent polishing. There is nothing offensive about the well-washed faces of the children. A few favorite flowers are growing on the window-sill. The room contains a book-shelf with a few popular volumes. A bird-cage hangs from the ceiling ; the little songster seems to feel that his music is appreciated in this tenement-kitchen, and pours forth more rich and tender notes than are ever heard in the silent chambers of the wealthy. In such homes the oft-recurring motto, " God Bless Our Home," is not an idle mockery.

A large number of tenement-houses in the lower portion of New York are only a little below the common up-town flat. It is often difficult to tell where the flat leaves off and the tenement begins. You get about as little air and sunshine in the one as in the other. The main difference lies in the number of rooms and the location. If some down-town tenement-houses stood up-town they would be called flats.   The word *tenement* is becoming unpopular down-town, and many landlords have dubbed their great caravansaries by the more aristocratic name of "flat," and the term "rooms" has been changed to "apartments."

There are three distinct classes of homes in the tenement-houses ; the cheapest and humblest of these is the attic home, which usually consists of one or two rooms, and is found only down-town. These are generally occupied by old persons. Occasionally three or four attic rooms are connected and rented to a family, but as small single rooms are sought after by lonely old people, the landlord often rents them separately. An old lady who has to earn her bread with the needle finds the attic at

Pig Alley.

once the cheapest and best place for her needs.   The rent of one or two unfurnished attic rooms ranges from $3 to $5 per month.

A large number of very poor people live in three rooms—a kitchen and two dark bedrooms. Where the family is large the kitchen lounge is opened and converted into a double bed at night. The rent for three rooms is generally from $8 to $12 per month.

The vast majority of respectable working people live in four

4

rooms—a kitchen, two dark bedrooms, and a parlor. These parlors are generally provided with a bed-lounge, and are used as sleeping-rooms at night. The best room is always carpeted and often provided with upholstered chairs. The walls are generally decorated with family photographs and inexpensive pictures, and in some of them I have found a piano. These parlors compare very favorably with the best room in the house of the average farmer. The rent for four rooms is from $12 to $16 per month.

The rent is an ever-present and unceasing source of anxiety to a great many poor people. The family is sometimes obliged to go half clothed and live on the cheapest and coarsest food in order to provide the rent money. The monthly rent is a veritable sword of Damocles. To a poor woman who dreads the coming of the land-lord, the most enticing and attractive description of heaven which I have been able to give is a place where they pay no rent. The landlords are of necessity compelled to be peremptory and some-times arbitrary in their demands. If a landlord were even a little too lenient his tenement property would certainly prove a losing investment. The apparently unreasonable harshness of many land-lords is often justifiable, and the only means of securing them against loss. Generally where a good tenant is unable to pay the rent on account of sickness or lack of work the landlord is willing to extend the time a few weeks. I frequently find families who are two or three months in arrears. In the majority of cases where dispossess papers are served, the landlord does not know his tenant sufficiently well to trust him, or the tenant is unworthy of trust. Very few of those who are evicted are compelled to take to the street. In most cases sufficient money is collected from friends, neighbors, and charitable people to procure another place of shelter. Oc-casionally, however, all the worldly possessions of an unfortunate tenant are placed on the street. It is a pathetic sight to see a small heap of poor household stuff standing on the sidewalk guarded by the children, while the distressed mother is frantically rushing from one charitable organization to another in search of help.

A NEW TENEMENT OF THE BETTER SORT.

One of many recently erected by private enterprise.

A poor German woman came to me on one occasion and informed me that her furniture was standing on the sidewalk, and she knew not what would become of her. She had with her a beautiful little girl. The child cried continually, but the mother's distress was too great for tears. She begged me in God's name to help her. I gave her but little encouragement, and dismissed her with a few kind words. She left without heaping abuse on me or cursing the church for its neglect of the poor. A little later I went to the place where she informed me her furniture was and found all her earthly goods on the sidewalk. I inquired of some of her former neighbors about her character, and on being convinced that she was a worthy woman, rented two small rooms in a rear tenement. I found some young street-corner loafers, told them about the woman, and asked them to lend a hand in getting the furniture moved. There is no man so bad that he will not do a good turn for another if you approach him properly. These young roughs went to work with a will, and when the poor woman returned from her last fruitless attempt to collect enough for a new home she found everything arranged. She was thankful and happy. I did not see her until two months later. Then she appeared in as great distress as before, and showed me a new dispossess paper. She informed me that she had failed to find work, everything had been against her, but she hoped to get on her feet if I would once more help her. I told her it was impossible for me to do anything more for her ; so she thanked me for my former kindness and departed. That afternoon I heard of a lady in Orange, N. J., who wanted a house-servant and a little girl as waitress. I immediately thought of the German woman and promised if possible to send her out to Orange as soon as arrangements could be made. I was soon in the little rooms of the widow and her daughter and expected to be the bearer of joyful tidings. When I finished she looked sadly at the few scanty pieces of furniture and said:

"If I go to the country what shall I do with the stuff?"

"My good woman," I said, "the stuff is not worth fifty

cents ; give it to the boys to make a bonfire, and do what I tell you."

"But I have not money enough to leave the city."

I provided the fare, the boys had a glorious time around their fire, and that night, instead of sleeping in her comfortless room, the poor woman was on Orange Mountain. It would have been a losing investment for any landlord to give an extension of time to that woman, and yet she was a thoroughly worthy person, as the sequel proved ; her old misery and trouble were at an end. She found a good home and gave perfect satisfaction.

Many other experiences like this, and my constant association with the conditions of tenement-house life, have, of course, led me to certain conclusions as to the best remedies, which I shall reserve for specific mention in the latter part of this paper.

The population of the tenement-houses in lower New York is continually changing. There is a constant graduation of the better element. As soon as the circumstances of the people improve they want better homes. A foreigner who took up his abode in a tenement-house fifteen or twenty years ago may be perfectly contented with his surroundings, but when his children grow up and earn good wages they are not satisfied with a tenement-house, and give the old people no peace until a new home is found. Sometimes a man who has led a bad life reforms and immediately seeks a better home for his wife and children. I know several men who were at one time low and degraded drunkards, who would have been satisfied with a pig-sty, who had torn the clothes from their children's backs, the blankets from their beds, and taken them to the pawnshop to get money for drink ; but through the good influences that were thrown around them, the wise counsel of friends, and the saving power of the gospel they became changed men. Their circumstances began to improve, the children were provided with clothes, one piece of furniture after another was brought into the empty rooms, until the place began to look like a home again. These men were charmed with the new life. Home became so dear a place that they are willing to travel an hour each morning and evening in order to make it still more attractive. They began to see the disadvantages of life in a tenement and found a new home on Long Island or in New Jersey.

A Grandfather Cutting Carpet-rags.

This constant sifting of the best elements makes religious and philanthropic work in lower New York exceedingly difficult and apparently unfruitful, but none the less encouraging and necessary. The fact that the people leave the tenements in search of better homes is the best proof that a good work is being accomplished. A few months ago we celebrated the tenth anniversary of the dedication of one of our city mission churches. There were six hundred present, and out of this number there were only twenty-four who were at the dedication ten years before. While the better class is being constantly sifted out of the tenements, a steady stream of new-comers flows in to take their places.

Successive waves of population follow each other in rapid succession. It is often impossible to tell what the character of the population will be in the next ten years. In 1830 the agents of the New York City Mission visited 34,542 families. Among this number there were only 264 who desired foreign tracts, showing that the population was then almost exclusively American or English-speaking. Now the English language is rarely heard in some of the lower parts of New York, except by the children. That section of the city between the Bowery and East River, Grand and Houston Streets, has been successively occupied by Americans, Irish, Germans, and is now fast coming into the possession of Russian and Polish Jews. The Jewish invasion has been remarkably rapid. Eight years ago I used to see occasionally a Jewish face on the streets or a Jewish sign over the stores. Now the streets swarm with them.

In 1892 I made a careful canvass of a typical block and found 300 families composed of 1,424 individuals. The nationalities of the families were as follows: 244 German, 16 Irish, 11 American, 13 Hungarian, 6 Polish, 4 Russian, 2 Bohemian, 1 English, 1 Dutch, and 2 Chinese. Among the 244 German families there were 192 Jews, 38 Protestants, and 14 Roman Catholics. The German Jews are the most highly respected, and on this account many call themselves German who are in reality Russian or Polish Jews. These 300 heads of families are engaged in 72 different trades, occupations, and professions. There are 73 tailors, 17 cigarmakers, 17 storekeepers, 12 pedlars, 11 painters, 9 butchers, and 9 shoemakers in the block. The remaining 65 trades and professions are represented by 148 different persons. Thirty of the heads of families are Roman Catholics, 47 Protestants, and 221 Jews, and 2 have no religion. The Jews do not as a rule mingle to any great extent with the Christians. When they come in large numbers into a street, the Christians gradually withdraw, and the neighborhood finally becomes a Jewish quarter. There are streets in New York where it is a rare thing to find a Christian family.

During the transition period, when a locality is neither Christian nor Jewish, an interesting state of things prevails—a Jewish family, a Roman Catholic family, a pious Protestant family, and a heathen family, as far as religion is concerned, frequently live on the same floor. Suffering appeals to our common humanity. In trouble and sickness these neighbors render each other assistance and often become warm friends. I have seen a Jewish woman watching anxiously by the bedside of a dying Christian. A Roman Catholic or Jewish woman will often stand as godmother at the baptism of a Protestant child. A pretty, black-eyed Jewess occasionally captures the heart of a young Roman Catholic or Protestant, and they have come to me to perform the marriage service. Persons of various nations and religious beliefs are sometimes present at a tenement-house funeral. Bigotry and national prejudice are gradually broken down and the much-abused tenement becomes a means of promoting the brotherhood of man and the union of Christendom. You may hear daily from the lips of devout Roman Catholics and Jews such words as these: "We belong to a different religion, but we have the same God and hope to go to the same heaven." Such confessions are not often heard in small towns and country districts, but they are frequent in the tenement-houses.

The Jews, who in all ages have been noted for their exclusiveness, are affected by this contact with Christians in the tenement-house. In De Witt Memorial Church, with which I am connected, an audience of three or four hundred Jews assembles every week to hear Christian instruction. From the stand-point of social science such a gathering every week for two or three years past is significant. The Jew in every land has preserved his identity. Per-

Poverty and Death.

secution has isolated him; when he has been most hated he has flourished, when he has been despised he has prospered. Like the symbolic burning bush, the fires of persecution have not destroyed him. It remains to be seen whether he will preserve his identity in this country, where, as a citizen, he enjoys equal rights, and where the doors of the public school and the Christian church stand open to Jew and Gentile alike.

Whatever may be the nationality of the parents the children are always thorough Americans. The blond-haired, blue-eyed German children; the black-haired, dark-eyed Italians; the little Jews, both dark and blonde, from many lands, are all equally proud of being Americans. A patriotic Irishman gave a beautiful edition of "Picturesque Ireland" to one of the boys in my Sunday-school. The lad looked disappointed. His father asked him why he was not pleased with the present. He answered: "I want a history of the United States." We have a circulating library, patronized almost exclusively by foreigners. The librarian informs me that four boys out of every five call for United States histories.

The most powerful influence at work among the tenement-house population is the public school. Every public school is a great moral lighthouse, and stands for obedience, cleanliness, morality, and patriotism, as well as mental training. When the little children begin to attend the schools their hands and faces are inspected, and if they are not up to the standard, they are sent home for a washing. A boy who is especially dirty is sometimes sent down-stairs with the cleanest boy in school, and told to wash himself until he looks as well as his companion. Such lessons are not soon forgotten, and the result is the public-school children in lower New York present a very respectable appearance. The fresh-air excursions, with many other benefits, promote cleanliness. The heads of the children must be examined before they can enjoy a trip into the country. There is no more beautiful and beneficent charity than this fresh-air work.* In two or three weeks the pale-faced children return to the crowded city with renewed health and with larger and better views of life. I know boys who became so enraptured with green fields, running brooks, waving grain, and life on the farm that they have fully resolved to leave the city when they become men. One little fellow was so anxious to become a farmer that he ran away because his parents would not permit him to leave home.

The fresh-air work usually closes in October, but the young ladies connected with the "College Settlement" have added a new feature, which will commend itself to everyone who is acquainted with the condition of life around us. Every Saturday afternoon during the winter two of the ladies take a small party of children to their summer home. Saturday evening is spent in playing various

* See The Story of the Fresh-air Fund, page 131.

games, or enjoying a candy-pull, and having a general good time. On Sunday the children attend the country church, and Sunday evening, seated before a blazing open fire, a good book is read, or the ladies in charge give some practical talk to the children. On Monday the little party returns to the city and the house is locked until the following Saturday. Such a visit to the country will be indelibly impressed upon these children. You cannot do people very much good at long range. Hand-picked fruit is the best.

In the summer of 1891 I took my first party of boys from my mission church to Northfield, Mass., and attended Mr. Moody's students' conference. We pitched our tents in the forest, cooked our own food, and sang college songs around our camp-fire at night. In ten days I became thoroughly acquainted with the boys, and was able to help them in many ways. I believe if every minister, priest, rabbi, and Sunday-school superintendent would select eight or ten young men and spend two weeks with them under canvas by the side of a mountain-lake or trout-stream, more good might be done in permanently influencing their lives than by many weeks of eloquent preaching.

To keep the boys off the streets, and to train them to habits of cleanliness, obedience, and manliness, military companies have been formed in several of our down-town Sunday-schools. It is astonishing how well a number of wild boys will go through military tactics after a few months' drilling. The hope of our great cities lies in the children of the poor. If we can influence them to become upright, honorable men and women, we shall not only save them, but produce the most powerful lever for lifting up those of the same class who are sinking. I know scores of children and young people who are far better than their parents. Some of the noblest young men I have ever known have worthless, drunken parents. Some of the most beautiful flowers grow in mud-ponds, and some of the truest and best young women in our city come from homes devoid of good influences; but in all such cases uplifting outside help has moulded their characters.

While the people in tenement-houses are compelled to sleep in rooms where the sunlight never enters, and suffer many discomforts from overcrowding, especially in summer, there are certain compen-

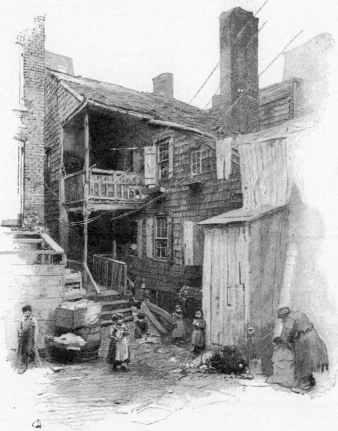

A Hovel in the Italian Quarter.

sations which must not be overlooked.   The poor in large cities who have steady work are, as a rule, better fed and clothed than the same class in rural districts.   Fresh vegetables, raised in hot-houses, or sent from Southern markets, are sold throughout the winter at reasonable prices, and in the early spring strawberries and various

other fruits are for sale on the streets in the tenement district long
before they reach the country towns and villages. In the poorest
quarter of the city you find the so-called "delicatessen" shops,
where the choicest groceries, preserves, and canned meats are sold.
The clothing, too, worn by the young people is stylish and sometimes expensive ; anyone who walks through these districts will be
astonished at the number of well-dressed young people. A young
woman who earns from $6 to $8 a week will often be dressed in
silk or satin, made according to the fashion. The teeth, finger-
nails, and shoes are often the only signs of her poverty. When
visiting a stylish young woman's plain mother, I have sometimes
seen all the finery in which the daughter appeared at church on
Sunday hanging on the wall of a bare, comfortless bedroom not
much larger than a good-sized closet.

The tenement-house people are not all thriftless, as the records
of the down-town savings-banks clearly prove. Seven hundred out
of every thousand depositors in one of the banks on the Bowery live
in tenement-houses, and if it were not for tenement-house depositors several of our down-town savings-banks would be compelled to
give up business. An abundance of cruel and bitter poverty, however, can always be found. The "submerged tenth" is ever present.
A widow, for instance, with three or four young children who is
obliged to earn her bread by sewing, is in a most pitiable and ter-
rible position. Hundreds of such weary mothers continue their
work far into the night, with smarting eyes, aching backs, and breaking hearts. There is nothing which makes a man who has any feeling for the suffering of his fellows so dissatisfied with our present
social system as the sight of such a poor woman sewing shirts and
overalls for twenty-nine cents a dozen. There are good people in
all our large cities who live just above the starving-point. The
average earnings of the unskilled laborers with whom I am acquainted is not over $10 per week. When a man is obliged to
spend one-fourth of this for rent, and feed and clothe his family on

EVICTED—ON THE SIDEWALK.

the remainder, it is impossible to lay by anything for a rainy day. When the father is out of work for a considerable time, or when sickness or death enter the home, distress, hunger, and an urgent landlord stare him in the face.

It is easy for those who have never felt it to overlook the constant strain of poverty and the irritation which it causes in families which in circumstances of ordinary comfort would be contented. In such cases particularly can great good be accomplished by a visit from some clear-sighted and sympathetic person.

Not very long ago I was invited to act as referee between a husband and wife. There were three little children and a grandmother in the family. The man worked in a cigar-box factory; business was slack and he was employed only half time. His average weekly earnings were $5. They had a debt of $11 at a grocery-store and another of $35 at an undertaker's shop. I knew the family; both husband and wife were honest, sober, and industrious people. The wife wanted to break up housekeeping; the husband was opposed to this plan, and they had agreed to abide by my decision. I examined each one separately. I began with the husband and said:

"When a physician prescribes a remedy he must first know the disease. I want you, therefore, to tell me plainly why your wife wants to break up the home. There may be good reasons why her plan should be adopted. If you two cannot possibly agree, and are fighting like cats and dogs, then I may be in favor of breaking up. Tell me just how the matter stands."

He informed me that he and his wife had always lived in perfect peace. They never had any trouble except poverty. The wife had become completely discouraged, and the only way she saw out of the difficulty was to put the children into an orphan asylum and go out as a house-servant until she could earn enough to clear off the debt, after which she hoped to get her home together again. The wife and grandmother gave me the same account. The perpetual strain of poverty was the only reason for breaking up the home.

5

For the sake of the three little children I decided that the home must not be broken up and promised to see that the debt at the grocery-store was wiped out and the family clothing was taken out of the pawn-shop. The grandmother was so pleased with the decision that she determined to become a servant and begged me to find a place for her.

In our large cities there is too much isolation between the rich and the poor. The charitable societies are often the only link between them. If the mother of every well-to-do home in our large cities would regularly visit, once a month, a needy family, a vast amount of good would be accomplished among the worthy poor, and distress would be unknown. Human nature is too selfish for such a happy state of things ever to be realized, but it is possible to bring the givers and receivers of charity closer together than they are. If some of the wealthier ladies who now give a few dollars each year to the charitable societies would seek through these societies to come into direct personal contact with the recipients of their charity, they would experience a deeper happiness and fully realize the blessedness of giving. Business men are too much occupied to make a monthly visit to the tenement-houses, but if their wives and daughters would undertake this work a new day would dawn for many a poor, heartbroken mother who is now hopeless and longing for death to end her misery. We are frequently asked, "Is it safe for a lady to visit these great tenement-houses?" We answer unhesitatingly, perfectly safe. The young ladies connected with the City Mission go unmolested into the darkest portions of New York. The first visit to a tenement-house might be made in the company of a city missionary, after which the most timid could go alone.

Nothing is easier than to make paupers out of the poor. Great discretion must be exercised, but the Charity Organization Society, the Society for Improving the Condition of the Poor, the City Mission, the Children's Aid Society, and other equally worthy institutions are ever ready to give direction to individuals who

The Monroe Model Tenement.

desire to do personal work. A few persons have through the City Mission come into personal contact with the poor, and the results are most gratifying.

While in a small town the distress of the poor is easily made known through friends and neighbors or the clergyman, in our large cities the most deserving are often overlooked and suffer most intensely ; and it is these cases which are reached by personal visitation. The worthy poor are generally the silent poor. Their sufferings must be extreme before they make their wants known. There are many poor, upright, God-fearing old people who struggle against fearful odds to keep body and soul together, and yet they drift daily toward the almshouse on Blackwell's Island, the last and most dreaded halting-place on the way to Potter's Field. I have nothing to say against the administration of the almshouse or the treatment of its inmates, but I do not wonder that old men and women who have led a good moral life would rather die than be stranded on the island and take up their abode among the broken wrecks of humanity which fill that institution.

It is very unwise to give aid without a thorough investigation. Some time since a Polish Jew asked me the way to a certain street. I directed him, and he said : " Dear sir, I am in great distress ; my furniture is standing on the sidewalk in Essex Street, and my children are watching the stuff, while I am trying to collect a little money to get another place." He drew from his pocket a few coppers, and asked me to add my gift. I said: "I do not know you, and I am acquainted with a great many poor people whom I would like to help, but I have not the means ; how, then, can you expect any help from me ? " Two streams burst from his eyes. The big tears rained down his beard and coat. "It is hard," he said, and bowed his head, buried his face in a red handkerchief, wiped off the tears, and passed on. I crossed the street. The tears of that sad man touched me. I turned, ran after him, and said: " Where is the stuff ? " " In Essex Street." " What have you ? " " A table, bureau, bed, and looking-glass," he replied. " Have you nothing small that I can take with me and loan you money on ? " He pointed to his well-worn greasy coat, and said : " I have this." " Show me the stuff," I said. We walked together, and I endeavored to carry on a conversation with the stranger in German, for he was ignorant of English, but suddenly he seemed to have lost all knowledge of the German tongue in which he had before addressed me, and was perfectly dumb. When we reached Ridge Street he finally spoke, and asked me to wait for him a moment while he went to see a friend. I said: "Look here, I want you to take me to the stuff immediately." He looked amazed and said: "What have I to do with you?" "A good deal," I replied; "you either take me to the stuff or I take you to the police station." "Do you think I am a liar?" I said: "You must take me to the stuff or you are a liar." "Come," he said, "I will take you to the stuff." It was wonderful to see how that old man, who had moved so slowly before, walked through the crowded streets. I had all I could do to keep up with him. We soon reached Essex Street. It was Friday afternoon and Essex Street was in all its glory—old clothes, decayed meat, pungent fish, and stale fruit abounded. The Ghetto in Rome and the Jewish quarters in London and Amsterdam are nothing compared with Essex Street. At one place it was almost impossible to get through the crowd, and I left the sidewalk and took the street. In a moment my new acquaintance disappeared, and I have not seen him since. I have no doubt this man and many others like him are making a good deal of money by playing on the sympathies of poor people.

I have made it a rule never to give a homeless man money, but when his breath does not smell of whiskey I give him my card containing the name and address of a lodging-house. The card must be used the same day it is given. As some of those who ask for a lodging never use the cards, my bill is always less than the number of cards given out. One night a man told me he was tired of his bad life and he wanted to become a better man. I spoke a few encouraging words to him and was about to dismiss him, when he told me he was sick and needed just five cents to get a dose of salts. I took him at his word and immediately sent for the drug and made him take it on the spot. It is needless to say that he never troubled me again.

There remain many cases where charity is of no avail. Where

poverty is caused by crime, no relief can come except by breaking
up the home. Not long since I was called to take charge of the
funeral of a little child. I groped my way up the creaking, filthy

An Invalid Supporting His Family by Making Lace.

stairs of a small, old-fashioned rear tenement. I knocked, but heard
no response ; I pushed the door open, but found no one in the room,
yet this was the place—"Rear, top floor, left door." I made no

mistake. I entered the room and found a dead baby wrapped in an old towel lying on a table. I learned from the neighbors that the father and mother had been out collecting money to bury the child and both had become beastly drunk. I returned to the dead child, read the burial service, and thanked God that the little one was out of its misery. A little later a man came and took the body to Potter's Field. The parents had buried (it would be more accurate to say starved to death) six children before they were two years old. Very little can be done for such people. Cumulative sentences ought to be imposed upon them each time they are arrested for drunkenness, so that prison-bars may prevent them from bringing the little sufferers into the world.

A great deal is done by the various charitable societies for the relief of distress, but as far as my observation goes the most effective charitable work is done by the poor themselves. Thousands of dollars are given away in the tenement districts every year by the inhabitants of the tenements, of which no charitable society makes a record. I have never related a peculiarly distressing case of poverty to a poor person but there was a ready response, and out of their own poverty the poor have ministered to those who were in need of relief. The children of our City Mission school, who come from the tenement-houses, contribute every Thanksgiving-Day from $80 to $100 for the poor in our immediate neighborhood. A club of fifty small boys and girls saved their pennies one year and bought thirty-five Thanksgiving dinners for the poor, consisting of chickens, potatoes, beans, turnips, and cabbages. The original plan was to have a head of cabbage go with each chicken, but the money gave out ; this did not in any way disconcert the children, for they quickly solved the difficulty by cutting a cabbage into four parts, and putting a quarter into each bag. The children worked from 7.30 to 11 P.M. distributing the provisions. The members of this club visit the hospitals, sing to the patients, and furnish them with reading matter. In ten months they distributed as many as 27,901 booklets and illustrated papers. One summer the children noticed that the flies troubled the sick people and there were no fans in some of the hospitals. They saved their pennies, which in most cases would have gone to the candy-store, and bought a lot of palm-leaf fans at a wholesale house. They bound the fans with variously colored ribbons and decorated them with scripture texts appropriate to the sick, and on Sunday afternoon presented them to the delighted patients. The poor give that which costs them something, and their joy is correspondingly greater. That the most spontaneous and beautiful charity flourishes in the tenement-houses will undoubtedly be a surprise to many, but it is a fact well known to all who have any large acquaintance with the poor in our great cities.

It is equally true that there is more virtue in tenement localities than is commonly supposed. Darkness and sin have much in common. The dark halls and crowded homes are not favorable to virtue, but nevertheless virtue is the rule and vice the exception. The people who live in tenement-houses are not fastidious about rules of etiquette and propriety. Young women sometimes allow young men to address them and caress them in a manner which would offend well-bred people, and yet these girls would indignantly resent any liberties which they consider dishonoring. Young people occasionally desire to be married secretly, and timidly ask if it is not possible for me to date back the wedding certificate three or four months ; such cases, however, are not common. There are many hasty marriages where the consent of the parents has not been obtained ; these sometimes end in a speedy separation. Young girls occasionally come to me accompanied by young men half drunk and ask me to perform the marriage ceremony. There are self-styled clergymen who put up conspicuous signs advertising the fact that they make a business of uniting young people in marriage. These hungry sharks are ever ready to give their services for one or two dollars, thus plunging thoughtless young people into misery. I have succeeded in breaking up matches which I knew would have brought certain ruin to the parties concerned. I always refuse to marry a young couple when I am not permitted to consult the parents before performing the ceremony. If a law were passed making it obligatory on young people to get a license

The Poor Helping the Poor—Distributing Thanksgiving Dinners.

from the civil courts before a clergyman could perform the marriage, some unfortunate marriages would be prevented. A few hours of sober reflection would bring both parties to their senses.

The young people in our cities are extravagant. Very few of them save anything. Many of them put all they earn on their backs, and sometimes have not enough to pay the wedding fee, and all the furniture for the new home has been bought on the instalment plan. When the young husband is sober and industrious the married life generally moves on smoothly. It frequently happens, however, that from the day of her marriage a girl begins to fade like a flower. In three or four years a bright young girl will degenerate into a careworn, ill-tempered, slovenly middle-aged woman, surrounded by two or three pale, ragged, ungoverned children. She spent her girlhood in a store or shop, and was never initiated into the art of housekeeping. Her husband finds the saloon a far more comfortable place than his home. When industrial training shall have been introduced into every public school and the girls get a thorough training in housekeeping we may look for improvement in the home life of the poor in our cities. The cooking classes in connection with the girls' clubs, the Young Women's Christian Association, and those opened in some of the City Mission churches are doing excellent service in training young women to assume the responsibilities of home-makers.

The influence of the church on the tenement population is not as great as it probably will be in the near future. The strongest churches have followed their constituents and moved up-town; those which remained have languished, and in some cases have been compelled to close for want of active support. A new era has dawned. All religious denominations are interested in the churchless masses. New churches and chapels are being erected down-town, and there is a strong feeling in every quarter that the old stations must be maintained. The wisest men fully recognize the fact that if the churches among the tenement population are to do efficient work they must be well manned, richly endowed, and run at high pressure all through the year. Wherever church work has been pursued on these lines the results have been most gratifying. The workingmen, although not hostile, are generally extremely indifferent to religion. They are concerned about food, clothing, and a place of shelter for the present, and trouble themselves but little about the future. The fact that the church is beginning to take an active interest in the temporal welfare of the working people is already producing beneficial results.

The daily press exerts as great an influence over the parents as the public school does over the children. The workingmen in the tenement-houses constantly read the newspapers, and they read almost nothing else. What we need is not more learned lectureship foundations on the evidences of Christianity, but endowments to secure a large number of short, concise, popular prize essays on moral and religious subjects, especially adapted in language and style to the working people. If these prize essays were published

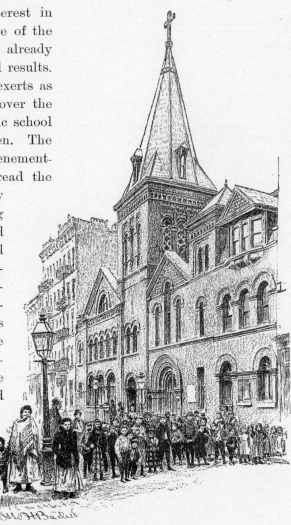

A Missionary Workshop—De Witt Memorial Church (non-sectarian).

in the Sunday papers they would be read by tens of thousands of workingmen, and be a most powerful means of doing good.

There are a great many things which might be done to improve the conditions of the poor, but most of the schemes proposed are altogether impracticable. If we could make the poor sober and industrious, and the rich unselfish and generous, poverty would soon disappear; unfortunately we can do neither. We must take the world as we find it, and employ the best means to reach the desired end. I have seen a great deal of wretchedness and poverty in lower New York, and for some of these evils I can offer no remedy; but if the following suggestions could be carried out I believe something would be done toward improving "darkest New York:"

First.—There is nothing the inhabitants of the tenement-houses need so much as more room, sunshine, and fresh air. At present the sun never shines in the bedrooms of three-quarters of the people of New York City. In some parts of our city the population is nearly twice as dense as in the most crowded part of London. Nowhere on the wide earth are human beings so crowded as in the tenement districts. The suffering in July and August is often intense. The bedrooms become unbearable, and the roofs, fire-escapes, and empty wagons are used as sleeping-places. Thousands of little children do not see green grass during the entire summer; they are virtually prisoners in their own homes. The only true remedy can come in a complete system of cheap rapid transit. If the happy day ever comes when a poor man can be carried to the green fields of Long Island, New Jersey, or Westchester County for five cents, then a wonderful change will take place. It is commonly supposed that the poor enjoy herding together like dumb brutes on a cattle train, but nothing is further from the truth. The only reason why so many people put up with the numerous inconveniences of a tenement-house is simply that stern necessity compels them to live in this way. At the present time, with all the inconveniences of travel, many persons are leaving tenement-houses and seeking better homes in Brooklyn, Jersey City, and upper New York. If the North and East Rivers were spanned with railroad bridges, so that in twenty minutes a workingman might be ten miles distant from the factory or store, there would be a great exodus from the tenement-houses, and many places now used as homes would be turned into shops and warehouses.

Second.—A great blessing will be conferred on the crowded multitudes of the East Side when the long-promised and eagerly-desired small parks are opened. There are stone, coal, and lumber yards on the river-front on the East Side which would make attractive breathing spots for the children of the poor. If the Park Commissioners would bestir themselves, and with all possible haste provide the children of the poor with small parks and play-grounds they would confer an inestimable blessing upon the city.

Third.—Great improvements have been made in the construction and sanitary arrangements of tenement-houses, but still more must be done in the same direction. There are scores of horrible, pestilential rat-holes which are utterly unfit for human habitation. All such places ought to be condemned, and the Board of Health must be backed up by public sentiment in its endeavor to root out these plague-spots. Our city lots are not of the proper size to erect the large rectangular European tenements with a court in the centre, from which light and air can be conveyed into every room. A few such model tenements, however, have been built by associations of philanthropists and private individuals. More of these model tenements are needed. They will bring down the exorbitantly high rents which are now exacted from the poorest people. The model tenement will confer a great boon upon large families. It is often exceedingly difficult for a man who has seven or eight children to get rooms in the better class houses. The first question asked is, "How many children have you?" I know families who have been compelled to pay a high rent for poor accommodations on account of the large number of children. A poor woman searched all day for rooms ; wherever she saw a place that suited her the old question, "How many children have you?" was asked, and she was obliged to look elsewhere. One morning she sent all her children to Greenwood Cemetery, put on a black dress, and began the search of rooms. When she had found a suitable place the landlord asked, "How many children have you?" "Six," answered the woman, sadly; "but they are all in Greenwood." The landlord was satisfied that the children would do his place no harm. The woman paid a month's rent and took possession. There was a scene at night, but during the month the woman proved to be such a good tenant that she was allowed to remain permanently.

Fourth.—The saloon is the poor man's club, and flourishes most vigorously in the poorest sections of the city. Instead of denouncing the saloon on account of the numerous evils it afflicts on the poor, something better must be supplied to take its place. "Home is the sacred refuge of our life," but notwithstanding all that poets have sung and moralists have spoken, many workingmen are perfectly convinced that two dark bedrooms and a kitchen is not an attractive place in which to spend a pleasant evening with a friend. The saloon is the only substitute. When Orpheus passed by the cave of the siren he took his lyre and made such wondrous melody that sailors, enraptured by the music, spurned the seductive strains that were wafted from the dangerous cave. The fable has its application—give the workingmen something they will like as well as the saloon and you will strike at the root of the evil. There are excellent places, like Cooper Union and the Young Men's Institute; but these institutions cannot expect to draw those who live one or two miles away in another part of the city. If the workingmen were fully alive to the advantages afforded them they would undoubtedly be willing to walk a long distance, but the majority of them have no ambition to improve themselves. They spend their evenings in the saloons because they are always within easy reach and form agreeable meeting-places. It is absurd to denounce the saloon in unqualified terms. The multitudes who patronize them are not all absolute fools. Many simply seek to satisfy the craving after fellowship which the Creator has implanted in their natures. The saloons are well-lighted, conveniently located social clubs, provided in some cases with a pleasant reading-room, and

BOTH OVER SEVENTY. "WOOD FOR SALE."

always with obliging proprietors. Wise men are beginning to see that a substitute must be supplied to take the place of the saloon which shall retain all its good features and simply discard its evil elements. The churches of various denominations are taking a deep interest in providing attractive, well-lighted reading and club-rooms for the workingmen in our large cities. A great and beneficent work might be done by the Board of Education if free reading rooms and libraries were opened in connection with every public school in the crowded portions of the city.

Fifth.—Good old John Wesley said, " Cleanliness is next to god-liness ; " but bathing in tenement-houses is exceedingly difficult and sometimes impossible. On pleasant days, when vast numbers of young men prefer the street-corner to the saloon, I have often stopped among a group of young fellows and said : " Boys, suppose a first-class swimming-bath were opened somewhere in this neighborhood, where you could for five or ten cents dive from a spring-board and plunge into a tank 50 feet wide and 100 feet long, full of warm, clean water, would you patronize such a place ? " and the spontaneous and united answer always is : " You bet your life we would." I am fully convinced that if a first-class natatorium, with reading-rooms, library, and restaurant attached, was opened in some crowded district, the result would surpass all expectation. The baths have been remarkably successful in London. In one of these institutions over two hundred thousand baths were taken in a single year, and the receipts were more than $3,000 over the expenditures. Every humanitarian effort which is successful across the ocean does not succeed here, but from the sights which I witness every summer, when hundreds of young men plunge from the docks, lumber-yards, and shipping, at the risk of being arrested and having their clothes stolen, I am convinced that a swimming-bath would at once become immensely popular. The old Romans were wise in this respect. One of their great baths in our modern cities would be an effective means of aiding all forms of good work.

At the Christian conference held in Chickering Hall, in 1888, I

6

endeavored to impress upon the audience the need of public baths. The good work begun at that time by the City Mission has been completed by the Society for Improving the Condition of the Poor. The first bath was opened in August, 1891, and the results are most satisfactory. Sixteen thousand baths were taken during the first one hundred and fifteen days. One day in the latter part of August, 1891, there were six hundred and sixty-nine bathers.*

Sixth.—There has been great need of a universal loan association. The poor, as well as the rich, are frequently compelled to borrow money. Unfortunately the poor, until lately, have not been able to get it at a reasonable interest. There is no bank in the city that will loan a poor man money and take his old clothes, his wife's wedding-ring, or some little household treasure as security. Yet the poor man is forced to borrow. He has been out of work a few weeks. The landlord will come to-morrow. The children are hungry and call loudly for bread. In the dark bedroom lies a child with a burning fever. A physician has been to see the child. He is a kind-hearted man, he knows the hardships of the poor and does not expect his fee to-day; but of course the father cannot be expected to pay for the prescription he has just written. How shall the man get bread for those hungry children and medicine for this one who is sick? They have one last resort left—the household idols must be sacrificed. All the valuables are brought together. These little rings and lockets, and the silver cup which a proud uncle presented to the first baby boy; the father's overcoat and Sunday suit, with the mother's best dress, are all needed to make up the $10 for the landlord, and to get food and medicine for the children. The pawnbroker is ready to devour everything which has any value. The pawn-tickets are carefully put away, and the parents confidently hope that they will soon be able to redeem the things they have "put away." They redeem them at three per cent. a month, or else they finally lose them, not having received more than one-fifth of the actual value

---

* Nearly one hundred thousand baths are now taken every year.

of the articles. I sent a boy to an East Side pawn-shop with a gold watch, the original cost of which was $150; its actual present value was certainly not less than $40. The boy received $5, and this was as much as he could get. I redeemed the watch the next day, much to the disgust of the pawnbroker. What has proved a great blessing to many people in distress, was the opening of the offices of the Provident Loan Society, in the United Charities Building on Fourth Avenue and Twenty-second Street.* I fear that heretofore, no charitable society has undertaken this work, from the mistaken idea many people have that such an institution would foster thriftless habits among the poor. Such persons forget that it is not a question of pawn-shops or no pawn-shops, but whether we shall have one large, reputable loan association, where the poor man's clothing and jewelry shall be as good as the rich man's real estate at a banking-house, or a vast number of little pawn-shops—those whirlpools in which the valuables of many poor families are swallowed. Thieves who want to get rid of stolen property, and thriftless drunkards who go to the pawnbroker to dispose permanently of their property at the highest prices, will continue to visit the pawn-shop; but persons who need a temporary loan to help them through a period of enforced idleness or sickness will be greatly benefited by a wisely managed loan association.

Seventh.—There is great need of trained nurses for the sick. Hundreds of mothers who are obliged to care for their homes during the day, are sitting at night by the bedside of sick children. If the sickness is of a temporary nature these periods of broken rest and double duty are passed without disaster. It frequently happens, however, that two or three children are sick at the same time. The mother is compelled to work night and day until nature gives way and she breaks down under the strain. Sickness brings increased expenses, therefore it is impossible for the husband to stay at home to take care of his family. If he does not work there will

* Other loan associations have been opened since this paper was written.

be no money next week for food, rent, and medicine. When the physician tells him that the end is near for wife or child, then he gives up his work. I have visited homes where I found the mother and all the children sick, and if it had not been for the occasional visit of a neighbor there would have been no one to give a cup of water to the sick or dying. Into such homes the trained nurse comes like a ministering angel. She lights a fire in the cold stove, bathes the sick, provides clean bedding, dresses the little children, puts in order the rooms, and when the place looks like home again, she takes from her basket some beef-tea, a little jelly, or some other tempting morsel for the sick. The mother, who has been lying hopeless in the dark bedroom, begins to revive, and watches with deep interest the ministering stranger, and with wet eyes says: "God bless you and reward you for what you have done this day." The nurse not only aids the sick, but is able by her counsel to help the mother when she has recovered. The friendly talks on housekeeping and the care of the children are often of the greatest value. The nurse also forms the connecting link between the hospitals and the invalids hidden away in the tenement-houses, many of whom would have been left to rot and finally to die on their filthy beds if the nurses had not found them and sent them to the hospital. The nurse does not stop to ask what the nationality or creed of the sufferers is. The only recommendation required to receive her services is sickness and distress. The nurses of the City Mission are doing a noble work, but their number is too small and they must be constantly restrained lest they break down from overwork. Here is a work which can be done at once. Anyone who desires to relieve the suffering poor in the most direct and effective way can do it through a trained nurse. It would be a source of the purest happiness to many a man and woman, when they go to rest in their beautiful and luxurious homes, to know that $600, the saving, perhaps, of some needless luxury, is keeping a faithful nurse at work the entire year, moistening the fevered lips of the sick, or soothing the last hours of the dying. The Great

Teacher of men consigned Dives to hell, not because of erroneous theological opinions, but because he neglected the beggar, who lay at his gate full of sores. Dives is among us to-day. He is clothed in the finest robes and fares sumptuously every day. Lazarus is also here. He lies in the cheerless bedroom of a tenement-house, hungry, sick, and full of sores. The two have been brought together for a purpose. The only salvation for our modern Dives lies in Lazarus.

Eighth.—There is need of greater co-operation among all good men. When we see anyone endeavoring to cast out social demons among us, let us not forbid him because he does not accept our creed or follow our party. Prejudice, narrow-mindedness, and bigotry have too long stood in the way of social reform. Wise men must recognize that whatever is good is of God. It makes no difference from what source it comes. When all good men shall work together on the broadest lines of social reform, great and beneficent changes will be brought about, and New York will continue to be a great, happy, and prosperous city.

THE CHILDREN OF THE POOR

By JACOB A. RIIS,

AUTHOR OF "HOW THE OTHER HALF LIVES," ETC.

"ONE OF GOD'S CHILDREN" — PROGRESS IN THE CARE OF POOR CHILDREN IN NEW YORK—THE CHILDREN'S AID SOCIETY—ITALIANS IN MULBERRY BEND—THE SCHOOLS—SOME TYPICAL CHILDREN OF THE EAST SIDE—CHILD POPULATION OF THE JEWISH TENEMENTS—CHILD LABOR IN THE TENEMENTS—SOME SOLUTIONS OF THE PROBLEM—AMBITION AMONG THE SCHOOL CHILDREN—THE FLAG IN THE SCHOOLS—STREET GAMINS AND THEIR FUTURE—BOYS' CLUBS —LITTLE HOUSEKEEPERS—THE STORY OF "BUFFALO."

UNDER the heading "Just One of God's Children," one of the morning newspapers told the story not long ago of a newsboy at the Brooklyn Bridge, who fell in a fit with his bundle of papers under his arm, and was carried into the waiting-room by the Bridge police. They sent for an ambulance, but before it came the boy was out selling papers again. The reporters asked the little dark-eyed newswoman at the bridge entrance which boy it was.

"Little Maher it was," she answered.

"Who takes care of him?"

"Oh! no one but God," said she, "and he is too busy with other folks to give him much attention."

Little Maher was the representative of a class that is happily growing smaller year by year in our city. It is altogether likely that a little inquiry into his case could have placed the responsibility for his forlorn condition considerably nearer home, upon someone who preferred giving Providence the job to taking the trouble himself. There are homeless children in New York. It is certain that we shall always have our full share. Yet it is equally certain that society is coming out ahead in its struggle with this problem. In ten years, during which New York added to her population one-fourth, the homelessness of our streets, taking the returns of the Children's Aid Society's lodging-houses as the gauge, instead of increasing proportionally has decreased nearly one-fifth; and of the Topsy element, it may be set down as a fact, there is an end.

"I scrubs."—Katie, who keeps house in West Forty-ninth Street.

If we were able to argue from this a corresponding improvement in the general lot of the poor, we should have good cause for congratulation. But it is not so. The showing is due mainly to the perfection of organized charitable effort, that proceeds nowadays upon the sensible principle of putting out a fire, viz., that it must be headed off, not run down. It is possible also that the Bowery lodging-houses attract a larger share of the half-grown lads with their promise of greater freedom, which is not a pleasant possibility. The general situation is not perceptibly improved. The menace of the Submerged Tenth has not been blotted from the register of the Potter's Field, and though the "twenty thousand poor children who would not have known it was Christmas," but for public notice to that effect, be a benevolent fiction, there are plenty whose brief lives have had little enough of the embodiment of Christmas cheer and good-will in them to make the name seem like a bitter mockery. If indeed, New York were not what she is; if it were

possible to-morrow to shut her door against the immigration of
the world and still maintain the conditions of to-day, I should
confidently predict a steady progress that would leave little of the
problem for the next generation to wrestle with. But that is only
another way of saying "if New York were not New York." It
is because she is New York that in reviewing our own miseries we
have to take into account half the poverty, the ignorance, and the
helplessness of the cities of the Old World, that is dumped at our
door while the procession of the strong and of the able moves on.
And that is what makes our problem.

Heretofore the assimilation of these alien elements has been
sufficiently rapid. Will it continue so? There has been evidence
lately that we are entering upon a new stage of metropolitan development that might have fresh difficulties on this score. Anyone
who will sit an hour at a meeting of the Police Board, for instance,
when candidates for appointments are questioned as to their knowledge of the city, will discover that a generation of young men has
grown up about us who claim, not New York as their birthplace,
but this or that section of it—the East Side, the Hook, Harlem, and
so on, and outside of that immediate neighborhood, unless their
employment has been of a character to take them much about, know
as little of the city of their birth as if the rest of it were in Timbuc-
too. These were the children of yesterday, when the population
was, so to speak, yet on the march. To-day we find it, though drift-
ing still, tarrying longer and crystallizing on race-lines in settlements some of which have already as well-defined limits as if they
were walled in, to all intents and purposes separate towns. The
meaning of this is that our social fabric is stiffening into more permanent forms. Does it imply also that with its elasticity it is losing its old power of assimilation, of digestion?

I think not. The evidence is all to the contrary. Its vitality
seems to me not only unimpaired, but growing plainly stronger as
greater claims are made upon it by the influx of races foreign alike
of speech, of tradition, and of sentiment. Fresh problems are pre-

sented, fresh troubles foreshadowed, fresh prejudices aroused only to receive in their turn the same orderly, logical, and simple solution that discovers all alarm to have been groundless. Yesterday it was the swarthy Italian, to-day the Russian Jew that excited our distrust; to-morrow it may be the Arab or the Greek. All alike they have taken, or are taking, their places in the ranks of our social phalanx, pushing upward from the bottom with steady effort, as I believe they will continue to do, unless failure to provide them with proper homes arrests the process. The slum tenement bears to it the same relation as the effect the rags of an old tramp are said to have upon the young idler in his company. He has only to wear them to lose all ambition and become himself a tramp; the stamp is on him. But in the general advance the children are the moving force, the link between the past that had no future and the present that accounts no task too great in the dawning consciousness of a proud manhood. Their feeble hands roll away in play the stone before which the statecraft of our wise day stood aghast. The one immigrant who does not keep step, who, having fallen out of the ranks, has been ordered to the rear, is the Chinaman, who brought neither family nor children to push him ahead. He left them behind that he might not become an American, and by the standard he himself set up he has been judged.

I recall, not without amusement, one of the early experiences of a committee with which I was trying to relieve some of the child misery in the East Side tenements by providing an outing for the very poorest of the little ones, who might otherwise have been overlooked. In our anxiety to make our little charges as presentable as possible, it seems we had succeeded so well as to arouse a suspicion in our friends at the other end of the line that something was wrong, either with us or with the poor of which the patrician youngsters in new frocks and with clean faces, that came to them, were representatives. They wrote to us that they were in the field for the "slum children," and slum children they wanted. It happened that their letter came just as we had before us two little lads from the Mulberry Street Bend, ragged, dirty, unkempt, and altogether a sight to see. Our wardrobe was running low, and we were at our wits' end how to make these come up to our standard. We sat looking at each other after we had heard the letter read, all

The Late Charles Loring Brace, Founder of the Children's Aid Society.

thinking the same thing, until the most courageous said it : "Send them as they are." Well, we did, and waited rather breathlessly for the verdict. It came, with the children, in a note by return train, that said : "Not *that* kind, please !" And after that we were allowed to have things our own way.

The two little fellows were Italians. In justice to our frightened friends, it should be said that it was not their nationality, but their rags, to which they objected ; but not very many seasons have passed since the crowding of the black-eyed brigade of "guinnies," as they were contemptuously dubbed, in ever-increasing numbers into the ragged schools and the kindergartens, was watched with regret and alarm by the teachers, as by many others who had no better cause. The event proved that the children were the real teachers. They had a more valuable lesson to impart than they came to learn, and it has been a salutary one. To-day they are gladly welcomed. Their sunny temper, which no hovel is dreary enough, no hardship has power to cloud, has made them universal favorites, and the discovery has been made by their teachers that as the crowds pressed harder their school-rooms have marvellously expanded, until they embrace within their walls an unsuspected multitude, even many a slum tenement itself, cellar, "stoop," attic, and all. Every lesson of cleanliness, of order, and of English taught at the school is reflected into some wretched home, and re-hearsed there as far as the limited opportunities will allow. No demonstration with soap and water upon a dirty little face but widens the sphere of these chief promoters of education in the slums. "By'm by," said poor crippled Pietro to me, with a sober look, as he labored away on his writing lesson, holding down the paper with his maimed hand, "I learn t' make an Englis' letter; maybe my fader he learn too." I had my doubts of the father. He sat watching Pietro with a pride in the achievement that was clearly proportionate to the struggle it cost, and mirrored in his own face every grimace and contortion the progress of education caused the boy. "Si! si!" he nodded eagerly ; "Pietro he good-a boy ; make Englis', Englis'!" and he made a flourish with his clay-pipe, as if he too were making the English letter that was the object of their common veneration.

Perhaps it is as much his growing and well-founded distrust of the middle-man, whose unresisting victim he has heretofore been, and his need of some other link to connect him with the English-speaking world that surrounds him, as any personal interest in book-learning, that impels the illiterate Italian to bring his boy to school early and see that he attends it. Whatever his motive, the effect is to demonstrate in a striking way the truth of the observation that real reform of poverty and ignorance must begin with the children. In his case, at all events, the seed thus sown bears some fruit in the present as well as in the coming generation of toilers. The little ones, with their new standards and new ambitions, become in a very real sense missionaries of the slums, whose work of regeneration begins with their parents. They are continually fetched away from school by the mother or father to act as interpreters or go-betweens in all the affairs of daily life, to be conscientiously returned within the hour stipulated by the teacher who offers no objection to this sort of interruption, knowing it to be the best condition of her own success. One cannot help the hope that the position of trust in which the children are thus placed may, in some measure, help to mitigate their home-hardships. From their birth they have little else, though Italian parents are rarely cruel in the sense of abusing their offspring. It is the home itself that constitutes their chief hardship. Theirs are the poorest tenements, the filthiest hovels in the city. It is only when his years offer the boy an opportunity of escape to the street, that a ray of sunlight falls into his life; in his back-yard or in his alley it seldom finds him out. Thenceforward most of his time is spent there, until the school claims him. Since the sewing-machine found its way, with the sweater's mortgage, into the Italian slums also, his sweet-faced sister has been robbed to a large extent of even the freedom of the dump, where she used to pick cinders for her mother's kitchen fire, and she has taken her place among the wage-earners when not on the school-bench. Sickness, unless it be mortal, is no excuse from the drudgery of the tenement. When, recently, one little Italian girl, hardly yet in her teens, stayed away from her class in the Mott Street Industrial School so long that her teacher went to her home to look her up, she found the child in a high fever,

THE MOTT STREET BARRACKS.

in bed, sewing on coats with swollen eyes, though barely able to
sit up.

But neither poverty nor abuse have power to discourage the
child of Italy; for though he be born to the succession of the White
House, if fate and the genius of politics so will it, he is in looks, in
temper, and in speech, when among his own, as much an Italian as
his father, who could not even hold real estate if there were any
chance of his getting any. His nickname he pockets with a grin
that has in it no thought of the dagger and the revenge that come
to solace his after-years. Only the prospect of immediate punishment eclipses his spirits for the moment. While the teacher of the
sick little girl was telling me her pitiful story in the school, a characteristic group appeared on the stairway. Three little Italian culprits in the grasp of Nellie, the tall and slender Irish girl who was
the mentor of her class for the day. They had been arrested " fur
fightin'," she briefly explained as she dragged them by the collar
toward the principal, who just then came out to inquire the cause
of the rumpus, and thrust them forward to receive sentence. The
three, none of whom was over eight years old, evidently felt that
they were in the power of an enemy from whom no mercy was to be
expected, and made no appeal for any. One scowled defiance. He
was evidently the injured party.

"He hit-a me a clip on de jaw," he said in his defence, in the
dialect of Mott Street, with a slight touch of " the Bend." The
aggressor, a heavy-browed little ruffian, hung back with a dreary
howl, knuckling his eyes with a pair of fists that were nearly black.
The third and youngest was in a state of bewilderment that was
most ludicrous. He only knew that he had received a kick on the
back and had struck out in self-defence, when he was seized and
dragged away a prisoner. He was so dirty—school had only just
begun and there had been no time for the regular inspection—that
he was sentenced on the spot to be taken down and washed, while
the other two were led away to the principal's desk. All three
went out howling.

Perhaps of all the little life-stories of poor Italian children I have come across in the course of years—and they are many and sad, most of them—none comes nearer to the hard every-day fact of those dreary tenements than that of my little friend Pietro of whom I spoke, exceptional as was his own heavy misfortune and its effect upon the boy. I met him first in the Mulberry Street police station, where he was interpreting the defence in a shooting case, having come in with the crowd from Jersey Street, where the thing had happened at his own door. With his rags, his dirty bare feet, and his shock of tousled hair, he seemed to fit in so entirely there of all places, and took so naturally to the ways of the police station, that he might have escaped my notice altogether but for his maimed hand and his oddly grave, yet eager face, which no smile ever crossed despite his thirteen years. Of both, his story, when I afterward came to know it, gave me full explanation. He was the oldest son of a laborer, not " borned here " as the rest of his sisters and brothers. There were four of them, six in the family besides himself, as he put it : " 2 sisters, 2 broders, 1 fader, 1 mother," subsisting on an unsteady maximum income of $9 a week, the rent taking always the earnings of one week in four. The home thus dearly paid for was a wretched room with a dark alcove for a bed-chamber, in one of the vile old barracks that still preserve to Jersey Street the memory of its former bad eminence as among the worst of the city's slums. Pietro had gone to the Sisters' school, blacking boots in a haphazard sort of way in his off-hours, until the year before, upon his mastering the alphabet, his education was considered to have sufficiently advanced to warrant his graduating into the ranks of the family wage-earners, that were sadly in need of recruiting. A steady job of " shinin' " was found for him in an Eighth Ward saloon, and that afternoon, just before Christmas, he came home from school and, putting his books away on the shelf for the next in order to use, ran across Broadway full of joyous anticipation of his new dignity in an independent job. He did not see the street-car until it was fairly upon him, and then it was too late.

They thought he was killed, but he was only crippled for life. When, after many months, he came out of the hospital, where the company had paid his board and posed as doing a generous thing, his bright smile was gone; his shining was at an end, and with it his career as it had been marked out for him. He must needs take up something new, and he was bending all his energies, when I met

2 a.m. in the Delivery Room in the "Sun" Office.

him, toward learning to make the "Englis' letter" with a degree of proficiency that would justify the hope of his doing something somewhere at some time to make up for what he had lost. It was a far-off possibility yet. With the same end in view, probably, he was taking nightly writing lessons in his mother-tongue from one of the perambulating schoolmasters who circulate in the Italian colony peddling education cheap in lots to suit. In his sober, submissive way he was content with the prospect. It had its compen-

7

sations. The boys who used to worry him now let him alone.
" When they see this," he said, holding up his scarred and mis-
shapen arm, " they don't strike me no more."   Then there was his
fourteen months' old baby brother, who was beginning to walk and
could almost " make a letter."   Pietro was much concerned about
his education, anxious evidently that he should one day take his
place.   " I take him to school sometime," he said, piloting him
across the floor and talking softly to the child in his own melo-
dious Italian.   I watched his grave, unchanging face.

" Pietro," I said, with a sudden yearning to know, " did you ever
laugh ? "

The boy glanced from the baby to me with a wistful look.

" I did wonst," he said, quietly, and went on his way.   And I
would gladly have forgotten that I ever asked the question, even
as Pietro had forgotten his laugh.

I said that the Italians do not often abuse their children down-
right ; but poverty and ignorance are fearful allies in the homes of
the poor against defenceless childhood, even without the child-
beating fiend.   Two cases which I encountered in the East Side
tenements this past summer show how the combination works at
its worst.   Without a doubt they are typical of very many, though
I hope that few come quite up to their standard.   The one was
the case of little Carmen, who at this writing lay between life and
death in the New York Hospital, the special care of the Society
for the Prevention of Cruelty to Children.   One of the summer
corps doctors found her in a Mott Street tenement, within a stone's-
throw of the Health Department's office, suffering from a wasting
disease that could only be combated by the most careful nursing.
He put her case into the hands of the King's Daughters Committee
that followed in the steps of the doctors, and it was then that I saw
her.   She lay in a little back-room, up two flights, and giving upon
a narrow yard where it was always twilight.   The room was filthy
and close, and entirely devoid of furniture, with the exception of a
rickety stool, a slop-pail, and a rusty old stove, one end of which

was propped up with bricks. Carmen's bed was a board laid across the top of a barrel and a trunk set on end. I could not describe, if I would, the condition of the child when she was raised from the mess of straw and rags in which she lay. The sight unnerved even the nurse, who had seen little else than such scenes all summer. Loathsome bed-sores had attacked the wasted little body, and in truth Carmen was more dead than alive. But when, shocked and disgusted, we made preparations for her removal with all speed to the hospital, the parents objected and refused to let us take her away. They had to be taken into court and forced to surrender the child under warrant of law, though it was clearly the little suffer- er's only chance for life, and only the slenderest of chances at that.

Carmen was the victim of the stubborn ignorance that dreads the hospital and the doctor above the discomfort of the dirt and darkness and suffering that are its every-day attendants. Her par- ents were no worse than the Monroe Street mother who refused to let the health officer vaccinate her baby, because her crippled boy, with one leg an inch shorter than the other, had " caught it "—the leg, that is to say—from his vaccination. She knew it was so, and with ignorance of that stamp there is no other argument than force. But another element entered into the case of a sick Essex Street baby. The tenement would not let it recover from a bad attack of scarlet fever, and the parents would not let it be taken to the coun- try or to the sea-shore, despite all efforts and entreaties. When their motive came out at last, it proved to be a mercenary one. They were behind with the rent, and as long as they had a sick child in the house the landlord could not put them out. Sick, the baby was to them a source of income, at all events a bar to expense, and in that way so much capital. Well, or away, it would put them at the mercy of the rent-collector at once. So they chose to let it suffer. The parents were Jews, a fact that emphasizes the share borne by desperate poverty in the transaction, for the family tie is notoriously strong among their people.

How strong is this attachment to home and kindred that makes the Jew cling to the humblest hearth and gather his children and his children's children about it, though grinding poverty leave them only a bare crust to share, I saw in the case of little Jette Brodsky, who strayed away from her own door, looking for her papa. They were strangers, and ignorant and poor, so that weeks went by before they could make their loss known and get a hearing, and meanwhile Jette, who had been picked up and taken to Police Headquarters, had been hidden away in an asylum, given another name when nobody came to claim her, and had been quite forgotten. But in the two years that passed before she was found at last, her empty chair stood ever by her father's at the family board, and no Sabbath eve but heard his prayer for the restoration of their lost one. The tenement that has power to turn purest gold to dross digs a pit for the Jew through this, his strongest virtue. In its atmosphere it becomes his curse by helping to crowd his lodgings to the point of official intervention. Then follow orders to " reduce " the number of tenants, that mean increased rent which the family cannot pay, or the breaking up of the home. An appeal to avert such a calamity came to the Board of Health recently from one of the refugee tenements. The tenant was a man with a houseful of children, too full for the official scale as applied to the flat, and his plea was backed by the influence of his only friend in need —the family undertaker. There was something so cruelly suggestive in the idea that the laugh it raised died without an echo.

When it comes to the child population of the poor Jewish tenements, we have at last something definite to reckon with. We know from the police census that there were, in 1890, 160,708 children under five years in all the tenements of the city, which is not saying that there were so many poor children by a good many thousand. But how many of them were Italians, how many Bohemians, how many of Irish or German descent, we are yet left to guess. It is different with these. A census, that was taken for a special purpose, of the Jews in the East Side sweaters' district, several years ago, gave a total of 23,405 children under six years, and 21,285 between six and fourteen, in a population of something over a hundred and eleven thousand that inhabited forty-five streets in the Seventh, Tenth, and Thirteenth Wards. All of these were for-

Pietro Learning to Make an Englis' Letter.

eigners, most of them Russian, Polish, and Roumanian Jews, and they are by all odds the hardest-worked and, barring the Bohemians, as a class, the poorest of our people. According to the record, scarce one-third of the heads of families had become naturalized citizens, though the average of their stay in the United States was between nine and ten years. The very language of our country was to them a strange tongue, understood and spoken by only 15,837 of the fifty thousand and odd adults enumerated. Seven thousand of the rest spoke only German, five thousand Russian, and over twenty-one thousand could only make themselves understood to each other, never to the world around them, in the strange jargon that passes for Hebrew on the East Side, but is really a mixture of a dozen known dialects and tongues, and of some that were never known or heard anywhere else. In the census it is down as just what it is—jargon, and nothing else.

Here, then, are conditions as unfavorable to the satisfactory, even safe, development of child life in the chief American city, as could well be imagined, more unfavorable even than with the Bohemians, who have at least their faith in common with us, if safety lies in the merging through the rising generation of the discordant elements into a common harmony. A community set apart, set sharply against the rest in every clashing interest, social and industrial; foreign in language, in faith, and in tradition; repaying dislike with distrust; expanding under the new relief from oppression in the unpopular qualities of greed and contentiousness fostered by ages of tyranny unresistingly borne. But what says the record of this? That of the sixty thousand children, including the fifteen thousand young men and women over fourteen who earn a large share of the money that pays for rent and food, and the twenty-three thousand toddlers under six years, fully one-third go to school. Deducting the two extremes, little more than a thousand children of between six and fourteen years, that is, of school age, were put down as receiving no instruction at the time the census was taken; nor is it at all likely that this condition was permanent in the case of the greater number of these. The poorest Hebrew knows—the poorer he is, the better he knows it—that knowledge is power, and power as the means of getting on in the world that has spurned him so long, is what his soul yearns for. He lets no opportunity slip to obtain it. Day- and night-schools are crowded with his children, who learn rapidly and with ease.

Every synagogue, every second rear tenement or dark back-yard, has its school and its school-master, with his scourge to intercept those who might otherwise escape. In the census there are put down 251 Jewish teachers as living in these tenements, nearly all of whom probably conduct such schools, so that, as the children form always more than one-half * of the population in the Jewish quarter, the evidence is, after all, that even here, with the tremendous inpour of a destitute, ignorant people, the cause of progress along the safe line is holding its own.

It is true that these tenement schools which absorb several thousand children are not what they might be from a sanitary point of view. It is also true that heretofore they have mainly been devoted to teaching East-Side Hebrew and the Talmud. But to the one evil the health authorities have recently been aroused; of the other, the wise and patriotic men who are managing the Baron de Hirsch charity are making a useful handle by gathering the teachers in and setting them to learn English. Their new knowledge will soon be reflected in their teaching, and the Hebrew schools become primary classes in the system of public education. The school in a Hester Street tenement that is shown in the picture is a fair specimen of its kind—by no means one of the worst—and so is the back-yard behind it, that serves as the children's playground, with its dirty mud-puddles, its slop-barrels and broken flags, and its foul tenement-house surroundings. Both fall in well with the home lives and environment of the unhappy little wretches whose daily horizon they limit. Missionaries though they truly be, like their Italian playmates, in a good cause, they have not even the satisfaction of knowing it. Born to toil and trouble, they claim their heritage early and part with it late. What time they do not spend on the school-bench is soon put to use in the home workshop. When, in the midnight hour, the noise of the sewing-machine was stilled at last, I have gone the rounds with the sanitary police and counted often four, five, and even six of the little ones in a single

* Fifty-four per cent. in the census.

bed, sometimes a shake-down on the hard floor, often a pile of half-finished clothing brought home from the sweater, in the stuffy rooms of their tenements. In one I visited very lately, the only bed was occupied by the entire family, lying lengthwise and crosswise, literally in layers, three children at the feet, all except a boy of ten

or twelve, for whom there was no room. He slept with his clothes on to keep him warm, in a pile of rags just inside the door. It seemed to me impossible that families of children could be raised at all in such dens as I had my daily and nightly walks in. And yet the vital statistics and all close observation agree in allotting to these Jews even an unusual degree of good health. Their freedom from enfeebling vices and the marvellous vitality of the race must account for this. Their homes, or their food, which is frequently of the worst because cheapest, assuredly do not.

The Backstairs to Learning.
(Entrance to a Talmud School in Hester Street.)

I spoke of the labor done in tenement homes. Like nearly every other question that has a bearing on the condition of the poor and of the wage-earners, this one of the child home-workers has recently been up for discussion. The first official contribution to it was a surprise, and not least to the health officers who furnished it. According to the tenement-house census, in the entire mass of nearly a million and a quarter of tenants, only two hundred and forty-nine children under fourteen years of age were found at work in living rooms by the Sanitary Police. To anyone acquainted with the ordinary aspect of tenement life the statement seemed preposterous, and there are some valid reasons for believing that the policemen missed rather more than they found. They were seeking that which, when found, would furnish proof of law-breaking against the parent or employer, a fact of which these were fully aware. Hence their coming, uniformed and in search of children, into a tenement where such were at work, could scarcely fail to give those a holiday who were not big enough to be palmed off as fifteen at least. Nevertheless, I suspect the policemen were much nearer right than may be readily believed. Their census took no account of the tenement factory in the back-yard, but only of the living-rooms, and it was made chiefly during school hours. Most of the little slaves, as of those older in years, were found in the East Side tenements just spoken of, where the work often only fairly begins after the factory has shut down for the day and the stores have released their army of child-laborers. Had the policemen gone their rounds after dark, they would have found a different state of affairs. The record of school-attendance in the district shows that forty-seven attended day-school for every one who went to night-school.

The same holds good with the Bohemians, who are, if anything, more desperately poor than the Russian Jews, and have proportionally greater need of their children's labor to help eke out the family income. The testimony of the principal of the Industrial School in East Seventy-third Street, for instance, where there are some three hundred and odd Bohemian children in daily attendance, is to the effect that the mothers "do not want them to stay a minute after three o'clock," and if they do, very soon come to claim them, so that they may take up their places at the bench, rolling cigars or stripping tobacco-leaves for the father, while the evening meal is being got ready. The Bohemian has his own cause for the reserve that keeps him a stranger in a strange land after living half his life among us ; his reception has not been altogether hospitable, and it is not only his hard language and his sullen moods that are to blame. Yet, even he will "drive his children to school with sticks," and the teacher has only to threaten the intractable ones with being sent home to bring them 'round. And yet, it is not that they are often cruelly treated there. The Bohemian simply proposes that his child shall enjoy the advantages that are denied him—denied partly perhaps because of his refusal to accept them, but still from his point of view denied. And he takes a short cut to that goal by sending the child to school. The result is that the old Bohemian disappears in the first generation born upon our soil. His temper remains to some extent, it is true. He still has his surly streaks, refuses to sing or recite in school when the teacher or something else does not suit him, and can never be driven where yet he is easily led; but as he graduates into the public school and is thrown there into contact with the children of more light-hearted nationalities, he grows into that which his father would have long since become, had he not got a wrong start, a loyal American, proud of his country, and a useful citizen.

But when the State has done its best by keeping the child at school, at least a part of the day—and it has not done that until New York has been provided with a Truant Home to give effect to its present laws—the real kernel of this question of child labor remains untouched yet. The trouble is not so much that the children have to work early as with the sort of work they have to do. It is, all of it, of a kind that leaves them, grown to manhood and womanhood, just where it found them, knowing no more and therefore less than when they began, and with the years that should have prepared them for life's work gone in hopeless and profitless drudgery. How large a share of the responsibility for this failure is borne by the senseless and wicked tyranny of so-called organized labor in denying to our own children a fair chance to learn honest trades, while letting in foreign workmen in shoals to crowd our market, a policy that is in a fair way of losing to labor all the respect due it from our growing youth, I shall not here discuss.

SALUTING THE FLAG.

(Morning Exercise in the Industrial Schools.)

The general result was well put by a tireless worker in the cause of improving the condition of the poor, who said to me : " They are down on the scrub-level ; there you find them and have to put them to such use as you can. They don't know anything else, and that is what makes it so hard to find work for them. Even when they go into a shop to sew, they come out mere machines, able to do only one thing, which is a small part of the whole they do not grasp. And thus, without the slightest training for the responsibilities of life, they marry and transmit their incapacity to another generation that is so much worse off to start with." She spoke of the girls, but what she said fitted the boys just as well. The incapacity of the mother is no greater than the ignorance of the father in the mass of such unions. Ignorance and poverty are the natural heritage of the children.

I have in mind a typical family of that sort which our committee wrestled with a whole summer in Poverty Gap. Suggestive location ! The man found his natural level on the Island, where we sent him first thing. The woman was decent and willing to work, and the girls young enough to train. But Mrs. Murphy did not get on. " She can't even hold a flat-iron in her hand," reported her first employer indignantly. The children were sent to good places in the country, and repaid the kindness shown them by stealing, and lying to cover up their thefts. They were not depraved, they were simply exhibiting the fruit of the only training they had ever received—that of the street. It was like undertaking a job of original creation to try to make anything decent or useful out of them.

Another case that exhibits the shoal that lies always close to the track of ignorant poverty, is even now running in my mind, vainly demanding a practical solution. I may say that I inherited it from professional philanthropists, who had struggled with it for more than half a dozen years without finding the way out they sought. There were five children when they began, depending on a mother who had about given up the struggle as useless. The

father was a loafer. When we took them the children numbered
ten, and the struggle was long since over. The family bore the
pauper stamp, and the mother's tears, by a transition impercepti-
ble probably to herself, had become its stock in trade. Two of the
children were working, earning all the money that came in ; those
that were not lay about in the room, watching the charity visitor
in a way and with an intentness that betrayed their interest in
the mother's appeal. It required very little experience to make
the prediction that shortly ten pauper families would carry on the
campaign of the one against society, if those children lived to
grow up. And they were not to blame, of course. I scarcely know
which was most to be condemned—when we tried to break the
family up by throwing it on the street as a necessary step to getting possession of the children—the politician who tripped us up
with his influence in the court, or the landlord who had all those
years made the poverty on the second floor pan out a golden interest. It was the outrageous rent for the filthy den that had been
the most effective argument with sympathizing visitors. Their
pity had represented to the owner, as nearly as I could make out,
for eight long years, a capital of $2,600 invested at six per cent.,
payable monthly. The idea of moving was preposterous ; for
what other landlord would take in a homeless family with ten children and no income ?

Naturally the teaching of these children must begin by going
backward. The process may be observed in the industrial schools,
of which there are twenty-one scattered through the poor tenement
districts, with a total enrolment of something over five thousand
pupils.* A count made last October showed that considerably
more than one-third were born in twelve foreign countries where
English was not spoken, and that over ten per cent. knew no word
of our language. The vast majority of the rest were children of
foreign parents, mostly German and Irish, born here. According

---

* These schools are established and managed by the Children's Aid Society, as a
co-ordinate branch of the public-school system.

to the location of the school it is distinctively Italian, Bohemian, Hebrew, or mixed, the German, Irish, and colored children coming in under this head and mingling without the least friction. Whatever its stamp of nationality, the curriculum is much the same. The start, as often as is necessary, is made with an object-lesson—soap and water being the elements and the child the object. The alphabet comes second on the list. Later on follow lessons in sewing, cooking, carpentry for the boys, and like practical " branches," of which the home affords the child no demonstration. The prizes for good behavior are shoes and clothing, the special inducement a free lunch in the dinner hour. Very lately a unique exercise has been added to the course in the schools, that lays hold of the very marrow of the problem with which they deal. It is called " saluting the flag," and originated with Colonel George T. Balch, of the Board of Education, who conceived the idea of instilling patriotism into the little future citizens of the Republic in doses to suit their childish minds. To talk about the Union, of which most of them had but the vaguest notion, or of the duty of the citizen, of which they had no notion at all, was nonsense. In the flag it was all found embodied in a central idea which they could grasp. In the morning the star-spangled banner was brought into the school, and the children were taught to salute it with patriotic words. Then the best scholar of the day before was called out of the ranks, and it was given to him or her to keep for the day. The thing took at once and was a tremendous success.

Then was evolved the plan of letting the children decide for themselves whether or not they would so salute the flag as a voluntary offering, while incidentally instructing them in the duties of the voter at a time when voting was the one topic of general interest. Ballot-boxes were set up in the schools on the day before the last general election. The children had been furnished with ballots for and against the flag the week before, and told to take them home to their parents and talk it over with them. On Monday they cast their votes with all the solemnity of a regular election, and with as much of its simple machinery as was practicable. As was expected, only very few votes against the flag were recorded. One little Irishman in the Mott Street school came without his ballot. "The old man tore it up," he reported. In the East

A Synagogue School in a Hester Street Tenement.

Seventy-third Street school five Bohemians of tender years set themselves down as opposed to the scheme of making Americans of them. Only one, a little girl, gave her reason. She brought her own flag to school: "I vote for that," she said, sturdily, and the teacher wisely recorded her vote and let her keep the banner.

I happened to witness the election in the Beach Street school, where the children are nearly all Italians. The minority elements were, however, represented on the board of election inspectors by a colored girl and a little Irish miss, who did not seem in the least abashed by the fact that they were nearly the only representatives of their people in the school. The tremendous show of dignity with which they took their seats at the poll was most impressive. As a lesson in practical politics, the occasion had its own humor. It was clear that the negress was most impressed with the solemnity of the occasion, and the Irish girl with its practical opportunities. The Italian's disposition to grin and frolic, even in her new and solemn character, betrayed the ease with which she would, were it real politics, become the game of her Celtic colleague. When it was all over they canvassed the vote with all the gravity befitting the occasion, signed together a certificate stating the result, and handed it over to the principal sealed in a manner to defeat any attempt at fraud. Then the school sang Santa Lucia, a sweet Neapolitan ballad. It was amusing to hear the colored girl, and the half-dozen little Irish children, sing right along with the rest the Italian words of which they did not understand one. They had learned them from hearing them sung by the others, and rolled them out just as loudly, if not as sweetly, as they.

The first patriotic election in the Fifth Ward Industrial School was held on historic ground. The house it occupies was John Ericsson's until his death, and there he planned nearly all his great inventions, among them one that helped save the flag for which the children voted that day. The children have lived faithfully up to their pledge. Every morning sees the flag carried to the principal's desk and all the little ones, rising at the stroke of the bell, say with one voice, "We turn to our flag as the sunflower turns to the sun!" One bell, and every brown right fist is raised to the brow, as in military salute: "We give our heads!" Another stroke, and the grimy little hands are laid on as many hearts: "And our hearts!" Then with a shout that can be heard around the corner: "—— to our country! One country, one language,

8

one flag ! " No one can hear it and doubt that the children mean every word, and will not be apt to forget that lesson soon.

The earliest notion of order and harmless play comes to the children through the kindergartens, to which access is now made easier every day. Without a doubt this is the longest step forward that has yet been taken in the race with poverty ; for the kindergarten, in gathering in the children, is gradually but surely conquering also the street, with its power for mischief. Until it came, the street was the only escape from the tenement—a Hobson's choice, for it is hard to say which is the most corrupting. The opportunities rampant in the one were a sad commentary on the sure defilement of the other. What could be expected of a standard of decency like this one, of a household of tenants who assured me that Mrs. M——, at that moment under arrest for half-clubbing her husband to death, was " a very good, a very decent woman indeed, and if she did get full, he (the husband) was not much ? " Or of the rule of good conduct laid down by a young girl, found beaten and senseless in the street up in the Annexed District last autumn : "Them was two of the fellers from Frog Hollow," she said, resentfully, when I asked who struck her ; "them toughs don't know how to behave theirselves when they see a lady in liquor." Hers was the standard of the street, that naturally stamps what belongs to it, the children's games with the rest. Games they always had. It is not true, as someone has said, that our poor children do not know how to play " London Bridge is falling down " with as loud a din in the streets of New York, every day, as it has fallen these hundred years and more in every British town, and the children of the Bend march " all around the mulberry bush " as gleefully as if there were a green shrub to be found within a mile of their slum. It is the slum that smudges the game too easily, and the kindergarten's work comes in helping to wipe off the smut. So far from New York children being duller at their play than those of other cities and lands, I believe the reverse to be true. They lack neither spirit nor inventiveness. I watched a crowd of them having a donkey party in the street one night, when those parties were all the rage. The donkey hung in the window of a notion store, and a knot of tenement-house children, with tails improvised from a newspaper and dragged in the gutter to make them stick, were staggering blindly across the sidewalk trying to fix them in place on the pane. They got a heap of fun out of the game, quite as much, it seemed to me, as any crowd of children could have got in a fine parlor, until the storekeeper came out with his club. Every cellar-door becomes a toboggan-slide when the children are around, unless it is hammered full of envious nails; every block a ball-ground when the policeman's back is turned, and every roof a kite-field; for that innocent amusement is also forbidden by city ordinance " below Fourteenth Street."

It is rather that their opportunities for mischief are greater than those for harmless amusement; made so, it has sometimes seemed to me, with deliberate purpose to hatch the "tough." Given idleness and the street, and he will grow without other encouragement than an occasional "fanning" of a policeman's club. And the street has to do for his playground. There is no other. Central Park is miles away. The small parks that were ordered for his benefit five years ago, exist yet only on paper. Games like kite-flying and ball-playing, forbidden but not suppressed, as happily they cannot be, become from harmless play a successful challenge of law and order that points the way to later and worse achievements. Every year the police forbid the building of election bonfires, and threaten vengeance upon those who disobey the ordinance; and every election night sees the sky made lurid by them from one end of the town to the other, with the police powerless to put them out. Year by year the boys grow bolder in their raids on property when their supply of firewood has given out, until the destruction wrought at the last election became a matter of public scandal. Stoops, wagons, and in one place a showcase containing property worth many hundreds of dollars, were fed to the flames. It has happened that an entire frame house has been carried off piecemeal and burned up on election night. The boys, organized in gangs, with the one condition of membership that all must "give in wood," store up enormous piles of fuel for months before, and though the police find and raid a good many of them, incidentally laying in supplies of kindling wood for the winter, the pile grows again in a single night as the neighborhood reluctantly con-

Night School in the Seventh Avenue Boys' Lodging House.
(Edward, the little pedlar, caught napping.)

tributes its ash-barrels to the cause. The germ of the gangs that terrorize whole sections of the city at intervals, and feed our courts and our jails, may, without much difficulty, be discovered in these early and rather grotesque struggles of the boys with the police.

Even on the national day of freedom the boy is not left to the enjoyment of his firecracker without the ineffectual threat of the law. I am not defending the firecracker, but arraigning the failure of the law to carry its point and maintain its dignity. It has robbed the poor child of the street-band, one of his few harmless delights, grudgingly restoring the hand-organ, but not the monkey that lent it its charm. In the band that, banished from the street, sneaks into the back-yard, its instruments hidden under bulging coats, the boy hails no longer an innocent purveyor of amusement, but an ally in the fight with the common enemy, the policeman. In the Thanksgiving-Day and New-Year parades, which he formally permits, he furnishes them with the very weapon of gang organization which they afterward turn against him to his hurt.

And yet this boy who, when taken from his alley into the country for the first time, cries out in delight, " How blue the sky and what a lot of it there is! "—not much of it at home in his barrack—has, in the very love of dramatic display that sends him forth to beat a policeman with his own club or die in the attempt, in the intense vanity that is only a perverted form of pride capable of any achievement, a handle by which he may be most easily grasped and held. It cannot be done by gorging him *en masse* with apples and gingerbread at a Christmas party.* It can be done only by individual effort, and by the influence of personal character in direct contact with the child—the great secret of success in all dealings with the poor. Foul as the gutter he comes from, he is open to the reproach of "bad form" as few of his betters. Greater even than his desire eventually to " down " a policeman, is his ambition to be a "gentleman," as his sister's is to be a "lady." The street is responsible for the caricature either makes of the character. On a play-bill in an East Side street, only the other day, I saw this *répertoire* set down: "Thursday—'The Bowery Tramp;' Friday—'The Thief.'" It was a theatre I knew newsboys and the other children of the street who were earning money to frequent in shoals. The

---

* As a matter of fact I heard, after the last one that caused so much discussion, in an alley that sent seventy-five children to the show, a universal growl of discontent. The effect on the children, even on those who received presents, was bad. They felt that they had been on exhibition, and their greed was aroused with their resentment. It was as I expected it would be.

play-bill suggested the sort of training they received there. Within sight of the window where it hung was a house occupied by a handful of courageous young women, who settled there a couple of years ago, to see what they could do among the children on the other tack. They had a different story to tell. Having once gained their confidence they had found boys and girls most eager to learn from them the ways of polite society. Perhaps that may be thought not the highest of aims ; but it will hardly be denied that to find a girl who was fighting in the street yesterday, to-day busying herself with the anxious inquiry whether it is proper, at table, to take bread from the plate with the fingers or with the fork, argues progress ; or to see the battle-scarred young tough who a month ago sat on the table with cigar in his mouth, hat on the back of his head, and kicked his heels, who was ashamed to own where he lived, and so terrorized the others with his scowl that the boy who knew said he would get killed if he told—to see this product of the street with carefully brushed clothes, a clean collar, and a human smile inviting the lady manager to the foot-ball game because he knew she was from Princeton and a partisan, and what is more, escorting her there like a gentleman.

In the wise plan of these reformers the gang became the club that weaned the boys from the street. The " Hero Club " and the " Knights of the Round Table " took the place of the Junk Gang and its allies. They wrote their own laws, embodying a clause to expel any disorderly member, and managed them with firmness. True knights were they after their fashion, loyal to the house that sheltered them, and ever on the alert to repel invasion. Sinful as it was in their code not to " swipe " or " hook " a chicken or anything left lying around loose within their bailiwick, if any outsider employed their tactics to the damage of the house, or of anything befriended by it, they would swoop down upon him with swift vengeance and bring him in captive to be delivered over to punishment. And when one of their friends hung out her shingle in another street, with the word " doctor " over the bell, woe to the urchin

The " Soup-House Gang."
Class in History in the Duane Street Newsboys' Lodging-house.

who even glanced at that when the gang pulled all the other bells
in the block and laughed at the wrath of the tenants. One luckless
chap forgot himself far enough to yank it one night, and immediately an angry cry went up from the gang: "Who pulled dat
bell?" "Mickey did," was the answer, and Mickey's howls an-

nounced to the amused doctor the next minute that he had been
"slugged" and she avenged. This doctor's account of the first
formal call of the gang in the block was highly amusing. It called
in a body and showed a desire to please that tried the host's nerves
not a little. The boys vied with each other in recounting for her
entertainment their encounters with the police enemy, and in exhibiting their intimate knowledge of the wickedness of the slums
in minutest detail. One, who was scarcely twelve years old, and
had lately moved from Bayard Street, knew all the ins and outs of
the Chinatown opium dives, and painted them in glowing colors.
The doctor listened with half-amused dismay, and when the boys
rose to go told them she was glad they had called. So were they,
they said, and they guessed they would call again the next night.

"Oh! don't come to-morrow," said the doctor, in something of a
fright; "come next week!" She was relieved upon hearing the
leader of the gang reproving the rest of the fellows for their want
of style. He bowed with great precision and announced that he
would call "in about two weeks."

I am sorry to say that the *entente cordiale* of the establishment
was temporarily disturbed recently by a strike of the "Hero Club,"
or the "Knights," I forget which. The managers received their
first intimation that trouble was brewing in the resignation of the
leader. It came by letter, in very dignified form. "My apprehen-
sions is now something eligible," he wrote. The ladies decided,
after thinking the matter over, that he meant that he was looking
for something better, and they translated the message correctly.
There came shortly, from the disaffected element he had gathered
around him, a written demand for the organization of a new club to
be called "the Gentlemen's Sons' Association;" among the objects
this: "Furthermore, that we may participate hereafter to commem-
orate with the doings of a gentleman." The request was refused,
and the boys went on strike, threatening to start their club elsewhere. The ladies met the crisis firmly. They sent a walking
delegate to the boys with the message that if they could organize a

strike, they, on their side, could organize a lock-out. There the matter rested when I last heard of it.

The testimony of these workers agrees with that of most others who reach the girls at an age when they are yet manageable, that the most abiding results follow with them, though they are harder to get at. The boys respond more readily, but also more easily fall from grace. The same good and bad traits are found in both ; the same trying superficiality, the same generous helpfulness, characteristic of the poor everywhere. Out of the depth of their bitter poverty I saw the children in the West Fifty-second Street Industrial School, last Thanksgiving, bring for the relief of the aged and helpless, and those even poorer than they, such gifts as they could —a handful of ground coffee in a paper bag, a couple of Irish potatoes, a little sugar or flour, and joyfully offer to carry them home. It was on such a trip I found little Katie, aged nine, in a Forty-ninth Street tenement, keeping house for her older sister and two brothers, all of whom worked in the hammock factory, earning from $4.50 to $1.50 a week. They had moved together when their mother died and the father brought home another wife. Their combined income was something like $9.50 a week, and the simple furniture was bought on instalment. But it was all clean, if poor. Katie did the cleaning and the cooking of the plain kind. She scrubbed and swept and went to school, all as a matter of course, and ran the house generally. In her person and work she answered the question sometimes asked, why we hear so much about the boys and so little of the girls ; because the home claims their work much earlier and to a much greater extent, while the boys are turned out to shift for themselves, and because therefore their miseries are so much more common-place, and proportionally uninteresting. It is woman's lot to suffer in silence. If occasionally she makes herself heard in querulous protest; if injustice long borne gives her tongue a sharper edge than the occasion seems to require, it can at least be said in her favor that her bark is much worse than her bite. The missionary who complains that the wife nags her husband to

the point of making the saloon his refuge, or the sister her brother
until he flees to the street, bears testimony in the same breath to
her readiness to sit up all night to mend the clothes of the scamp
she so hotly denounces. Sweetness of temper or of speech is not a
distinguishing feature of tenement-house life, any more among the
children than with their elders. In a party sent out by our committee for a summer vacation on a Jersey farm, last summer, was a
little knot of six girls from the Seventh Ward. They had not been
gone three days before a letter came from one of them to the
mother of one of the others. "Mrs. Reilly," it read, "if you have
any sinse you will send for your child." That they would all be
murdered was the sense the frightened mother made out of it. The
six came home post haste, the youngest in a state of high dudgeon
at her sudden translation back to the tenement. The lonesomeness
of the farm had frightened the others. She was little more than a
baby, and her desire to go back was explained by one of the rescued ones thus : " She sat two mortil hours at the table a stuffin' of
herself, till the missus she says, says she, ' Does yer mother lave ye
to sit that long at the table, sis ? ' "

Not rarely does this child of common clay rise to a height of
heroism that discovers depths of feeling and character full of unsuspected promise. Two or three winters ago a midnight fire,
started by a fiend in human shape, destroyed a tenement in Hester
Street, killing a number of the tenants. On the fourth floor the
firemen found one of these penned in with his little girl and helped
them to the window. As they were handing out the child she broke
away from them suddenly and stepped back into the smoke to what
seemed certain death. The firemen, climbing after, groped around
shouting for her to come back. Half-way across the room they
came upon her, gasping and nearly smothered, dragging a doll's
trunk over the floor.

"I could not leave it," she said, thrusting it at the men as they
seized her ; "my mother——"

They flung the box angrily through the window. It fell crash-

Present Tenants of John Ericsson's Old House, now the Beach Street Industrial School.

ing on the sidewalk, and, breaking open, revealed no doll or finery, but the deed for her dead mother's grave. Little Bessie had not forgotten her, despite her thirteen years.

It is the tenement setting that stamps the child's life with the vicious touch which is sometimes only the caricature of the virtues of a better soil.   Under the rough burr lie undeveloped qualities of good and of usefulness, rather perhaps of the capacity for them, which, if the testimony of observers on the other side be true, one shall vainly seek in their brothers and sisters of the Old-World slums.   It may be, as I have had occasion to observe before, that the reason must be sought in the greater age of the breed over there, and that we are observing here the beginning of a process of deterioration that shall eventually land us where they are, unless the inroads of the tenement be checked by the preventive measures of which I have spoken.   The testimony of a teacher for twenty-five years in one of the ragged schools, who has seen the shanty neighborhood that surrounded her at the start give place to mile-long rows of big tenements, is positive on this point.   With the disappearance of the shanties—homesteads in effect, however humble —and the coming of the tenement crowds, there has been a distinct descent in the scale of refinement among the children, if one may use the term.   The crowds and the loss of home privacy, with the increased importance of the street as a factor, account for it.   The general tone has been lowered, while at the same time, by reason of the greater rescue efforts put forward, the original amount of ignorance has been reduced.   The big loafer of the old day, who could neither read nor write, has been eliminated to a large extent. Nearly all the children get now some schooling, if not much ; and the proportion of child offenders annually arraigned in the courts has been materially reduced.   There is compensation in this ; whether enough to make up for what is lost, time and the amount of effort put forth to turn the scales for good will show.

Drunkenness is the vice that wrecks that half of the homes of the poor which do not cause it.   It is that which, in nine cases out of ten, drives the boy to the street and the girl to a life of shame. No end of sad cases could be quoted in support of this statement. I can here only refer those who wish to convince themselves of its truth to the records of the Society for the Prevention of Cruelty to Children, the Five Points House of Industry, the Reformatory, and a score of other charitable and correctional institutions. I have been at some pains to satisfy myself on the point by tracing back, as far as I was able—by no means an easy task—the careers of the boys I met in the lodging-houses that are set as traps for them, where they have their run, chiefly down around the newspaper of-fices. In seven cases out of ten it was the same story : a drunken father or mother made the street preferable to the home—never home in anything but name—and to the street they went. In the other cases death had, perhaps, broken up the family and thrown the boys upon the world. That was the story of one of the boys I tried to photograph at a quiet game of " craps " in the wash-room of the Duane Street lodging-house—James Brady. Father and mother had both died two months after they came here from Ire-land, and he went forth from the tenement alone and without a friend, but not without courage. He just walked on until he stumbled on the lodging-house and fell into a job of selling papers. James, at the age of sixteen, was being initiated into the mysteries of the alphabet in the evening school. He was not sure that he liked it. The German boy who took a hand in the game, and who made his grub and his bed-money, when he was lucky, by picking up junk, had just such a career. The third, the bootblack, gave his reasons briefly for running away from his Philadelphia home : " Me muther wuz all the time hittin' me when I cum in the house, so I cum away." So did a German boy I met there, if for a slightly different reason. He was fresh from over the sea, and had not yet learned a word of English. In his own tongue he told why he came. His father sent him to a gymnasium, but the Latin was " zu schwer" for him, and " der Herr Papa sagt' heraus ! " He was evi-dently a boy of good family, but slow. His father could have taken no better course, certainly, to cure him of that defect, if he did not mind the danger of it.

Two little brothers, who attracted my attention by the sturdy way in which they held together, back to back, against the world, as it were, had a different story to tell. Their mother died, and their father, who worked in a gas-house, broke up the household, unable to maintain it. The boys, eleven and thirteen years old,

A Warm Corner for Newsboys on a Cold Night.

went out to shift for themselves, while he made his home in a Bowery lodging-house. The oldest of the brothers was then earning three dollars a week in a factory; the younger was selling newspapers and making out. The day I first saw him he came in from his route early—it was raining hard—to get dry trousers out for his brother against the time he should be home from the factory. There was no doubt the two would hew their way through the world together. The right stuff was in them, as in the two other lads, also brothers, I found in the Tompkins Square lodging-house. Their parents had both died, leaving them to care for a palsied sister and a little brother. They sent the little one to school and went to work for the sister. Their combined earnings at the shop were just enough to support her and one of the brothers who stayed with her. The other went to the lodging-house, where he could live for eighteen cents a day, turning the rest of his earnings into the family fund. With this view of these homeless lads, the one who goes much among them is not surprised to hear of their clubbing together, as they did in the Seventh Avenue lodging-house, to fit out a little ragamuffin, who was brought in shivering from the street, with a suit of clothes. There was not one in the crowd that chipped in who had a whole coat to his back.

It was in this lodging-house I first saw Buffalo. He was presented to me the night I took the picture of my little vegetable-peddling friend, Edward, asleep on the front bench in evening-school. Edward was nine years old and an orphan, but hard at work every day earning his own living by shouting from a pedler's cart. He could not be made to sit for his picture, and I took him at a disadvantage—in a double sense, for he had not made his toilet; it was in the days of the threatened water-famine, and the boys had been warned not to waste water in washing, an injunction they cheerfully obeyed. I was anxious not to have the boy disturbed, so the spelling-class went right on while I set up the camera. It was an original class, original in its answers as in its looks. This was what I heard while I focused on poor Eddie:

The teacher: "Cheat! spell cheat."

Boy spells correctly.

Teacher: "Right! What is it to cheat?"

Boy: "To skin one, like Tommy——"

The teacher cut the explanation short, and ordering up another boy, bade him spell " nerve." He did it.

" What is nerve ? " demanded the teacher ; " what does it mean ? "

" Cheek ! don't you know," said the boy, and at that moment I caught Buffalo blacking my sleeping pedler's face with ink, just in time to prevent his waking him up. Then it was that I heard the disturber's story. He *was* a character, and no mistake. He had run away from Buffalo, whence his name, " beating " his way down on the trains until he reached New York. He " shined " around until he got so desperately hard up that he had to sell his kit. Just about then he was discovered by an artist, who paid him to sit for him in his awful rags, with his tousled hair that had not known the restraint of a cap for months. " Oh ! it was a daisy job," sighed Buffalo, at the recollection. He had only to sit still and crack jokes. Alas ! Buffalo's first effort at righteousness upset him. He had been taught in the lodging-house that to be clean was the first requisite of a gentleman, and on his first pay-day he went bravely, eschewing " craps," and bought himself a new coat and had his hair cut. When, beaming with pride, he presented himself at the studio in his new character, the artist turned him out as no longer of any use to him. I am afraid that Buffalo's ambition to be " like

" Buffalo."

folks" received a shock by this mysterious misfortune that will prevent his ever attaining the level where he may join the class in history that goes by the attractive name of the "Soup-house Gang" in the Duane Street lodging-house school. And it is too bad, for the class is proficient, if it *is* in its shirt-sleeves, and has at least a couple of members who will certainly make their mark.

In the summer a good many of the boys sleep in the street; it is coolest there, and it costs nothing if one can get out of the sight of the policeman. In winter they seek the lodging-houses or curl themselves up on the steam-pipes in the newspaper offices that open their doors after midnight. They are hunted nowadays so persistently by the police and by the agents of the Society for the Prevention of Cruelty to Children, that very few escape altogether. In the lodging-houses they are made to go to school. There are enough of them always whom nobody owns; but the great mass of the boys and girls who cry their "extrees!" on the street are children with homes, who thus contribute to the family earnings and sleep out, if they do, because they have either not sold their papers or gambled away the money at craps, and are afraid to go home. It was for such a reason little Giuseppe Margalto and his chum made their bed in the ventilating chute at the post-office on the night General Sherman died, and were caught by the fire that broke out in the mail-room toward midnight. Giuseppe was burned to death; the other escaped to bring the news to the dark Crosby Street alley in which he had lived. Giuseppe did not die his cruel death in vain. A much stricter watch has been kept since upon the boys, and they are no longer allowed to sleep in many places to which they formerly had access. The purpose is to corral the homeless element in the lodging-houses; and but for the neighboring Bowery "hotels" that beckon the older boys with their promise of greater freedom, it would probably be successfully attained.

Even with this drawback, the figures of the Children's Aid Society show that progress is being made. While in 1881 its

9

lodging-houses sheltered 14,452 children, of whom 13,155 were boys
and 1,287 girls, in 1891, though more than 500,000 had been added
to the city's population, the number of child-lodgers had fallen to
11,770, only 335 of whom were girls. The whole number of children sheltered in the six houses, in twelve years, to 1891, was 149,-
994, among them 8,820 girls. The problem is a great one, but the
efforts on foot to solve it are as great, and growing. That the beginning must be made with the children in the battle with poverty
and ignorance and crime was recognized long ago. It has been
made ; and we know now that through them the rampart next to
be taken—the home—is reached. It has been a forty years' war,
and it is only just begun. But the first blow, as the old saying
runs, is half the battle, and it has been struck in New York, and
struck to win.

THE STORY OF THE FRESH-AIR FUND

By WILLARD PARSONS

MANAGER

The Foundation of the Fund—The Post and Tribune—Statistics of the Fund—Excursions—The Provision for Entertaining the Children—How the Excursions are Managed—Typical Letters—Effect of the Children's Outings—Some "Fresh-Air Boys"—The Physician's Report—Fresh-Air Funds in Other Cities—Development of the Plan.

IN the summer of 1877, when pastor of a small church in Sherman, Pa., I came to New York and gathered a little company of the poorest and most needy children I could find. They were taken out among my people, who were waiting to receive them as their guests for a fortnight during the midsummer heat. Others took the place of the first company; and at the end of the season the good people had entertained sixty poor city children for a fortnight each; and that, too, without any compensation save the consciousness of having done a simple Christ-like act of charity to one in need. This somewhat novel experiment of taking little ones from the wretched city tenements to comfortable country homes was a most gratifying success.

The object first aimed at was the physical improvement of the poor. It was only after months of earnest thought and careful planning that the Fresh-Air project was launched, even in this small way. The work was started with the hope of proving that bodies diseased, enfeebled by poor and insufficient food and foul air, could be benefited by a two weeks' stay in better surroundings.

In the plan of carrying on this experiment, there were three main factors to be considered, viz.: 1. To get the money. 2. To find the temporary homes. 3. To select the children.

First, as to raising the money: It was an easy matter, after the success of the first season, to induce the New York *Evening Post* to take up the enterprise, and raise the necessary fund to carry on and enlarge it, which it did successfully for four years.

When the plan of continuing the enterprise was discussed in the spring of 1882, the friends of the "Fund" most heartily welcomed the willingness of the New York *Tribune* to take it up; and it was then transferred from the *Evening Post* to the *Tribune*. By the law of natural selection such a humane undertaking will best crystallize around a journal of the character of the *Tribune*. The large circulation of that newspaper and its well-known interest in philanthropic labors of like character, together with the high class people the journal reaches, have given the best possible support to the "Fresh-Air Fund."

Money in abundance for all possible needs has always been forthcoming. The mere statement in the *Tribune* that $3.00 would give a poor child a fortnight in the country has been all that was necessary to fill the treasury. It is a most significant fact that more than three hundred thousand dollars have been sent as *voluntary* contributions, and it has never been necessary to employ any collectors.

Every sort of entertainment has been given to swell the fund, from children selling pin-wheels and wild flowers by the wayside, netting, perhaps, a few coppers, to the more pretentious fair and festival, netting its hundreds of dollars; from the boys' circus in the barn to the finished entertainments in public halls. Children have pulled weeds in the garden and boys gone without their Fourth of July fire-crackers; the small savings-bank of the dead child has often been sent to bring life and happiness to the poor sick one; in fact, from Maine to California, from Canada to Florida, from South America, from the Old World, and even from Africa, have come voluntary contributions to carry on this most humane work among the poor of our overcrowded city.

Beginning in a very unobtrusive way—at first with a party of only nine children, and, as I have said, with sixty for the entire season—the work has grown steadily and rapidly till it has greatly exceeded the wildest dreams of its manager. The growth of the scheme from its inception is best illustrated by the following table:

	Number sent to the country for two weeks.	Number sent out for one day.	Total number of beneficiaries	Expenditures.	Average cost per capita.
1877.......	60	....	60	$187 62	$3 12
1878.......	1,077	....	1,077	2,980 29	2 77
1879.......	2,400	....	2,400	6,511 54	2 71
1880.......	2,500	600	3,100	8,519 71	3 55
1881.......	3,203	1,000	4,203	8,217 64	2 54
1882.......	5,500	....	5,500	21,325 06	2 85
1883.......	4,250	5,700	9,950	14,908 69	3 36
1884.......	6,253	1,000	7,253	18,756 14	3 00
1885.......	6,650	6,073	12,723	19,863 95	2 98
1886.......	8,336	1,600	9,936	24,092 09	2 89
1887.......	7,748	....	7,748	22,783 85	2 94
1888.......	10,920	...	10,920	25,636 64	2 35
1889.......	10,352	....	10,352	24,978 29	2 42
1890.......	11,193	18,029	29,222	23,804 11	2 12
1891.......	13,568	22,088	35,656	28,068 28	2 03
1892.......	15,236	25,560	40,796	27,925 51	1 83
1893.......	13,846	26,329	40,175	26,620 75	1 92
1894.......	10,171	28,432	40,850	22,809 60	2 24
Totals	133,263	136,411	269,674	$327,989 74	$2 46

It is thus seen that during its eighteen years 133,263 children have been sent to the country for a fortnight's vacation, at a total cost of $327,989.74, or at an average cost of $2.46 per capita. Besides this, 136,411 have been taken out for a day's trip, which makes the total number of beneficiaries 269,674. The entire expenses of the day excursions have been borne by one gentleman, and are not included in the table of expenditures.

The various transportation companies cheerfully make large reductions from the regular fare. No salaries or office expenses are ever paid from the fund, and many helpers voluntarily give their services. Who can instance a charity where $2.46 invested will do as much good?

The second question is most constantly asked: "How do you find the temporary homes for the children?" I have never found any value in circulars, and but very little response even to personal letters. I have only found success by personal appeals. Among my own parishioners a practical interest was aroused as soon as I had shown them something of the condition of the poor children in the tenements, and the simple plan of relief was most heartily adopted. After the success of the experiment, other communities were more easily interested and were quite ready to offer hospitality.

I begin early in April a systematic visitation from town to town. A call is made on the various clergymen, the editor of the local paper, and, if possible, a few of the leading citizens. A brief explanation of the work—a few words to show the condition and needs of the tenement-house children and the great benefit of a fortnight's trip, are usually sufficient to awaken a practical interest. Then a local committee is appointed and the success or failure in that community is due, to a large extent, to the zeal and earnestness of this committee. The local committee finds out how many children can be provided for, and, when ready for their company, reports the result and arranges with the manager the various details for their coming. Every possible opportunity for getting a knowledge of the work before the people is seized upon. At any and every sort of public meeting that can be heard of, permission is asked to present the cause. Almost without exception, a few minutes are granted.

Since the charity has grown to such proportions it is not possible for me to give much time to the country visitations, and several people who are thoroughly familiar with my methods, and in whom I have perfect confidence, have been most successful in arousing an interest in the cause in the country. A railway ticket given is often the only expense necessary to send some of the city missionaries, physicians, or clergymen into their native regions, where (with an extended acquaintance among the people) it is easy to induce them to throw wide open their hospitable doors. In every case there is a great deal in personal solicitation.

In answer to the third question, I may say that it is no easy matter to select the children for these trips. Everyone who has had the care of getting a band of children ready for the country will most readily testify to the truth of this statement. Last summer more than two hundred workers among the poor aided in the selecting and preparing the children for the country. These workers are from the Church Missions, Bible Missions, Hospitals, Dispensaries, Industrial Schools, Day Nurseries, Model Tenement Houses, and kindred organizations. When the local committee has reported the number they can receive their list is apportioned among those who have children to send. A record is kept of all organizations and individuals who apply for a share in the benefits, and the first one to apply is called upon for children for the first company to start. Before the season is over all have abundant opportunity to send their most needy ones. The children selected manifest all degrees of ignorance of the country—from those who imagine they know all about it, having played under the trees in a city square, to the boy who was shown a large herd of Alderneys by his farmer-host, and, after intently watching them chew the cud, asked, " Say, mister, do you have to buy gum for all them cows to chew ? "

Those who apply for a chance to send their children to the country are instructed that they must be poor and needy, without any infectious disease, clean, and free from vermin. A physician then inspects each child. Dr. C. C. Vinton was the examining physician in 1890, and he examined nearly fifteen thousand children, of whom about five thousand were sent into the country. Each day the Board of Health furnished a list of the houses where there was any contagious disease; which was of immense help. With that list before him, it was easy for the examiner to stop any child

who came from an infected house. The majority were refused on
account of their hopeless condition as to vermin. It is a herculean
task to get the average tenement-house child in a suitable condition
to be received into country families.

   What is the effect of entertaining these poor children upon their
country hosts ? Will they receive such guests a second time in
their homes ? Is there no danger in bringing children directly out
of their low surroundings into families where the children are so
differently trained ?

The danger is much less than would at first appear. Those who
select the children are, for the most part, trained workers who have
a personal knowledge of each child and its surrounding, and they
send only such as are considered somewhat fitted to enter the new
home. The judgment of these Christian workers is by no means
infallible, yet the average result is remarkably good. The children
are on their good behavior. Self-respect is engendered. The entirely new and comfortable surroundings usually bring out the
best in the child, and the fortnight's vacation is over before the
novelty has worn off.

A clergyman in northern New York, after having entertained one
hundred children, wrote as follows : "They have left a rich blessing behind them, and they actually gave more than they received.
They have touched the hearts of the people and opened the foun-
tains of love, sympathy, and charity. The people have read about
the importance of benevolence, and have heard many sermons on
the beauty of charity ; but these have been quickly forgotten. The
children have been an object-lesson that will long live in their
hearts and minds."

"We want to thank you," wrote another minister from Massachusetts, "for giving us this opportunity to do so much good.
Any inconvenience to which we have been put during the two
weeks is insignificant now, as we look at these thirty glad faces and
think of the purifying and strengthening influences that have come

into their young lives during these two weeks' stay with us."
These two letters are fair samples of hundreds of others I receive
every year.

Many people become strongly attached to the children, and follow them into their wretched homes with letters and substantial
gifts. These country letters are highly prized and religiously
guarded. Nearly two thousand of these letters were forwarded to
me last year, containing invitations for the child to repeat the visit.
I can now recall no community where hospitality has been given
once, but that some children have been invited back the following
years.

The success of the charity turns upon the country friends' willingness to receive the children into their homes, and as yet they
have shown no signs of being weary in this service; each year the
number of free places has increased. To the hospitable country
family the largest share of the work has fallen, both in practical
care and personal touch. To them belongs the greatest credit!
They have given hospitality and a rich personal service during the
busiest days of the year. It is given too—not grudgingly, but with
wonderful heartiness.

Nothing has ever so strengthened my faith in humanity as the
kind and loving way the country people have received these
stranger guests.

Is there in the fortnight's outing for the poor anything more
than a merely pleasant holiday? What good can accrue from taking a child out of its wretched home, and after two weeks of comfort and decent living, sending it back to its old surroundings?
One minister writes: "It will only make the child discontented
with the surroundings where God placed him."

I contend that a great gain has been made, if you can only succeed in making the tenement-house child thoroughly discontented
with his lot. There is some hope then of his getting out of it and
rising to a higher plane. The new life he sees in the country, the

contact with good people, not at arm's length, but in their homes; not at the dinner, feast, or entertainment given to him while the giver stands by and looks *down* to see how he enjoys it, and remarks on his forlorn appearance; but brought into the family and given a seat at the table, where, as one boy wrote home, " I can have two pieces of pie if I want, and nobody says nothing if I take three pieces of cake; " or, as a little girl reported, where " We have lots to eat, and so much to eat that we could not tell you how much we get to eat."

This is quite a different kind of service, and has resulted in the complete transformation of many a child. It has gone back to its wretchedness, to be sure, but in hundreds of instances about which I have personally known it has returned with head and heart full of new ways, new ideas of decent living, and has successfully taught the shiftless parents the better way. One little girl talked so much of her trip and described the country life in such glowing terms, that her father came to inquire where it was his child went, adding, " I should think it was Heaven, from the way she talks about it."

Many a girl has begun, immediately on her return, to persuade her mother to adopt the ways of the country mother. In scores of instances that have come under my personal observation, children have become so delighted with the country life, with its possibilities for the poor, that they have persuaded the family to migrate, the country friends gladly helping them to a home, and giving work to make them independent.

One of the most serious problems of country life is to get help for the necessary household work; to be sure the few hundred people that have been helped by this charity to locate permanently in the country is but a drop in the bucket, and does not go far toward solving the " help " question; still it is a little aid in the right direction.

Even supposing it was nothing but a bright and pleasant holiday, and that after the two weeks of good and wholesome food, with pure air to breathe, the children were to go back to their old life—that is no small gain. We who do not live in tenements and, perhaps, are not obliged to work till the cheek grows pale, never think of objecting, when it comes our time for a fortnight's rest, because after the holiday we must return to our toilsome place. The change is thought necessary for those who have everything to make it least necessary ; then certainly the holiday is none the less beneficial for those whose whole life has been simply an exhausting battle with fearful odds against them.

A physician tells us we must take the loved one to a different climate if we would save his life, and we lose no time in obeying his orders. To thousands of the poor the same words have been spoken. The same change was the only hope; and the only change possible was, perhaps, a ride on the ferry-boat. To thousands of poor mothers the physicians have said, "Your child only needs pure air, with wholesome and nutritious food." Perhaps delicacies to tempt the appetite have been ordered when only the plainest and coarsest necessaries are procurable. In thousands of such cases the Fresh-Air Fund has come to the rescue, and given both the pure air and the wholesome food, with results most happy.

Let me give two or three instances where the moral influences exerted by the simple and kindly life (sometimes with eccentric people), have resulted most happily on the child.

In 1878 a Mrs. Y——, who was noted far and wide for her penuriousness, wrote me : " Homes are ready with me for two boys and two girls, if your work is for the *virtuous class of unfortunate children*. Please be plain and frank in the matter, for I don't wish to have anything to do with a work that is not *all right*. *God give you wisdom.*" The italics are not mine. Someone had frightened her by the statement that all the poor city children were illegitimate.

One of the quartet sent to this place was a little fellow from one of the most wretched homes that drink has caused. The boy had never before known kind treatment, and the pure, simple, and wholesome life, with the abundant food of the hillside farm, stirred his nature to the very depths and called out all his latent energies. A few months ago, while in a bank, a well-dressed fellow immediately behind me in the line, reached out his hand, saying:

"I suppose you don't know me; but I am Henry C——."

"Why," said I, "you must be the boy that Mrs. Y—— spanked and fitted out with a complete suit of homespun, with the jacket sleeves of a different color!"

"Yes, I am the identical boy. I can't tell whether it was due to the spanking or to the Joseph - like coat, but that two weeks changed my whole life. I went to work when I came back, and have been with the same firm ever since. See here," said he, and he opened his bank-book, showing several thousand dollars he was about to deposit for the firm, "don't that look as though the firm had confidence in me? I literally came up out of the very lowest slums, and my present prosperous condition is due to the interest that family in the country has always taken in me since my visit with them in 1878."

In the earlier days of the work a bright boy of ten was one of a company invited to Schoharie County, N. Y. He endeared himself so thoroughly to his entertainers, who " live in a white house with green blinds and Christmas-trees all around it," that they asked and received permission to keep the lad permanently. The following is an exact copy of a part of the letter he wrote home after he had been for a few months in his new home:

DEAR MOTHER

i am still to Mrs. D—— and i was so Busy that i Could not Write Sooner i drive the horses and put up the Cows and clean out the Cow Stable i am all well i pick stones and i have an apple tree 6 Feet High and I have got a pair of new pants and a new Coat and a pair of Suspenders and Mr. D —— is getting a pair of New Boots made for me We killed one pig and one Cow i am going to plow a little piece of land and plant Some Corn. When Mr. D—— killed the Cow i helped and Mr. D—— had to take the Cow skin to be taned to make leather and Mr. D—— gave the man Cow skin for leather to make me Boots i am going to school to-morrow and i want to tell lizzie—pauline—Charlie— Christie—maggie—george and you to all write to me and if they all do when Christmas Comes i will send all of you something nice if my uncle frank comes to see yous you must tell him to write to me i Close my letter

From your oldest son A——.

A year after that time the mother died. Some time afterward an uncle began writing for the lad to come back to the city— he coveted his small earnings. But the little fellow had sense enough to see that he was better off where he was. Finally the uncle went after the boy, and told him his brother was dying in the hospital, and was calling constantly for him. Under such circumstances his foster parents readily gave him permission to return with the uncle for a visit. Before they reached the city, the uncle told him he should never go back. He sent him to work at Eleventh Avenue and Twenty-ninth Street, in a work-room situated in the cellar, and his bedroom, like those in most tenement-houses, had no outside window. The third day he was sent upstairs on an errand, and as soon as he saw the open door he bolted. He remembered that a car that passed Fourth Street and Avenue C, would take him to the People's Line for Albany. He ran with all his might to Fourth Street, and then followed the car-tracks till he saw on the large flag "Peoples' Line." He told part of his story to the clerk, and finally added, "I am one of Mr. Parsons' Fresh-Air boys, and I have got to go to Albany." That settled the matter, and the clerk readily gave him a pass. A gentleman standing by gave him a quarter for his supper. He held on to his appetite as well as his quarter; and in the morning laid his twenty-five cents before the ticket agent at Albany, and called for a ticket to R——, a small place fifty miles distant. He got the ticket. After a few miles' walk from R—— he reached his new home safely, and there he proposed to stay. He said he would take to the woods if his uncle came after him again. This transpired fourteen years ago.

Several years ago, a letter came from the young fellow. He is now an active Christian, married, and worth property, and expects in a few years to have his farm all paid for.

Not long ago I was stopped on Broadway by a well-dressed and prosperous-looking young man.

"I am one of your Fresh-Air boys—I am John ——." I readily recalled the boy. In 1878 he was one of a party taken to central New York. It had been a hot and very dusty ride, and at the end of the journey this Five Points boy looked so thoroughly disreputable, that the person who was to take him utterly refused to accept such a dirty and ill-looking boy. The tears of the lad, when he found that no one wanted him, flowed in streams down his dirty face, while the two tear-washed streaks, the red and white and black spots about his eyes and mouth, gave him a most unpromising look. Before I reached the hotel with the sobbing and "left over" boy a man came out of a small butcher shop, and so heartily and kindly invited the boy to stay with him that the tears ceased instantly. A thorough bath and a new suit made a wonderful transformation. The family took a great interest in and became strongly attached to him. The change from the wretched Cherry Street tenement, with its drunken and often brutal parents, to the clean and cheerful family of the butcher, where he was kindly treated, made a strong impression. The family kept track of the boy by corresponding with him, and have claimed a visit from him every year since. He is now married, lives in a comfortable flat, and has a good position as a commercial traveller.

Each child was chosen the first year on account of its physical needs. The late Dr. White, of Brooklyn, most carefully examined every child sent out, the entire sixty having passed through his hands. He kept a careful record, and the following extracts from a report which he submitted to a medical society will show the success of the undertaking on its physical side:

All were taken from the very poor, though not from the class that usually beg from door to door. They were selected mainly with reference to their physical condition, and were suffering more or less with some chronic disease, born of neglect, privation, filth, and foul air. Prominent among the diseases represented were scrofula, consumption, chronic bronchitis, asthma, hip-joint, and spinal troubles. Among them were confirmed cripples, as well as those in the incipient stage of more or less incurable diseases ; while others were simply in bad health, delicate, or sickly, the result of impure air or insufficient and improper food. Enfeebled by want and disease, bred in poverty and filth, no wonder their faces, for the most part, were thin, pale, and haggard, and even their smiles feeble and sickly.

Of the effects of the trips he says generally :

Appetites improved, coughs ceased to be troublesome, ulcers healed, growing deformities were arrested, cheeks filled out and grew ruddy, spirits became buoyant, the step elastic and childlike, while the sickly smile gave place to the hearty laugh of childhood; or, as very happily expressed by a friend, " They went out men and women—they came back little children."

To the educated physicians to whom the report was addressed this general statement meant a good deal more than the words indicate to most laymen. We who are not physicians do not understand as physicians do how important the general building up of the system is in the treatment of positive disease, and very few persons not trained in the medical schools would think of a hygienic vacation as an effective method of treating physical deformity. In such a case we should hope to make the unfortunate child happier, perhaps, by sending him to the country, but beyond that we should not venture to hope for good. Yet here is what the physician reported to his associates of such a case :

Another marked case of improvement was a boy, five years of age, who had been suffering more than a year with disease of the upper dorsal vertebræ. The disease had been detected in its earliest stages, and as the mother, a widow with five young children, was very poor and unable to give proper care or suitable food to the little patient, I had him sent to a hospital established for treating such cases, expecting he would receive such special treatment as his case required. After a residence of some months in the hospital, finding that nothing was done for him excepting allowing him to live there, and that he was constantly growing worse, the mother clandestinely brought him away. I found him in constant pain, nights restless and sleepless, appetite gone, emaciation extreme, and deformity increasing. In that condition he went to the country with his little brother, seven years old, for nurse and guardian. A few weeks' residence there produced a marvellous change. He came back hale and hearty, health completely established—his spinal trouble arrested—indeed, cured.

That little fellow's cure cost some contributor to the fund about three dollars, and a family in the country a fortnight's hospitality.

The following are additional extracts from Dr. White's interesting report:

The whole number selected under my own supervision was sixty. As to diseases, they were classified as follows:

General debility	31
Deformities	7
Hip-joint disease	5
Spinal disease	2
Knee-joint disease	1
Consumption	5
Bronchitis	4
Chorea	3
Chronic ulcers	2
Total	60

All those whose health was being slowly undermined by living in the impure air of crowded and badly ventilated apartments, or from insufficient and improper food, as well as those enfeebled by a previous attack of some acute disease, were classed under the head of General Debility, without reference to the cause of their physical condition. Nearly all of this class returned home completely restored to health. All others were greatly benefited by the trip, and, if not cured, in many cases with disease arrested for the time being at least. All the cases of consumption improved. One young woman, aged twenty-three, inheriting phthisis from her mother, and suffering for more than a year with hemorrhages, harassing cough, and profuse expectoration, was so exhausted by the trip on the Annex to the Erie Railroad depot that Mr. Parsons had misgivings about the propriety of her going on, fearing the result. She was carried through safely, though soon after arriving at her destination an attack of hemorrhage prostrated her still more. She returned, after an absence of six weeks, literally another being, resuming labor which sickness had interrupted, in the shop where she still continues to work.

I afterward learned that the family who had entertained this girl were straining every nerve to save enough to pay interest on borrowed money, and thus avert the sale of their farm. While writing this article I have heard that this girl is now living in a comfortable home of her own, apparently as well as any one ; and it was only last summer that the eldest of her four children enjoyed the farmer's hospitality. It may be of interest to add, that a lady, who had been interested in this girl, when she heard of the farmer's financial condition, made a most substantial gift to help him out of his difficulty.

Dr. White also says in his report that "very marked improvement was observed in nearly all cases of joint and spinal diseases."

I have given more space to this report of the first year of the work for the simple reason that when but few children were sent out, it was comparatively easy to watch the results closely. Now, while many thousands are sent each year, selected by about two hundred different workers, it is far more difficult and well-nigh impossible to have a personal knowledge of many of the children. Yet I am fully convinced that when the children are carefully chosen the same good results always obtain. The following brief reports from responsible people, thoroughly familiar with the work, surely support this conviction :

The superintendent of one of the missions that has sent a large number of children into the country says : "In the fall I can tell, by just looking in their faces, which of the children have been in the country. They are fatter, ruddier, and their whole expression is changed and improved."

The superintendent of another of the Church Missions, who is also a physician, told me that he selected the weakly ones each year for the country trip, and he found the benefit so great that they were the stronger ones during the winter. He instanced several cases where particularly puny children, predisposed to nervous and lung difficulties, had been entirely restored to robust health.

One of the missionary nurses said to me recently : "There are
10

about two hundred children sent to the country from our mission each year. These nearly all live in the crowded tenements where four families occupy each floor. I constantly visit among the sick in these poor families, and I notice that those children who had a fortnight in the country are much stronger physically, and the improved condition lasts during the winter."

The chairman of the local committee in one village community weighed every child in the party on arrival, and again after fourteen days in the country. The average age was ten years. The least gain was shown in a four-year-old boy, who added only one pound to his weight. The greatest by an eleven-year-old girl, who gained nine pounds. The average gain for the entire party was four and nine-tenths pounds.

A missionary from one of the City Mission chapels says: "During the eight years I have been connected with this chapel, we have sent out through the Fresh-Air Fund many hundreds of children. I believe this fortnight in the country to be of incalculable benefit, both educationally and physically. In a number of instances the entire family of a beneficiary of the fund has been led to move to the country. No small part of the good accomplished is the building up of health, and instances come constantly to my notice where the two weeks in the country have, I believe, saved the life."

Dr. Vinton says: "In my experience of several years I have seen much benefit received physically by children sent into the country for two weeks. The first child I sent under the *Tribune* Fresh - Air Fund was Annie ——, whom I had been treating throughout the summer for St. Vitus's dance, and for whom place was made in the last party of the year. She came back after two weeks, rosy - cheeked instead of pale, heavier by a number of pounds, and without any trace of her nervous trouble."

"In August, 1889," he adds, "I accompanied a party of about one hundred and twenty children to Franklinville, N. Y., and again took charge of them on their return to the city two weeks later. The improvement in the physical condition of many of these children was very noticeable, eyes and faces which had been wan and sunken, bearing the evidences of health. The same changes were noticed in a party I brought back from Waterville in the summer of 1888, most of whom I had examined two weeks previously."

Dr. Daniel, who has long taken a professional interest in the work, writes to me :

In 1890 I sent 235 children on excursions of the Fresh-Air Fund. I shall comment upon them under the following classification :

1. Thirty-five children re-invited by their hosts of former years. Of these not one had been ill during the preceding year, nor has been since. I have either seen or heard directly from all of these, and for obvious reasons these are the children who show the most physical improvement.

2. One hundred and four delicate children, *i.e.*, children who are weakly without recent acute illness. Of this number I can count thirty-five who were not at the time under treatment in the dispensary. These were sent either to care for younger children or because they were not very strong. All were benefited by the change, as far as I know. Of this class I can give the least positive evidence because I have seen possibly only one-half of them.

3. Forty-seven children recovering from acute illness. These included typhoid fever, measles, and acute pulmonary diseases, such as pneumonia and bronchitis. All were improved, except two, increased in weight and with better appetites.

4. Twenty-five chronic invalids. These included consumptives, those suffering from tuberculosis of the glands, chronic heart diseases and bone diseases. Of this class three were decidedly worse after the vacation, and the rest were slightly improved; the greatest improvement being in the appetite. All of this class are continually under my observation.

5. Twenty-four children of the striking cloak-makers. This class showed the most improvement, excepting only the first class. These children were taken into the country simply because they were hungry and had been for several weeks. All returned very much improved in appearance and evidently in weight; the pale face and the hungry appearance had disappeared. Doctor Brown took these children to the country and returned with them, and her testimony agrees with mine. I have seen at least one-half of these children since, and they still remain well.

I should classify the children again into the very poor, that is, those continuously poor, and children of a class who are able to have the actual necessaries of life. About one-half of the children I sent last summer (not including the cloak-makers' children) belong to the very poor class. These were not so much benefited as the better class, because, 1, they are in a state of chronic hunger; 2, the time is not long enough to make much of an improvement; and

3, the slight benefit derived is not permanent, because they return to the same mode of life.

Of the two hundred and thirty-five children twenty lived above Fourteenth Street, two west of Broadway, four in Hoboken, and the others lived east of the Bowery as far south as Chatham Square; fifty-seven lived in rear tenements, and twenty-eight in basements.

I have sent children for six or seven years, but have not definite statistics, yet my impression is that at least one-half of the children sent are improved physically. The most marked improvement is in appetite and general appearance. I can say that I believe the Fresh-Air Fund is the best plaster we have for unjust social conditions of the people.

One of the most gratifying results of this Fresh-Air enterprise has been the readiness with which the idea has been taken up by others, till to-day there are vacation societies for about every class of the poor. A great many of the city churches now provide fresh air for the sick poor. Various societies and hospitals have their country summer homes. Missions have their cottages by the sea. Working girls' vacation societies provide a fortnight in the country for working girls who need the change; other societies have sprung up which provide for mothers both with and without young children. King's Daughters' circles open houses for a few weeks or for the season, and send into the city for the quota of inmates.

The Bartholdi Crèche has been organized to help women with small children who are unable to leave home except for a few hours at a time. New York *Life* has started a summer village, where a deserted hamlet, containing a score of cottages beautifully shaded, is turned into a populous village, and where three hundred at one time can find ample accommodations. Unoccupied houses in many a town have been temporarily fitted up for the little city sufferers.

During the last few years there has been a number of permanent places fitted up for children. At these homes there are skilled people to manage and entertain children, and most excellent results are obtained.

The best results are obtained where the children are received into the country families, for there the great moral influences are best exerted, yet all these other plans do a vast amount of good.

There has also been a marked growth in the direction of day excursions. More than a score of times last summer invitations were sent from some of the suburban towns, for ten, twenty, or one hundred of the poor, to come as their guests for a day. Transportation and most abundant food were supplied. One gentleman, who only stipulated that his name should not be published, gives for the entire season the use of a grove on the Hudson. He also supplies all the money for barges, music, and milk. Through the generosity of this one man, more than one hundred and thirty-six thousand of the city poor have had a day's outing.

Not only have various organizations in New York been quick to seize hold of this Fresh-Air idea and adopt some phase of it for their own poor, but the interest has been very marked in other cities. Committees have waited upon the writer, from Boston and Philadelphia, or have sent for instructions, to aid them in starting a Fresh-Air Fund for the poor—in each of these cities they now have a prosperous Country Week. Also from Hartford, Troy, Albany, Buffalo, Chicago, St. Louis, Louisville, Cincinnati, Baltimore, and San Francisco, have inquiries and committees come. Quite a number of other cities of less importance have also sent to ascertain how such a work can be started.

Committees have also visited New York, to find out the *modus operandi*, from Toronto, Montreal, St. Johns, and London and Manchester. In London there is now a large work done for the poor, either in the way of day-trips or a week's stay in the country. Germany and Italy, too, have sent for information on the subject. Dresden, Stuttgart, Vienna, and Berlin have each joined the movement, and there is now a prosperous Fresh-Air work in each of these cities. Some time ago a lady from the Sandwich Islands wrote for full information concerning the work. She was to present the plans in detail at a large gathering in Honolulu. The latest call for reports and statistics came from Russia.

This Fresh-Air movement all began in a small hamlet in northeastern Pennsylvania; among a small flock, not one of whom was rich enough to purchase the most modest house in New York. The first band numbered only nine—since that eighteen cars have been necessary to accommodate a single party. The little enterprise so simply started in 1877, has made its influence felt from Canada to South America, from Boston to San Francisco. There has never been an organization or staff of officers. The constitution and by-laws are made and amended from day to day as required, and have yet to be written. Perhaps the time is near at hand when the work should be more systematically developed. I am quite certain that a large number of skilled and paid helpers could be employed with most satisfactory results.

BOYS' CLUBS IN NEW YORK

By EVERT JANSEN WENDELL

THE BOYS OF THE TENEMENTS—STREET LIFE—A BOYS' TEMPTATIONS—FIRST IDEA OF THE BOYS' CLUBS—THEIR MANAGEMENT—THE BOYS' CLUB OF ST. MARK'S PLACE—THE AVENUE C WORKING BOYS' CLUB—CLASSES AND AMUSEMENTS—BOYS' CLUB OF CALVARY PARISH—THE FREE-READING-ROOM FOR BOYS—THE MANOR CHAPEL BOYS' CLUB—THE NORTH SIDE, THE WEST SIDE, AND OTHER CLUBS—SOME CLUB DOCUMENTS—ENTERTAINMENTS—SONGS—THE RESULTS—THE NEEDS OF A SUCCESSFUL CLUB WORKER.

ANYONE who has been down to the tenement-house districts on either side of our city of New York, knows how overrun they are with boys of all descriptions, races, and sizes. Every doorway pours forth its little quota, and it is sometimes with difficulty that one can thread one's way through the crowds that literally swarm about the sidewalks. Some are playing quietly ; some are fighting ; some are " passing " ball when the policeman on the beat is not in sight ; and others are gathered in little groups smoking cigarettes, pitching pennies, or hatching some scheme for fun when night comes.

Night is the great time ! In the morning many of them are at school, and the streets are comparatively deserted ; but in the afternoon, when the schools let out, the children, with all the pent-up energy produced by six hours of repression, descend upon them and make them resound, only taking time to rush in for a few moments at supper-time, and then out again, to remain as late as is consistent with escaping a spanking when they finally come in for the night.

It is not strange that they seek the streets when one realizes
that the homes of many of them consist only of one or two small
rooms in a tenement-house, which have to serve as parlor, bedroom, and kitchen, for father, mother, and all the children—and
families are not apt to be small in the tenement-house district. A
few of the more sober-minded stay in at night to prepare their lessons for the next day, or to help the mother care for the smaller
children, or wash the dishes ; but often they would only be in the
way, and it is more convenient for the mother to have them off
somewhere, amusing themselves, than under her feet, as she sets
the little home to rights, and the father wants a quiet rest after his
hard day's work ; so the greater part of the children naturally seek
the streets at night—good and bad alike—and strong must the
character be that can long remain untarnished in the midst of all
that goes on there.

Many of them are children with instincts as pure and high-
minded as your own, if only they could be rightly trained ; children of honest and hard-working parents, whose influence on them
during the short time that their daily labor permits them to be together is all that need be asked. But these children, from force of
circumstances, have to play side by side with children low in mind
and expression, unwashed, whose home influences are of the worst,
and who drink, smoke, chew, swear, or steal, when they are not in
the gallery of some cheap theatre, in one of the many small gambling - dens in the rear of an innocent - looking candy or grocery
store, or "scrapping" in some dark corner far enough removed
from the glare of the saloons to render their movements indistinct.
All about, too, are groups of older boys just approaching manhood,
or its age, loafing about the corners, going in and out of the pool-
rooms, telling low stories, and making careless remarks to the
women who pass by ; while the not unusual spectacle of the men,
and sometimes women, rolling home from the grog-shops, com-
pletes a picture which makes it patent that if these boys are to
have a fair chance to develop good, wholesome characters, some

The Carpenters' Shop—Avenue C Working Boys' Club.

other alternative must be offered to them for the passing of their evenings.

Something must be provided which will attract them from the dirt and crime of the streets to places where they will, instead, be surrounded by simple cleanliness and good breeding ; where a cordial welcome will take the place of the rough greetings of their street companions, and where they will have every opportunity to pass an evening of innocent enjoyment, restrained only by having to consider the comfort and pleasure of the other boys about them.

It is from force of circumstances that many a small boy has found himself in court on a charge of theft, unmanageable conduct, or vagrancy—the three great heads under which our juvenile delinquents are arraigned! Many a boy has been taught to steal by an older companion of the streets, who draws a wily picture of how easy it will be for him to tap a till or snatch from the front of a store the coat or pair of shoes he can exchange at the pawnshop for the pennies he gets so few of at home; who shares the pennies, if the plan prove a success, and who leaves him to his fate if he is caught. Many a boy has become unmanageable at home because he has had so little home influence, and because on the street he has been continually surrounded by boys whose disregard for home restraint, and contempt for those who are bound by it, are very infectious when no one is by to say a word on the other side. Many a boy has been found sleeping in a box or a wagon because he has been beguiled by flaring advertisements to go with "the rest of the fellers" into the top gallery of a cheap theatre, and has emerged again, after having had his curiosity improperly satisfied, at so late an hour that he honestly feared to go to the home he ought to have gone to two or three hours earlier, and face his angry father—and in each case the trouble has been brought about by the influences of the street, with no one by to counteract them or to offer any proper alternative in place of their attractions.

Dirt and crime go hand in hand; and if you can teach a boy that cleanliness of body and courtesy of manner are preferable to unwashed hands and surliness of speech, you will have helped him forward farther than you know on his road to respectable manhood.

It was in the fall of 1878 that the small boys about Tompkins Square, having exhausted the ordinary methods of street enjoy-

"ANNIE ROONEY"—AT A BOYS' CLUB.

ment, began to amuse themselves by throwing stones through the windows of the Wilson Mission at No. 125 St. Mark's Place, and by jeering at the various people connected with it as they passed in and out of the building.   These customs proving in time both expensive and annoying to the ladies and gentlemen connected with the mission, and complaints to the Police Department only resulting in a temporary cessation of hostilities whenever the lynx-eyed policeman on the beat appeared, and as long as he remained in sight, one of the ladies determined to try the soothing effects of coals of fire, poured metaphorically upon the heads of the offending boys.   So one evening she answered an especially irritating volley of stones by appearing on the door-steps, and taking advantage of a momentary lull in the cat-calls which her appearance had excited, asked the boys if they would not come in and have some coffee and cakes.   Visions of "cops" with clubs behind the door naturally occurred to the minds of the prospective guests; but when a few of the more venturesome had sidled in, and no attacks, apparently, had been made on them, the others took courage and followed them, to find themselves quietly welcomed to the simple repast which the lady had plenteously provided as the most practical form in which to administer her coals of fire.   Everyone had as much as he wanted, no reference was made to the cause of the broken glass, and each boy was treated with a kindness and courtesy quite unexpected, in view of the fact that within a few moments he had been engaged in smashing his hostess's windows. When the supper had all been absorbed, the boys were sent forth with a pleasant good-night to ruminate on their evening's experiences, and to decide which part of the evening had been the more enjoyable—defacing the exterior of the mission building, or being treated with kindness and courtesy within its walls ; and their decision soon became apparent, for not only did the annoyances cease, but the boys were soon back again, not for coffee and cakes, but to ask if they could not come in and play games—though there was little in the room but an atmosphere of kindness and good-breeding.

Then more boys came and were welcomed, interested friends sent down chairs and tables and games, a board of managers was instituted, and so the first boys' club was started on the broad principle which should underlie them all, of hearty welcome for any boy, whatever his condition or belief, who prefers an evening of innocent enjoyment in a place where he must show respect and courtesy to all about him, to the thoughtlessness and hidden dangers of an evening in the street.

It makes no difference what a boy's religion is—or if he has any! That is a question which should never come up in a club drawn from all classes in a crowded district, where all beliefs and no beliefs are all about one. Make rules for the government of the clubs that will teach boys rather to be good citizens; that will teach them they have duties not only to themselves but to others; that will teach them to stick to their own ideas and yet to respect the ideas of other people, and to feel that they have not done their part if they have failed to show consideration and courtesy to everyone with whom they are brought in contact—be he millionaire or be he newsboy! This is Christian love and sympathy in its most practical sense; and its teaching does not breed dissension.

The Boys' Club is now in its seventeenth year of work, and an average attendance of over two hundred and fifty boys a night was the result of one season's first three months.

When boys first come to the club the dirt of the street has often rendered them quite unprepared to handle a book or a game without seriously damaging its condition; but the desire to join the other boys soon leads them to retire to the neat wash-room adjoining the club-room and to submit to the temporary discomfort of washing their hands; and after a short time they begin to prefer a condition of mild cleanliness, and either come with clean hands to the club, or retire at once to the wash-room on their arrival, without waiting for the superintendent's hint to do so.

Occasionally, too, you find a small boy who has been beaten at checkers or parchesi, and who has been asked by his victorious opponent if he can play any other game better, replying to the query by " batting " the other small boy over the head ; but the assault is usually committed with as much self-restraint as is possible under the circumstances, and with a feeling of considerable regret on the part of the assailant that he is forced to avenge the insult within the walls of the Boys' Club. A nicer, brighter lot of boys you will not find anywhere than you can see there of an evening. Their clothes are not made at Poole's, nor is their linen of the finest, when they substitute it for the cotton or flannel shirts in which they look so much more picturesque; but their bright smiles and cheery greetings show that their hearts are in the right place, and that the influences of the Boys' Club have not been exerted in vain.

There are classes in singing, writing, and book-keeping for those who care to avail of them. A class in modelling, a year or two ago, developed a latent genius who is now working at a good salary in an art museum, and has almost enough laid aside to go abroad and pursue his studies. There is a separate meeting-room for the older boys whose records at the club entitle them to use it; and a penny savings-bank is in active and successful operation. But the main object of the club has always been simply to provide quiet and innocent amusement sufficiently attractive to draw the boys away from the danger of the streets, and to put into their lives the softening influences they are not apt to find elsewhere.

Those who knew Tompkins Square before the club was started have only to walk through it now to see at once the different character of the boys there; and those who did not know it before need only talk with the neighbors and the policemen near by, to convince themselves of the splendid work it has accomplished.

The Avenue C Working Boys' Club, at No. 650 East Fourteenth Street, was started in 1884, under the name of the St. George's Boys' Club, and in its first two years of existence occupied the basement of the building No. 207 East Sixteenth Street, which was then pulled down to make room for the St. George's Memorial House that now stands upon the same site, when the club moved to

No. 237 East Twenty-first Street, still retaining the old name, though at that time it had no real connection with St. George's Church. This new house was of four stories, of which the basement was given to the janitor and his family, the parlor floor and the second story were devoted to club purposes, and the upper floor was rented to unhappy tenants.

Type-setting at the Avenue C Working Boys' Club.

At first the club was conducted on the principle of the Boys' Club of St. Mark's Place, and aimed only to offer counter-attractions to those of the street; but the signal success of a class in type-setting, which had been started as an experiment, so impressed the managers that they decided to concentrate their energies on the teaching of trades; and a kindly offer being made to them by the Avenue C Industrial Schools of the use of a beautifully appointed little carpenter shop, with benches and tools complete, in the new building at the corner of Fourteenth Street and Avenue C, they decided to leave the house in Twenty-first Street, after two very successful seasons, and moved to their new home, where classes were established in carpentering and type-setting.* There are fifty boys

* At present (1895) the club is carrying on its work most successfully in more commodious quarters at No. 269 Avenue C, near Sixteenth Street.

in the classes, each of whom receives two lessons a week in either one of these trades, from skilled and practical instructors.

The carpenter's shop is beautifully appointed, there being six benches, each one large enough to accommodate two boys; each boy has his kit of tools, as good in every respect as those used by regular carpenters; and the chairs and tables and book-cases they turn out, not to speak of brackets and smaller articles of furniture and decoration, many a man might well feel proud of having made.

The printing class is also in a flourishing condition, the boys having so far mastered the intricacies of setting and distributing type that they have been able to take in job printing, with most creditable results; and it is purposed before long to publish a small paper, to appear monthly, an experiment which had been instituted with success in the old Twenty-first Street house, but which had been discontinued on moving to the present quarters on account of so many of the boys being new to the work.

A number of the boys in the classes have regular work at these same trades in the daytime, and the instruction in the club has led, in many cases, to a decided increase in their weekly salaries. One of the managers takes charge of the savings of such boys as desire it, and, when they have enough, helps them to open accounts in a savings-bank; and some of the boys who have started in this way, now have two or three hundred dollars to their credit. There is always a list of boys waiting to get into the classes, and if a boy fails to attend regularly, or to do his best work, his place is filled by someone who will appreciate the advantages more; but these cases do not often occur. The boys like the classes too well to want to leave them. Medals are given at the end of each year to those who have done the best work in the classes; and on some holiday in the spring, usually on Decoration Day, the managers take the boys for an excursion to the country, the pleasure of which lasts in remembrance far into the winter.

On one of these excursions to Scarsdale, one of the oldest boys in the party, and one of the best workers in his class, appeared to

11

be especially happy, and finally confided to one of the managers that he never had seen a real green field before, excepting in the Park, his experience having been confined to the vacant lots in the city, filled with stones and broken bottles, in which the boys played ball ; and the idea of a natural field of green grass in which he could disport at pleasure with no sparrow policeman to chase him off, was an entirely new sensation. This was a boy nearly sixteen years old.

On another occasion when the boys of the old club were being taken in a special car to Rockaway, the candy and pop-corn boy on the train, under the impression that it was a demure Sunday-school picnic, entered, as usual, and tossed his packages right and left with that amiable lack of care so familiar to travellers on the suburban railways, and with every expectation of reaping a rich harvest. After allowing the usual two or three minutes for reflection, he again entered the car, to find every candy-box empty on the floor, and their contents being rapidly consumed by the boys, who proceeded at once to mob him when he attempted to collect the value of his indigestible confections. It was with difficulty that he was rescued, and with more difficulty that a small collection from the managers restored his equanimity, and consoled him for his broken hat and the total loss of his dignity.

Another of the excursions was by water to Staten Island, to see " Buffalo Bill," on a large excursion boat carrying several hundred passengers, the captain entering thoroughly into the spirit of the occasion, and taking a sort of parental interest in the boys, who were all gathered together in the bow of the boat, as quiet as lambs.

When the show was over and the excursionists began to return, the captain stood on the gang-plank, complacently patting his waistcoat, and wanting to know if " our boys " were all right, and not wanting to start quite on time for fear that some of them would be left behind—which it afterward turned out was the case with two or three. By the time this was discovered, however, it was no longer a source of regret to the captain, for the boys (who had become somewhat excited by two hours of guns and bucking-horses and Comanche Indians, and who were standing around the brass band that was playing on the deck), were somewhat more restless than they had been on the trip down ; and one of them attempted to relieve his pent-up emotions by sticking a button into the big

A Stereopticon Lecture—the Boys' Club of the Wilson Mission.

trombone, with the effect of nearly strangling the stout gentleman who was playing on it. The infuriated musician made a wild dive for the boy, who proceeded to defend himself with a chair, and in a moment there was as pretty a riot as one would care to see all over the forward deck—chairs flying, the bandmen swearing, and the boys yelling like steam-whistles. When quiet finally was restored by the extraction of the button from the trombone, and the relegation of the boys to the after-deck, the captain, whose ideas had undergone a sudden change, and who had become very red in the face, remarked that he " wouldn't take those d——d boys down to Staten Island again for ten dollars a head."

The question often is asked as to which kind of club is the more desirable—one in which trades are taught, or one in which the boys are simply entertained ; but they are so different in character that a fair comparison would be as difficult as it would be unnecessary.   There is no doubt that the teaching of trades is of great importance, and that the work done by a club of that character meets a very important need ; but, on the other hand, it is the boys who do not care to work who are much more apt to get into mischief at night on the street, and clubs devoted to drawing them in and providing them with innocent amusements fills a different need, but hardly a less important one.

The Boys' Club of Calvary Parish, at No. 344 East Twenty-third Street, was started about six years ago, shortly after the present Avenue C Working Boys' Club left that district; and it has met with great success, many of the boys of the old club, and no end of others, having enjoyed its privileges.   In addition to a room for books and games, they have a second room fitted up as a gymnasium, with trapezes, horizontal and parallel bars, and other gymnastic appliances, and the evening is usually divided between the two, the first half being devoted to the reading-room and the second half to the gymnasium, the boys forming in line at a given signal and being admitted one by one to the gymnasium on showing their tickets.   Then the rest of the evening is given up to exercise of all kinds, some going in for using the apparatus, and others preferring boxing, single stick, or wrestling, for which the gloves sticks, and mattresses are provided, if the superintendent has time to oversee the exercise and keep it within proper bounds.   Good-nature is the one thing insisted on, and many a boy receives there a valuable lesson in self - control, in connection with a mildly bruised nose.

They also have a small printing class, and it is purposed to issue periodically a small paper devoted to the interests of boys' clubs in general, which, if persisted in, will do much good to the cause.

I have devoted considerable space to these three clubs from their being the oldest and most complete of their respective classes ; but other clubs that are doing splendid work are the Free Reading-Room for boys, at No. 68–70 University Place, formerly at 18 West Seventeenth Street, and, later, at No. 8 West Fourteenth Street, which was founded in 1883, and at which the total attendance during the last twelve years has reached the enormous num-

Entrance to Boys' Club of the Wilson Mission, 125 St. Mark's Place.

ber of 316,913 boys; the Manor Chapel Boys' Club, at No. 348 West Twenty-sixth Street, which has an average attendance of about fifty boys a night, and would have as many more if its rooms were larger; the Boys' Club of St. George's Church, at the St. George's Memorial House in East Sixteenth Street, near Third Avenue, a flourishing organization with about three hundred members, open every night, but so arranged that different boys come on each evening, excepting on Wednesdays, when they all come together; the West Side Working Boys' Club, at No. 794 Tenth Avenue, formerly in West Forty-seventh Street; the Boys' Clubs of the University Settlement at No. 26 Delancey Street; and the Boys' Club of Grace Mission, at No. 540 East Thirteenth Street, which was started in 1891, and with which the Wayside Boys' Club, formerly in East Twentieth Street, and later at the Bible House, has been consolidated.

This consolidation, however, was not accomplished without some friction, as the following pathetic little letter, which is before me as I write, and which was received about a week after the new club had opened, by the former president of the Wayside Boys' Club, will show. It is given without change of any kind excepting the omission of the signers' names and the name of the lady to whom it is addressed:

New York, Dec. 15, 1890.

"Dear Mrs. ——— :

"Would you please come and see to our Wayside Boys' Club; that the first time it was open it was very nice, and after that near every boy in that neighborhood came walking in. And if you would be so kind to come and put them out it would be a great pleasure to us.

"Mrs. ———, the club is not nice any more, and when we want to go home, the boys would wait for us outside, and hit you.

"Mrs. ———, since them boys are in the club we don't have any games to play with, and if we do play with the games, they come over to us and take it off us.

"And by so doing please oblige,

———, *President,*
———, *Vice-President,*
———, *Treasurer,*
———, *Secretary,*
———, *Floor Manager.*

"Please excuse the writing. I was in haste.

"———, *Treasurer.*"

It is needless to state that the interests of the little fellows—for none of the signers are more than twelve years old, and most of them younger—were protected, and that the club is now running to the satisfaction of all.

All these clubs are open every night excepting in summer, and gladly receive as members any boys who are willing to conduct themselves properly while in the club-rooms—the only limit being space.

In addition there are the Covenant Chapel Boys' Club, at No. 310 East Forty-second Street; the Boys' Club of Bethany Church, on Tenth Avenue, between Thirty-fifth and Thirty-sixth Streets; and the Boys' Club of Christ Chapel, on West Sixty-sixth Street, near Tenth Avenue — each open two or three evenings in the week.

The membership of these clubs is largely composed of boys connected with the Sunday-schools of these churches—although, occasionally, some of the boys' friends are admitted also.

In summer, from June to October, all the clubs are closed, for no one wants to stay indoors during the hot weather, and the boys naturally seek the open air; but the streets then are much less dangerous, both on account of darkness coming on so much later than in winter, and because hundreds of respectable people, who in winter stay in their rooms, sit, in summer, out in front of their houses, and thus render questionable practices in the streets much less easy.

All the clubs have libraries, more or less good; some of them let the boys take books home, when they have shown themselves, by good behavior, to be worthy of confidence; many of them have a class in something, to interest the boys who care to work; several have penny savings-banks; all of them have games, excepting the Avenue C Working Boy's Club, which admits only the boys who come to attend the trade classes; a number have debating societies, in which weighty matters of world-wide interest are discussed and dismissed with a rapidity which would greatly expedite our national legislation if the system could be successfully introduced at Washington; two or three of them give their members an

excursion in summer; and they all give the boys periodical entertainments, some as often as once a week, and others once a month,
or at longer intervals.

An entertainment is the boys' greatest delight, especially when
it is accompanied by ice-cream, some of which a number always
wrap up in paper—or stick a piece into their pockets without

A Good-natured Scrap—Boys' Club, Calvary Parish, in East Twenty-third Street.

any wrapper—to take to the little brother or sister at home. I
only remember one boy who ever refused ice-cream at an entertainment, and he apologized by explaining that he had had the
colic all day, and his mother had told him " she'd lick him if he
took any."

They like anything in the form of an entertainment—magic-lantern, stereopticon lecture, banjo-playing, ventriloquism, legerdemain, any kind of instrumental music that is not too classical,

heroic or humorous recitations, and especially comic or sentimental songs in which they can join in the chorus. You have never
heard "Annie Rooney" or "McGinty" sung unless you have heard
it sung at a boys' club; nor have you ever heard "America" sung
as they can sing it. Thanks to the public schools, they know
nearly all the more familiar national and patriotic songs, "My
Country, 'tis of Thee," "The Red, White, and Blue," "Marching
thro' Georgia," "Hail, Columbia," and "The Star-spangled Banner;" and the life and earnestness they put into the singing of
them cannot but impress anyone who hears it with the importance
of surrounding them, so far as it can be done, with influences which
will tend to turn their enthusiasm into the right channels and
which will prevent their becoming the foes to society which the
roughness of street life is so apt to produce when they have not
had a fair chance to see the gentler side of life.

Sometimes they parody the sentimental songs very amusingly.
One of the popular favorites not long ago was a song with a very
taking air, called "Don't Leave your Mother, Tom," of which the
words of the chorus ran as follows:

> "Stick to your mother, Tom, when I am gone!
> Don't let her worry, lad; don't let her mourn.
> Remember that she nursed you when I was far away;
> Stick to your mother when her hair turns gray."

One night there seemed to be a certain disparity in the rhyming
of the chorus, and the gentleman who was playing on the piano
soon became aware that the boys were singing a different version
of it from the ordinary, which, on persistent investigation, he discovered to be

> "Stick to your mother, Tom, while she has wealth,
> Don't do a stroke of work; it's bad for the health;
> Be a corner loafer—roam around all day,
> And hit her with a shovel when her hair turns gray."

The boys are usually in fine form at an entertainment, especially an entertainment given by themselves, when solos on the har-

monica, piccolo, and clappers are interspersed by clog-dances, vocal solos, and recitations; and they guy each other unmercifully, though not more so than I have heard them guy other people who have come down to entertain clubs that are just starting.

I once heard a boys' club audience, which was being entertained by a lady playing on the banjo, take advantage of the fact that her dress did not quite reach to the ground to comment audibly upon the color of her stockings; and not long ago I heard a dignified missionary, who had been describing the spread of the Gospel in the Far East, and who proposed to illustrate Eastern customs by displaying some native costumes he had brought with him, instantly cautioned by one of the boys "to keep his shirt on."

Not many weeks back a distinguished financier in this city became possessed of a large magic lantern, with which on festive occasions he was wont to entertain the admiring children of his family; and after considerable difficulty he was induced one day by one of his daughters, who had become interested in a boys' club, to display it before the club's members.

The show was progressing famously, and the daughter was beaming with pride, when one of the boys suddenly beckoned to her, and pointing to the distinguished financier, remarked :

" What der yer call dat bloke ? "

" Whom do you mean ? " asked the proud daughter, in a tone of much surprise, being quite unaccustomed to hearing the distinguished financier described as a "bloke."

" I mean dat bloke over dere, settin' off dem picturs ! " replied the boy.

" What do you desire to know about him ? " inquired the proud daughter, with freezing dignity.

" I want ter know what yer call one of dem fellers dat sets off picturs ? " persisted the boy.

" That gentleman," said the proud daughter, in her most impressive tone, " is my father."

A Boys' Club Reading-Room.

"Well!" said the boy, surveying her with supreme contempt, "don't yer know yer own father's trade?"

After an entertainment given at the Boys' Club of St. Mark's Place, one of the managers discovered, when he came to go home, that his overcoat had been taken from the nail on which it had been hung. The boys had all gone, and there was no possible way of discovering the culprit, so the gentleman went home without his coat, and had gotten over his temporary annoyance and dismissed the matter from his mind when, one day, most unexpectedly, the overcoat was left at his house, accompanied by a communication signed by more than two hundred boys of the club, who, at the instance of the superintendent, had quietly taken the matter in charge, had traced the coat to a pawnshop where the thief had left it, and had taken up a collection among themselves to get it out of pawn and restore it to the owner, that the dignity and self-respect of the club members might be restored.

The gentleman lent me the communication, which also is before me as I write, and which reads as follows, again the only change being the omission of the names:

" January 15, 1891.

" Dear Sir :

" We, the undersigned members of the Boy's Club, have taken the matter regarding the overcoat which was taken from the club-rooms the night of the entertainment, into consideration, and regret to say that it makes a man of your rank feel very uncomfortable to have anything like that occur to him. We beg to state that one of the members of the club has succeeded in getting the pawn-ticket for same. This is the first time that anything of the kind has occurred in these rooms, and it was through the utmost work of Mr. Rivolta (the superintendent) that we succeeded in restoring the overcoat back to you.

"Trusting that anything of the sort will not occur again, we are,
" Very truly yours,"

and then follow two hundred and twenty-two signatures.

Could anyone ask a more striking example of the civilizing and elevating effects of boys' clubs on the characters of the little chaps who enjoy their privileges than is afforded by this letter!

The coat was gone, there was no way of getting it back, and the name of the thief was not known ; yet the boys could not stand the idea that anyone who had been kind to them had been shabbily treated, or that a stain should rest upon the reputation of their club ; and they left no stone unturned until their own exertions and pockets had made the wrong good and thus their self-respect had been restored.

The influences brought to bear upon the boys often are not merely temporary ones. Many of the managers become so interested in certain boys that the friendship is a lasting one ; and long after the boys have outgrown the clubs they come to see the managers or correspond with them, so that the active influence on their characters is often kept up until long after the age of young manhood has been passed. Several young men's clubs have been voluntarily formed, based on the broad principles of temperance and respectability, by boys who had become too old for the boys' clubs, but who were not willing to give up the quiet evenings of which they had become so fond ; and many of the assistants in the clubs to-day are boys who have graduated from them, and who often in their early days were among their most troublesome members.

Almost seven years ago there was a boy in one of the clubs in whom one of the managers took a great interest—though his natural wildness caused considerable anxiety at home—but who suddenly ceased to come to the club, and sent no word as to the cause of his sudden absence.

For several weeks the manager inquired for him and looked for him, but without success, until one day he heard from a companion that the boy had been committed to one of the public institutions for some especially unbridled demonstration of mischief, and was there serving out his term. The gentleman went to the institution and found the boy, who was delighted to see him, and who, after a time, confided to him the cause for which he had been sent there, which was of a much more serious nature than the gentleman had supposed. He talked to the boy, however, and wrote to him every little while, and though he continually got into harmless little scrapes, from his unbounded fund of animal spirits, still everything seemed to be going on most favorably until, on one of the gentleman's visits, he found the boy in a state of considerable

excitement (produced by having been punished, as he thought, un-
fairly), and with all his plans made to run away from the institution.

He detailed these plans to the gentleman, who told him, of
course, that he would consider the information confidential, and
certainly would not make use of it to stop him if the boy persisted
in his plan; that he advised him, however, very strongly, not to do
so, but to stay there, and so conduct himself as to leave behind

Lining Up to go into the Gymnasium.

him, when he should leave the institution, a record so clear that
anyone who ever should want to consult it afterward could find
nothing in it to his discredit.

In time the argument so impressed the boy that he determined
to follow the advice, and from that time forward he became as earnest a worker in the school and in the shops as any boy in the institution, and finally ended his term and left there with the hearti-
est good wishes of everyone connected with it, all having a good
word to say of him. Since leaving he has come constantly to the
gentleman for advice and counsel, and now is settling down into a
quiet, hard-working fellow, with every indication of becoming a
comfort to his parents and a useful member of society.

Some time ago the same gentleman found, in another institution of the kind, a bright little fellow, who had been sent there by his parents more than two years before for being unmanageable at home; and whose record there, both in work and in conduct, had been of too low a grade for him to get his discharge, although apparently he had no vicious traits. The gentleman took an interest in him, talked to him in a friendly way, and soon convinced him that it was a thing to be heartily ashamed of for a boy with his evident natural brightness to have so poor a record, as a result solely of his indifference.

Two or three times they talked together on the subject; and on coming for the fourth time the gentleman found the boy radiant at having attained the highest grade. For over five months he kept it, only losing it once for "slugging" a boy who had kicked him—an exhibition of spirit of which the gentleman heartily approved; and within a week of this writing, the boy received his honorable discharge from the institution, and went home to help his father at a trade, with a record of excellence behind him that he never would have attained had not his ambition been stirred by the evidence of friendly sympathy and the encouragement of feeling that some one else really cared whether or not he did himself and his abilities full justice—an impulse which the boys' clubs are giving to-day to hundreds of boys just like him. There is no doubt that they have been a most powerful factor in the encouraging decrease in juvenile delinquency during the last few years; and it is earnestly to be hoped that soon there may be a free club for boys in every ward of the city.

Every club has had trouble when it started; furniture has been upset, windows have been broken, and the managers have been assaulted with potatoes and onions and mud; but there is not one which has not the most satisfactory results to tell of as soon as it has become known that the managers had come there with no intention of patronizing the boys, but with every intention of being their friends. The boys will not stand patronage—and the more credit to them for it—but they quickly find out whether a man is really in sympathy with them or not.

Don't go in for boys' club work unless you can feel a genuine personal interest in the boys themselves; don't go in for it if occasional dirty hands and faces will hopelessly offend your taste; don't go in for it if ragged clothes and tattered shirts will antagonize you, for all these will continually confront you; but if you care enough for boys to look below the surface, you will find under those little breasts hearts as true and affections as deep as you will ever meet with anywhere, ready to be influenced by an interest they feel to be sincere, and eager to respond to the love and sympathy of which they get so little elsewhere, and which will do more than anything else ever can to counteract the dangerous influences of the streets, and make them honest, true, and law-abiding citizens.

THE WORK OF THE ANDOVER HOUSE IN BOSTON

By WILLIAM JEWETT TUCKER

PRESIDENT OF DARTMOUTH COLLEGE, FORMERLY PROFESSOR IN ANDOVER THEOLOGICAL SEMINARY

LOWER AND HIGHER PHILANTHROPY—GROWTH OF ORGANIZED CHARITY—ANDOVER HOUSE AND THE NEW PHILANTHROPY—ITS RELIGIOUS MOTIVE—TRAINING OF WORKERS—ORIGIN OF THE NAME—NOT DENOMINATIONAL—PEOPLE DEALT WITH—ROBERT A. WOODS—ADMINISTRATION—PRINCIPLES UPON WHICH WORK IS CONDUCTED—BOYS' CLUBS—THE QUESTION OF TENEMENTS—STUDY OF SOCIAL CONDITIONS—GREATER BOSTON—ANDOVER HOUSE ASSOCIATION—FIELD OF OBSERVATION—LECTURES—PLACE OF SYMPATHY IN SCIENTIFIC WORK—GROWTH OF THE MOVEMENT—AFTER FOUR YEARS.

THE distinction is now recognized, though not as yet very clearly defined in the public mind, between what is known as the lower and the higher philanthropy. The lower philanthropy meant the attempt "to put right what social conditions had put wrong." The higher philanthropy means the attempt "to put right the social conditions themselves."

Of course, no moral significance attaches to the use of the term "higher" as applied to philanthropy. The term, like the phrase, "the higher criticism," is entirely free from assumption. Nothing could have been nobler in motive or in practice than that first simple charity which went out to meet the early poverty of the cities, and which was always ready to run upon its errands of mercy without stopping to ask too many questions. It developed characters of rare sensitiveness. Charity became one of the fine arts, creating personal types of moral beauty. Men saw that it must be blessed to give, whatever it might be to receive. And when the problem of

12

suffering grew weighty and urgent, with the growth of the city, this same spirit of charity grew strong, watchful, and inventive. It proved to be able to deal with classes, as before it had dealt with individuals. It was quick to follow out every hint and suggestion of unrelieved want and distress. Charities multiplied as the objects of charity were detected. The relief of the poor brought to light the child of poverty, the child of poverty led the way to his crippled brother, the diseased child pointed to the suffering mother; and when the region of disease was once really discovered, it was quickly occupied with every variety of institutional relief.

I recall a characteristic example of the spirit and method of the old charity in the person of a well-known philanthropist of New York, who for more than half a century followed with an unerring instinct the subtle progress of distress and misery. When I knew him he had passed his three score and ten years. Yet each year seemed to add to the eagerness and intensity of his search. An incident, associated with his greatest personal bereavement, revealed to me the whole spirit of his life. As I called upon him in his sorrow, he took me, after a little, into the presence of his dead, and there talked, as only the voice of age and love could speak. Suddenly he stopped, put his hand into his pocket, and took out a check. "There," said he, "is a check for $25,000 from Mrs. Stewart for my woman's hospital." Then, resuming the conversation as if there had been no interruption—there really had been none—he covered the face of his dead and withdrew, to take up again in its time his now solitary, but joyous, work. My honored friend was the embodiment of that charity, to the credit of which must be placed the countless organizations and institutions which are the most conspicuous signs of a living Christianity.

But with the extraordinary multiplication and extension of charities, consequent upon the growth of poverty, disease, and vice, the question began to arise in some earnest minds, may there not be, after all, something better than charity, or, at least, may there not be a larger and better charity? Grant that the progress of Christianity has been marked by the relieving agencies and institutions which line its path, may not its progress be still more clearly marked by the relative decrease of these very agencies and institutions? May not Christianity be applied wisely, vigorously, and with better results at the *sources* of suffering? The serious asking of these questions gradually brought in the higher philanthropy, whose aim, as I have said, is not so much "to put right what social conditions have put wrong," as to "put right the social conditions themselves." The new philanthropy does not attempt to supersede entirely the old charity; it does offer itself as a much-needed helper and ally.

The intermediate step from the lower to the higher philanthropy was taken through the charity organization movement, the motive of which was to economize charity. The moral as well as financial waste of the current charity had become appalling. It was estimated that the "pauper, the impostor, and the fraud of every description, carried off at least one-half of all charity, public and private." The poor man, who preferred to work rather than to beg, was supplanted by the pauper, who preferred to beg rather than to work. It was a comparatively easy matter for a professional pauper to utilize the charity of several different societies, especially those which were religious, for the support of himself or his family; while shrewd knaves, who saw the market value of an infirmity or a deformity, organized an army of cripples of every sort, whom they stationed at the corners of the streets, or through whom they invaded the homes of the compassionate. The demoralizing effect of this traffic in charity was so evident that decisive measures were taken to break it up through reforms in the method of administration. In 1869 a society was organized in London under the title, "The Society for Organizing Charitable Relief, and for Repressing Mendicity," an organization which was quickly copied in the larger towns of the provinces. The first move in the same direction, in this country, was made in 1877, in the city of

Buffalo, through the establishment of a like organization, which has since been adopted in most of the cities of the country under the name of the " Associated Charities." Naturally these societies began their work as a crusade against indiscriminate charity. They brought together, as far as practicable, all the benevolent agencies which were at work in a given community, they introduced the scientific and systematic visitation of the poor, they sought out and exposed the iniquitous frauds which had been fostered by neglect, and in various ways decreased the growing volume of pauperism. And the work of the " Associated Charities " necessarily led to the study of social conditions. It was impossible to deal with pauperism in any scientific way without investigating the sources of it. Still the inherited object of the " Associated Charities " was charity—the relief of suffering—the special occasion for its action being the need of seeing to it that charity reached the actual sufferer, and only in the right way. It belonged by origin, and in part by method, to the agencies which were trying " to put right what social conditions had put wrong." It was evident that a new type of philanthropy was needed, with the one distinct object of trying " to put right the social conditions themselves."

The Andover House has its place and does its work within the sphere of this new philanthropy. It is one of the agencies which represent, in a simple and unostentatious way, the principles and methods through which the new philanthropy is beginning to make itself felt in society. While in sympathy with all charitable movements, and having representatives upon the boards of " Associated Charities " in its vicinity, it is not another charitable organization or institution. It has no moneys to disburse. As far as appears to a transient visitor, the House is simply a home where a group of educated young men live, study, and work. But the House is organized upon an idea, which the group is constantly working out, each man in harmony with his fellow. Evidently the great requisite in any attempt to modify wrong social conditions is the perfect understanding of those conditions. And the knowledge of any such conditions is best gained by practically subjecting one's self to them, at least to the extent of making them the daily environment of his life. Residence is the key to the situation in any locality. It is wonderful how many things come to one, in the way of the daily intercourse with his neighbors, which would entirely evade the most careful search from without. It is the unsought information which tells best the story of a neighborhood. And far beyond any gain in the way of knowledge is the sense of identification with others which comes through residence among them. One is conscious of breathing the same social atmosphere, and though he may retreat from the more disheartening surroundings of his work into the shelter and cheer of the group, yet the scenes in the midst of which he lives are in mind by day and by night. The constant strain upon the sympathies is the test of the real significance of living under wrong social conditions. I doubt if one person can well bear the strain. It is the group which saves the individual to his work, and supplies that fund of good cheer which is indispensable to it.

This resident group is made up of educated men, of men, that is, trained to think upon social problems. It represents the contribution of thought rather than of money toward their solution. Doubtless some of the theories held, though learned in the best schools, are found to need essential modification when tested by the actual fact. But they give intelligent approach to studies from life. And it should be said that much of the knowledge within recent books is based upon direct investigation, as with Charles Booth's "Labor and Life of the People," or is the result of reasoning upon ascertained facts. To call the present training of the schools in Sociology purely theoretical is a misnomer. It is in reality but one degree removed from life.

Further, the group represents the idea of special consecration on the part of its members. The work of the House proceeds from the religious motive. It is carried on without compensation, except in cases where expenses are met by fellowships. Some residents propose to make work of the nature there carried on their life-work. Others will take the spirit of it into their after-duties, whatever may be their special character. I doubt if there is any field which calls more clearly for the true missionary disposition and temper than resident work among the poor in the great cities.

The Andover House took its name from its origin. As might be supposed, a large number of the graduates of Andover Theological Seminary (about twenty miles from Boston) are in service in and around Boston. In October of 1891 a personal invitation was extended through these graduates, to all who were interested in establishing a settlement for social work in Boston, to form an association for that purpose. The invitation met with a quick and generous response, and an Association was at once formed which now numbers about three hundred members. This Association is made up of persons who are interested in this special type of work. No other qualification is asked for. Of course, the principles upon which the work is to be carried on are clearly stated in the constitution which was adopted by the Association. As has been stated, the religious motive pervades the whole movement, but it is in no sense sectarian. It is not even inter-denominational. No regard is paid to denominational distinctions. The Council, which is the administrative body in the Association, is made up of persons of various religious faiths, and this has come about not at all by design, but naturally according to personal interest. The work is supported partly by membership fees, and partly by annual subscriptions. The first year a considerable additional expense was incurred in the furnishing of the house, a task which was graciously fulfilled by a committee of ladies from the Association.

The House is located at No. 6 Rollins Street, a short street between Washington Street and Harrison Avenue, in Ward XVII., at the east end of the city. The street itself is quite exceptional in its appearance, being made up of two blocks of entirely respectable-looking dwelling-houses. Some of the houses still remain in the possession of the original owners. The general section covered by the House is a narrow strip of about half a mile in length, lying on the east side of Washington Street, and falling away toward what is known as the South Cove. The social movement in Boston is away from the south and east. Each street toward the west increases the social standing of its residents.

The population of the neighborhood is not the most picturesque in its poverty in the city. The most recent immigration—the Russian Jew, the Italian, and even the Arab—has not as yet really invaded the district, though it has made its appearance at the lower end. That stage of overcrowding has not been reached which discriminates in favor of the lowest and most degraded. And yet the population embraces some of the worst types to be found in the city. It is by no means homogeneous. Nearly all nationalities and races are represented in it. There is no social unity. The largest social unit is a group. Extreme social conditions are found in close contiguity. The visitor who passes from street into alley and court will quickly notice, but will not be apt to measure, the contrasts. The neighborhood is overshadowed by vice, though not as yet overwhelmed by it. The social evil is a more serious menace than drunkenness or gambling. In a word, the neighborhood is in precisely the condition in which some one section of a great city is always to be found, which has been left to take the chance of the future, with little or nothing to expect from business or social movements, and without the advantage of any kind of unity.

This general section of Boston was chosen with the purpose of attempting to stay the tide of poverty and vice which is flowing in upon it, and of arresting the social disintegration which, has already begun. While the section represents in some parts a family life of intelligence and purity, it represents in other parts most sorely the need of the three-fold work of development, recovery, and rescue.

The house accommodates at present six men. The head of the

House—Mr. Robert A. Woods—is a graduate of Andover, a former resident of Toynbee Hall, and now well known through his lectures upon social questions, and his book upon "English Social Movements." With him are associated five men, graduates of different colleges and seminaries, who give part or all of their time to the work. The "spare time" of men who are engaged in regular pursuits is not alone sufficient for the work in hand. Business life in this country is so intense, that all which can be asked of those in regular business is a certain amount of volunteer aid in special departments. No resident is received for less than six months, and the average term of service is more than a year. Naturally, the longer the time in residence the greater the results which may be expected. A certain element of comparative permanence among the residents is absolutely necessary to any success. And next to permanence among the residents is regularity among the associate workers. A very efficient staff of associates has already been organized of those who give one or two evenings of each week. Among these, at present, are some of the younger journalists, architects, and scientific and literary men of the city, some ladies of thorough interest and experience in work among girls and young women.

The local work of the Andover House rests upon certain well-defined principles, which it may be well at this point to carefully enumerate. The first principle is that the work is altogether personal, and in no sense institutional. None of the ordinary institutional results are to be expected. A thorough and consistent plan has been formulated, but no programme. The work of next year may not be that of this year. The one constant quantity is personal influence, personal invention, personal sympathy and courage, the individual and united purpose to increase the moral valuation of the neighborhood.

A second principle is that nothing should be done by the House which can be, or ought to be, done through existing organizations. All duplication of work is to be avoided. With this end in view, a careful estimate has been made of the various forces which are already in operation within the neighborhood, whether religious, moral, educational, or charitable. The aim is co-operation. Members of the House are identified with many of the organizations located in the vicinity. They serve on their committees, and are their agents and visitors. They report facts coming within their province, make suggestions, and in every way seek to increase their efficiency and usefulness. The Andover House does not crave notoriety in matters of reform, but it is intent upon securing such results affecting the public morals as may from time to time seem legitimate and practicable. It has already initiated some plans which have had a successful issue, but the work has been done through others. The object of the House is influence, not power.

A third principle, resolutely adhered to, is the avoidance of proselyting, not in appearance only, but in reality. The motive of the work, as I have said, is profoundly religious, admitting a consecration as deep as that attending any missionary enterprise, but the results arrived at are not specifically religious. Members of the House have the perfect freedom of their personal religious affiliations, and are encouraged to co-operate in every practicable way with the churches with which they may be identified. But the attempt to change the religious faith of those whom the residents may visit in their houses is not for a moment considered; and this, not as a matter of policy, but of principle. The one end and aim of the House is to create a true social unity, to which all may contribute who have anything of value to offer. Its chief object is not that of the churches. The religious motive permeates and informs its methods, but it does not seek chiefly religious results. Religion in and of itself, as illustrated in the various communions, will never give the social unity, in any community, which is now the most essential element in the change of social conditions.

A fourth principle is the development of the neighborhood from within rather than from without. The personal acknowledgment of this principle is through residence. That, however, is the only easy beginning of its application. The neighborhood must be in every way awakened, encouraged, and stimulated to work for itself. Perhaps the quickest appeal can be made through the needs of the children. Later, the appeals from more general needs can be made, needs which the neighborhood can fitly ask the city to satisfy, and the final outcome may be the development of a commendable pride, as true as that which sometimes shows itself in village communities. But the constant method is improvement through self-help, not by patronage. I cannot overestimate the advantage of co-operation between adjacent classes in society. To bring together the extremes, as in ordinary mission work, is not a sufficient result. It is the coming together of those who are separated by the slighter differences in conditions—which are often the greater barriers—the mutual helpfulness of those whose lives really touch, that constitutes the permanent hope of any neighborhood. It is the acknowledgment of neighborship which realizes that fine social ideal—the community.

Acting upon these principles, the residents of the House began their work about a year ago. It should be noted that for the first six months there were but four in residence, and two of these could give only a part of their time. Naturally, the first object sought was a general knowledge of the resources of the neighborhood, and then acquaintance with the people, as far as possible, through visitation in their homes. But access to one's neighbors in a city is not an altogether easy matter, whatever may be the intent. Fortunately, the small boy proved to be a natural medium of communication with the families whom the residents wished most to reach. As soon as the boys in the vicinage heard of the House, they began at once to investigate its possibilities. And as they came in increasing numbers, they were organized into clubs, till every night in the week, except Sunday, was given up to groups as large as could be accommodated.

A library of the best boys' books was generously provided by one of the Council for circulation, and the residents taxed their invention to provide interesting and profitable entertainment. The boy, thus become a friend, opened the door of the home, and the heart of the parent. Access to a considerable part of the neighborhood became simple and natural. Visitation, as far as there have been time and opportunity for it, has been conducive to the best results. Friendly relations have been established, which are simple and sincere. One of the more mature and experienced of the residents has gained a place in the confidence and affection of the families in an adjacent court, which any man might envy. He is known and trusted as their friend, to whom they turn in their temptations and trials, which are neither few nor light. And through him they are beginning to find themselves at home at the House.

After visitation came organization—so much, at least, as seemed necessary for the best development of those who had been reached. I have referred to the boys' clubs. These were transferred early in the autumn from the house to a hall near by, partly to allow the use of the house for the organization of other groups, and partly in accordance with the principle, which I have enunciated, that whatever can be done through other agencies should be done through them. The place of the boys' clubs in the house has been taken by clubs and classes of young men and young women, and by groups of girls and of children—these last under the care of special teachers. The residents and their associates still take the entire charge of the work among boys, and devote much time to it. The theory of work is to be lavish with personal influence, to put a great deal of one's self into the thing which one undertakes, whatever it may be. From four to six residents and associates are present on each evening with each group of boys. To the ordinary exercises and drill, of such clubs are added regular exhibitions through the microscope, instruction in drawing and carpentry, talks on electrical science, and a plentiful supply of good music. The clubs of young men and young women are furnished with fit objects of entertainment and study. One class in current events is under the charge of an accomplished journalist. The following schedule of evenings illustrates this kind of work :

Monday.—Boys' Club (thirty boys under eleven years of age), at hall.

Tuesday.—Boys' Club (twenty boys over twelve years of age), at hall.

Wednesday.—Boys' Club (twenty-five boys from eleven to twelve years of age), at hall ; Young Women's Class (fifteen young women), at house.

Thursday.—Monday night Boys' Club repeated, at hall.

Friday.—Tuesday night Boys Club repeated, at hall ; Children's Club (thirty children), 3 P. M., at house; Young Men's Class (fifteen young men), 8 P.M., at house.

Saturday.—Wednesday night Boys' Club repeated, at hall ; Girls' Club (thirty girls), 2.30 P.M., at house; Young Men's Club (ten young men), 8 P.M., at house.

Sunday.—8.30 P.M., music hour, at house.

At the present time organization has not advanced beyond these limits, but it will be extended among older persons if it seems the natural method of procedure ; otherwise some other means of mutual aid will be devised. It may prove to be better to establish entirely different relations with the working-men of the district. The residents have been cordially welcomed in their intercourse with the leaders of labor organizations, and it is hoped that there may soon be a conference between some representatives of these organizations and the members of the Council.

The house is frequently used for receptions, sometimes for the association, sometimes for workers in the various societies, temperance or charitable, in the ward, and sometimes for the families in different parts of the neighborhood. It is becoming more and more a true social centre. The table is found to be a fitting place where the residents may discuss with guests all questions of order or progress affecting the community. Much more is accomplished by the social than by merely official intercourse with those who may in various ways represent the political, or educational, or philanthropic affairs of the neighborhood.

While these more personal methods have been in operation, attention has been steadily directed toward the opportunity for material improvement, where it seemed to be necessary to moral development. I have said that the last stage of overcrowding has not been reached in the district. But the tenement-house question presents here, as everywhere where it exists, the dilemma, how to improve the tenement and keep the tenant. Little is gained morally by the erection of new and better buildings, if the old dwellers are driven out into even lower surroundings. Doubtless the beginning must be made in the elevation of the tenant through a certain amount of improvement in the tenement ; but after a little the process must be reversed and the further improvement of the tenement effected through the elevation of the tenant. It has seemed, therefore, to some of the business men on the Council, that it is necessary that control, by rental or purchase, should be gained of some of the worst tenements in the district, that the work of internal and external improvement may be carried on together. There is reason to hope that the methods of tenement-house reform developed by Miss Octavia Hill may be applied at no distant day to some one house, at least, as an object-lesson.

Without entering further into the local work of the House, which from the nature of the case cannot be fully forecast or even described in detail, I will refer to its more general scientific work. One object of the House is the study by the residents of social conditions. There are three sources of this study—observation in the field, conversation with experts, and books. The residents bring to their work a certain amount of attainment in the theoretical study of Sociology. Through the generosity of a friend of the House, residing in another State, a sociological library has been begun, which will enable the residents to continue their economic studies.

There are unusual opportunities in Boston for conference with experts on social questions. The value of the services of the Hon.

Carroll D. Wright, as Chief of the Bureau of Statistics of Labor in Massachusetts, was recognized by his appointment as United States Commissioner of Labor, and the work which he inaugurated has been vigorously maintained by his successor, the Hon. Horace G. Wadlin. The city has in its employ experts skilled in educational and economic affairs, and sanitation. The same remark applies to several of the educational and charitable institutions in and around Boston. And not a few private citizens, who have consecrated their leisure as well as their wealth to the service of humanity, have become authorities upon many questions of social urgency.

The field of observation open to the residents of the House is far wider than the limits of their actual work. Subjects reaching quite outside these limits are already before them for individual study and investigation. I am confident that no *general* field is so inviting to the student of questions which are partly social and partly political, as that of municipal politics. For the present, more questions of this sort await solution from the municipality than from the State. Boston has now reached that stage in its municipal growth when the most interesting and vital problems are pressing for solution. The Greater Boston, which Mr. Sylvester Baxter has described in his intelligent study, comprising the adjacent towns and cities, is nearly double the population of the city proper. But this greater city is already a fact in some particulars, especially as so recognized by the general Government in the postal service, and by the State in the system of sewerage. It is fast becoming a question, how long interests which are so closely related can be kept apart by political boundaries. An absorption of territory by Boston, corresponding to that already accomplished by Philadelphia and Chicago, would precipitate many moral and social issues which are to-day held in uncertainty. The time is opportune, whether changes are imminent or not, for the student of municipal questions to inquire into the social and political life of Boston.

Little reference has been made to the Andover House Association, which supports the House. Thus far its chief business has been the support of the House. The main return from the House to the Association has been in the bulletins, which from time to time show the progress of the work. Something has been done in the way of lectures, delivered at the house for the benefit of all the members. These lectures were furnished altogether from the Association itself. A course of six lectures is inserted to show the nature of the subjects treated by the lecturers, and afterward in general discussion : 1. "The Housing of the People," by Hon. Robert Treat Paine. 2. "Sanitary Improvement," by Professor Dwight Porter. 3. "The Temperance Problem in Massachusetts," by Rev. William E. Wolcott. 4. "Women's College Settlements," by Miss Vida D. Scudder. 5. "Working Girls' Clubs," by Miss O. M. E. Rowe. 6. "The Child Problem," by Mr. C. W. Birtwell.

The House serves, through its residents and library, the much-needed purpose of a bureau of information on social questions. Preparations are also being made for lectures to be given, as desired, in the neighboring towns, according to the methods of University extension. Social clubs are being organized in many towns, some in connection with churches and some independently, for serious investigation and discussion. Eastern Massachusetts, with its large urban and suburban population, with its manufacturing centres, representing various and changing nationalities, and with its small village communities retaining still something of the original type of the early settlement, offers rare facilities for social study. More than this, it makes its appeal to the new philanthropy. The social problem of New England is as grave as that of any part of the country. Charity certainly cannot solve it. Something as true in spirit, but far broader and deeper in method, is necessary to effect safely the transfer from the old individualism to the future state of social unity.

The work of the Andover House has been set forth in this chapter as an illustration of certain principles and methods which characterize a new type of philanthropy. The general features of the type are unmistakable. Details vary according to the agencies employed. Some of the agencies are purely scientific and express little or no sentiment. But all depend in part for their scientific value upon the sympathy which attends their working. There are facts in social life which will not yield their entire content except under the sympathetic approach. Science, which is unsympathetic, does not find what it is searching after. Sentiment may be lacking, but not sympathy. Still the fact remains that the new philanthropy is making its strongest appeal to young men and young women, especially to those who have the best intellectual and moral training. It is impossible to overestimate the seriousness and the enthusiasm with which the incoming generation is attacking what it believes to be the problem of its time. There is a fervor about this consecration to the work of social Christianity like that which characterized the work of Christian missions at the beginning of the century. It may well be so, for the only cry in our time which compares in intensity with that which caught the ear of Carey and Mills, is the cry from the Christian cities. We are beginning to understand how much the apparently simple command of Christ meant, " Thou shalt love thy neighbor." The perfect obedience has not yet been rendered, but enough has been attempted to show that it requires careful study, invention, patience, sympathy, and practical heroism. Resident work " among the poor in great cities " has its reliefs, like missionary work in foreign lands, chief of which is the fact that it is work in a group. Like that, too, it has its grateful surprises, or perhaps, one should better say, its grateful certainties, in individual results. The outcome is always found in some lives rescued, recovered, enlarged, with the possibility that one, at least, may be reached who may prove a greater blessing to his kind than all his benefactors. And the social result, while more undefined, is still appreciable to those who, as they work, can see in it the promise of the future society.

The growth of the movement represented by the Andover House is quite as rapid as its best interests allow. Three houses are already established in Boston working upon the same principles: one connected with Boston University, made up of graduate students and their wives; Denison House, one of the Women's College Settlements; and Dorothea House, named after Miss Dorothea Dix, and composed of unmarried women; and there are two others in immediate prospect. Similar work in other cities is fully described in other pages of this volume. The general movement is a remarkable illustration of the value of the contribution of the personal element, when fully trained and consecrated, to a noble cause.

POSTSCRIPT BY ROBERT A. WOODS, HEAD OF THE ANDOVER HOUSE

THE plan of work as explained by Dr. Tucker in this chapter has been quite consistently followed during the four years since the Andover House opened its doors. Whatever change of emphasis experience may have brought about in the details of the plan, the residents have held with especial firmness to the principle of being "lavish of personal influence." In several ways—though this art is very long, and results come not with observation—the House has justified the hopes of those who inaugurated it.

It has succeeded in keeping together a group of five or six college men representing a variety of tasks and of callings in life. The average stay of all the residents has been over a year. For the present staff, the average stay has been nearly two years. Thus the residents become identified in feeling with the neighborhood life, and several of them have developed original and valuable lines of social work such as would be suggested by their individual interests and talents.

In a perfectly gradual and natural way the House has been coming into relation with the people and the social institutions of its neighborhood and district. This is accomplished at the House by informal hospitality and by a great variety of clubs, classes, lect-

13

ures, concerts, entertainments, and parties, in all of which there is
the touch of simple fellowship on a basis of common humanity; and
throughout the district by visiting in the homes of the people and
by sharing in the work of all sorts of organizations and institutions
—charitable, philanthropic, reformatory, political, educational, religious—that are making for the better life of the district. The
plan is still to accomplish results not by creating new agencies, but
by co-operating with those already at work. This has been possible
for nearly everything but the ministry of beauty. That had to be
developed out of nothing. The House has taken the lead in organizing free art exhibitions and an annual series of concerts, through
which the best art and music that Boston can supply has become
available to South End people.

Much work has been done in the way of the careful and sympathetic study of social conditions. Some of the residents have
come into relations of friendly understanding with the trades-union-
ists of the city, and have come to have knowledge of, and influence in, the labor movement in its changing phases. Each resident
is encouraged to take up the special investigation of some practical social question. The results of these studies are published in
a series of bulletins which are sent out to members of the Andover
House Association. Some of their titles are: " A Guide to Evening
Classes in Boston," "The Number of the Unemployed," "The
Anatomy of a Tenement Street," "A Study of Beggars and their
Lodgings." One of the best uses of the House is its now well-rec-
ognized function of serving as a kind of moral and intellectual exchange through which busy men may acquaint themselves with the
social situation, at which they may meet on neutral ground other
men who under all ordinary circumstances would never cross their
paths, and may even be separated from them by great gulfs of
social distinction and prejudice.

August, 1895.

AMONG THE POOR OF CHICAGO

By JOSEPH KIRKLAND

AUTHOR OF "ZURY," ETC.

PECULIARITY OF CHICAGO'S CONDITIONS — WIDE DISTRIBUTION OF THE POOR POPULATION—THE GREATEST POVERTY AMONG FOREIGN ELEMENTS—"THE DIVE "—TYPICAL FAMILIES—THE "BAD LANDS "—CHINA-TOWN—THE CLARK STREET MISSION — THE WOMAN'S CHRISTIAN TEMPERANCE UNION — THE PACIFIC GARDEN MISSION — STATISTICS—THE UNITY CHURCH, ST. JAMES'S CHURCH AND CENTRAL CHURCH MISSIONS — VOLUNTEER VISITORS—A VETERAN—HULL HOUSE—CHARITY ORGANIZATIONS—THE JEWS' QUARTER—THE LIBERTY BELL AND FRIENDSHIP BUILDINGS—STATISTICS OF A SWEAT SHOP—THE ANARCHISTS—SOCIALISTS.

CHICAGO'S plague-spots are rather red than black ; blotches marking excess rather than insufficiency. Vice and crime are more characteristic of a new, young, busy, careless, prosperous city than is any compulsory, inevitable misery. An English philanthropist who visited Hull House (Rev. Mr. Barnett, Warden of Toynbee Hall) remarked, in taking his leave, that the prevalent dirt and flagrant vice in Chicago exceeded anything in London ; but that he had seen scarce any evidence of actual want.

The West is the paradise of the poor. " And the purgatory of the rest of us," adds some fine lady who agonizes over the servant problem. Well, even if this were true (which it is not), it would be better than the reverse. The paradise of the rich, based on the purgatory of the poor, has endured long enough in the older lands.

"How the other half lives," in Chicago, is " pretty much as it chooses." Americans born, and the better natures among the foreign born (supposing them to have physical strength), can select their own kind of happiness. If they choose the joy which springs from sobriety, they can have it in plenty. If they prefer the delight of drink, that also is abundant. A solid devotion to work and saving gives a house and lot, a comfortable and well-taught family, and a good chance for children and grandchildren, who will take rank among the best, employing laborers of their own, and perhaps, alas! looking back with mortification on their laboring ancestors. An equally solid devotion to drink gives vice, crime, want, and (what we should call) misery; but this is a free country. The latter class, like the former, are exercising their inalienable right of self-government. They absolutely do not want our cleanliness, our savings-accounts, our good clothes, books, schools, churches, society, progress, and all that, unless they can have them without paying the price—temperance; and they cannot so have them. Half of the "other half" belong strictly to the first-named class, a tenth to the last-named, and the rest pursue a middle course. Some rise from the middle to the upper; the others live along, having ups and downs and furnishing the recruits to keep up the numbers of the lower, the "submerged tenth" which, happily, has not the faculty of maintaining itself by direct reproduction.

The city has no "East End," "Whitechapel," or "Mulberry Street" region; no locality given over to great hives of helplessness, since there is no quarter which was built up for fine residences or business blocks and afterward deserted and turned over to baser uses. The most ancient house in town (but one) is not fifty years old, and the average scarcely twenty. Therefore "the tenement-house evil," as it is known in New York and London, shows almost no trace in the new, spacious mart on the edge of the Grand Prairie. Rooms are sublet to individuals and families, yet it is not in tall, huge rookeries built for the purpose, but in smaller, lower structures, outside the limits of the Great Fire, which destroyed the whole middle district—cleared it of weeds to make way for a sturdier and healthier growth. If ever the time comes when the sky-scraping structures of to-day are deserted by the uses for which they are now occupied because they are in the geographical and business centre of the city, then there may be in Chicago gigantic human hives of wretchedness such as exist in London and New York. But as Chicago can spread north, south, and west, it is difficult to imagine a state of things when the present business district shall not be what it is.

The "lay of the land" is against local congestion. The river, with its main stem running east and west and its sprawling branches running north and south, trisects the whole plain into North Side, South Side, and West Side. These in turn are dissected into smaller patches by the railways, which come to the very centre of population, and radiate thence in all directions except due east, where the lake maintains a glorious ventilation, moral and material.

There is no "Sailors' Quarter," no place where Jack ashore hastens to spend in a week the savings of a year; gets drunk as soon as possible, and stays drunk as long as possible, to balance his weeks or months of enforced abstinence. The sailors here have only a week or less afloat at one stretch, and they spend, every winter, several months on shore, when they go mining or lumbering or pursuing whatever calling suits their fancy. Many of them are family men — good, sturdy fellows, not distinguishable from the average of intelligent tradesmen.

Familiar Scene in an Underground Lodging.

For depth of shadow in Chicago low life one must look to the foreign elements,* the persons who are not only of alien birth but of unrelated blood—the Mongolian, the African, the Sclav, the semitropic Latin. Among them may be found a certain degree of isolation, and therefore of clannish crowding; also of contented squalor, jealous of inspection and interference. It is in the quarters inhabited by these that there are to be found the worst parts of Chicago, the most unsavory spots in their moral and material aspects.

Twelfth Street is encumbered by a long viaduct, reaching from Wabash Avenue, westward, across the south branch of the river, ending on the west side very near the starting-point of the Great Fire of 1871. The viaduct nearly fills the street, and from it one

---

* Of Chinamen there are about two thousand in Chicago, living, as a general rule, in one quarter of the city—South Clark Street, adjoining the line occupied by the Lake Shore and eastern Illinois Railways, running eastward and southward, and the Rock Island, running westward. Of Italians Chicago has many thousands, part of whom live in the South Clark Street neighborhood, and a larger number only a few squares away, on the West Side, across the south branch of the river. Besides the light common labor of street-cleaning, scavengering, etc., they control, practically, all the great fruit-business of the city, and some of them are getting rich at it. Yet the homes of the majority are among the most lowly and squalid in the city. Educated Italians of the upper classes are handsomely housed in some of the fashionable streets. The Poles and Bohemians inhabit a southwestern quarter, where their impossible names occupy the sign-boards and their unbeautiful faces strike the eye and haunt the memory. They are hard workers and not extravagant, and though crowded they are not congested, though poor they are not in want. The colored people have done and are doing remarkably well, considering the disadvantages and discouragements under which they live. They are not largely the supporters of the grog-shops. Their besetting sin is gambling. They are industrious rather than hard-working, docile rather than enterprising, and economical rather than acquisitive. There are impediments to any accumulation such as their white neighbors engage in. For instance, suppose one of them to invest his savings in a " Building Society," he would find, when his lot was ready for him, that he would be unwelcome to his neighbors of a lighter skin. Even as a renter he is only acceptable in regions devoted to his race. As one of them said to me : " Nobody thinks a colored man fit for anything above being a porter." Still, as I said, there is a very perceptible advance in the race ; and it shows but little of poverty or dependence, and still less of crime.

looks into the second stories of the taller houses, and over the roofs of the shorter. One has there the advantages for observation possessed by the fabled "devil on two sticks." This is the habitation of the Italian proletariat.

To get to the main floors of these squalid habitations one must climb down many steps; hence the name of the locality, "The

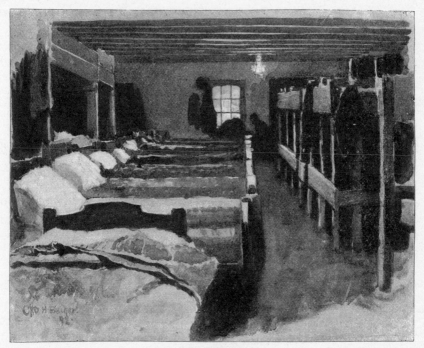

A Chicago Underground Lodging.

Dive." I once saw men carrying into one of the darkened entrances here an immense bunch of green bananas, which hung down between them like the "grapes of Eshcol" in the old primer. One can only fancy the atmosphere in which this wonderful fruit would hang to ripen, and hope that the ripening process is one of exhalation, not of inhalation, during the week or more which must elapse before it appears, yellow and mellow, to be sold from the wayside fruit-stand, or be dragged slowly about the streets in the wagons attended by the dark-skinned pedlers as they troll forth, in the sonorous Italian tones, "Banano-o! Fi, Ri, Banano-o-o-o!"

A bad state of things exists under the shadow of this viaduct, and under the inclined planes by which the traffic of each street it crosses is raised to its level. This is easy to believe, but it is hard to imagine just how filthy, how squalid, how noisome, how abhorrent it all is. Walking along between inhabited houses and the brick abutments of the raised way is like walking between the walls of a sewer—like it to every sense—sight, smell, hearing, and feeling.

The adjacent buildings are mostly of wood—small, low, rotten, and crowded. In no case have I found one family occupying more than two rooms—often only one. Here and there would be seen an attempt at cleanliness of floor and bedclothing, but nowhere even a pretence of sweeping of halls and stairways, or of shovelling out of gutters and other foul conduits. What squalor, filth, crowding! The constant feeling of the visitor is, "how dreadfully wretched these people—ought to be."

Ought to be, but are not. They are chiefly the lower class of Italians, born and bred, probably, to the knowledge of actual hunger, which here they must rarely feel. I went among them recently; there were scarcely any men visible; the swarms were chiefly of women and children. The men were away, largely, no doubt, attending to the fruit business and scavenger work which have been mentioned. The women were universally caring for their innumerable children, and these latter, especially the boys, played, shouted, careered about the halls and stairways, yards and roofs, in uncontrolled freedom and gayety. Two or three of them had found a great turnip, or some such vegetable, and split it in pieces, which they displayed in a row on a board beside a gutter; no pretence of having any customers—it was merely the exhibition of an inherited instinct for keeping an Italian fruit-stand!

In the corner of a squalid hallway, just outside of the maternal door (there not being an inch of spare room within), a bright-eyed little girl had arranged a quite respectable imitation of a floor-bed (both coverlet and stuffing being rags), and on it lay a dirty, dilapidated, flaxen-haired doll. The girl's instinct, too, was showing itself. Within the room the mother, with head bound up, as is the universal custom of her kind, was attending to some duties; a child of two or three years sat staring at the intruder, and on the floor stood a wash-tub over which was bending (and really working) a mite of a girl not more than six years old. Her little arms could scarcely reach the grimy liquid in the bottom of the tub, but she did the best she could, and up and down the tin wash-board sounded her tiny knuckles, handling some dingy, dripping stuff or other, she scarcely pausing to look up and notice who had opened the door.

Here were a few men, more women, and most children; but no young unmarried women. One wonders where are the grown girls. They are not in service in private families; such a thing is unknown here; and they are not adapted to the business of shop-girls. It is to be hoped that they are engaged in the innumerable handicrafts that prevail; paper-box and paper-bag makers, tobacco-handlers, book-folders and stitchers, etc. The Hull House ladies say that they marry early in their teens, and that many of them do bits of plain sewing—the mere finishing of trouser-legs, etc.—at wonderfully low rates, and in wonderfully large quantities, often in the so-called "sweat-shops" of the tailoring trade. The clothing of all has been (apparently) bought at Chicago second-hand clothing stores; or, if imported from Italy, has a common and familiar aspect, which anew illustrates the levelling and averaging hand of modern commerce and intercourse, whence it comes that all mankind is growing to look alike—each individual to be a "composite photograph" of all the rest.

Every person, of whatever sex or age, is clothed sufficiently for decency and for warmth; and seems to be provided with all food necessary to sustain life, though perhaps not the rudest health.

Emerging on a second-story balcony at the back of one of these Italian houses one comes upon a long vista of house rears and tumble-down back - sheds, squalid beyond conception. Neighboring windows are filled with faces peering out with interest and amusement at the stranger. Here and there are bits of rope stretched

Sunday Afternoon in the Italian Quarter.

from one nail to another—from house to shed, from fence to banister, from window-sill to door-post — carrying forlorn arrays of washed clothing. Each is the effort of some lowly woman to preserve a little cleanliness in the garments of herself and her household. At least a forlorn hope is keeping up the battle against vileness.

On a hot summer night every roof and every balcony in sight is covered with sleeping men, women, and children, each with only a single blanket or coverlet for all purposes of protection and decency. All winter the cook-stove of each family supplies warmth to the little household. (The cheapest coal is always to be had at $3 a ton or less.)

"The Bad Lands" is a quarter more repellent because more pretentious than "The Dive," but, being the abode of vice and crime rather than of poverty, it can be properly omitted here. Women of the town are not molested so long as they stay within doors, except on occasion of the frequent rows, fights, robberies, and murders. The men about are, if possible, more repulsive than the women. Some have showy clothes, more are "bums," wrecks of humanity; slouching, dirty, sneaking, hangdog tramps. They do not want work, could not get it if they wanted it, and could not do it if they got it. All they want is a dime a day. With that they can get a great big "schooner" of beer and a chance at the free-lunch counter. They sleep on the floor till the place closes up and then crawl into some doorway or hallway, or go to the police station for a bunk.

One recognizes Chinatown by the curious signs over the shops. The Chinese are industrious and economical and peaceable—never molest anybody who lets them alone. Opium they take just as our people take whiskey, and it does not seem to hurt them any more. But when the police find them taking in whites as well as Chinamen, they "run them in." It is death, and worse than death, to the others, especially to women. In a typical Chinese shop all is scrupulously neat and clean. It seems as if, by some magic, the smoky, dusty atmosphere of Chicago had been excluded from this unique interior, which looks like the inside of a bric-à-brac cabinet, with bright colors, tinsel, and shining metals. On the walls are colored photographs, showing the proprietors beautifully dressed in dove-colored garments. In a kind of shrine stands a "Joss table" or altar, with what is probably a Confucian text hanging

over it, and lying on it some opium pipes. In a room behind the
shop a "fan-tan" game is going on upon a straw-matted table,

Italian Mothers.

around which gather interested Celestials three deep.
In the shop is a freshly opened importation, barrels
and boxes of Chinese delicacies, pickled fish of various kinds, with
the pungent odor which belongs to that kind of food
the world round and the seas over. The men are
clothed in heavy, warm cloth, cut in Chinese fashion—
great, broad cloaks, loose trousers, felt-soled shoes, etc.—
but in American felt hats.

At 406 Clark Street, in the very
midst of all that is alien to our better nature, rises the Clark Street
Mission.* Here are daily gathered, in a free kindergarten, some
scores of the little unfortunates whom a cruel fate has planted in
this cesspool. It is a touching sight; they are so innocent as yet,

* The mission is now on Wabash Avenue, between Fourteenth and Fifteenth Streets.

mere buds springing up in the track of a lava-stream. There is a crèche here as well as kindergarten, and tiny creatures, well fed and cared for, swing in hammocks, or sit, stand, walk, or creep all about in charge of kind, devoted young women. Curiously enough, many of the little ones are born of Arabian mothers. There are some hundreds of Arabs housed near by. The attendant thinks they are Christian converts, in charge of church folk who were formerly missionaries in Arabia. The women are occupied in peddling small wares and trinkets, which they carry about in packs and baskets.* In the same hall are evening and Sunday religious meetings; and not long ago there was a series of midnight prayer-meetings held here, with how much success I do not know.

The whole enterprise is in charge (and at the charge) of the great Woman's Christian Temperance Union. This is an institution of wonderful strength and beauty; a giantess, throned in intelligence and honor; stretching her strong hands toward the weak, sinking thousands of the "submerged tenth," and all who are on the edge of the submergence. The W. C. T. U. numbers more than 200,000 members in all, of whom 16,000 are in Illinois, and their activity is tireless, their ability wonderful. It is one of the phenomena marking the elevation of the sex under the sunshine of Western freedom and prosperity. The building, planned, erected, and paid for by this body, is the most perfect and (as it should be) the most sightly of all Chicago's new "sky-scrapers." It is named "Temperance Temple;" its cost was $1,100,000. Its spare room is fully occupied, and it will earn rentals amounting to $200,000 a year.

The Pacific Garden Mission has a large hall, opening directly on Van Buren Street, within five hundred feet of the Grand Pacific Hotel, yet within a scarcely greater distance of some of the worst of the "bad districts" of the city. "The Dive" is only half a mile south of it, and "The Levee," "The Bad Lands," "Chinatown,"

---

* A year ago I met a party of Arabians on the San Juan River, in Nicaragua, and they too were peddling trinkets carried in packs and baskets.

etc., are still nearer. The single big room is vast and dingy—the latter characteristic inseparable from every apartment in Chicago which is not the object of constant, laborious cleaning and renovation. The walls are covered with Scripture texts in large letters, " Blessed are ye poor, for yours is the kingdom of God," etc. " Welcome," "God is love," and other cheering mottoes are embossed in Christmas greens over the platform. A little collection of hymns is upon each seat, and notices of the hours of services are suspended in various places, among the rest some announcing the Salvation Army meetings. No effort at ornament for ornament's sake appears anywhere ; nor any outward gayety to suggest inward joy and peace. Colonel Clark * is the moving and controlling spirit of the Mission, as well as its chief money supporter. The meetings on Sunday are often full to the doors; a few front seats being filled by the "workers" and particular friends, and the rest by the chance-comers, gathered from adjacent slums to hear the music and look on at the devotional exercises. It is one of the simply religious efforts to elevate the debased and reform the bad, by offering to them "Christ and him crucified;" by the direct interposition of heaven it must succeed, but without such miracle it cannot. The "news of salvation" no longer surprises and charms the world, for the world has ceased to fear the opposite. One is reminded of the plaint made two hundred years ago by the French missionaries sent to the savages of this very region (their skin was red in those days) when they said, in effect : "Surely we are in nowise to be compared with the Holy Apostles ; yet the world must have changed since they went forth among the heathen who heard them gladly, and, rejoicing to receive the glorious news of salvation, flocked forward, one and all, demanding baptism. Here we sail the floods and scale the mountains in pursuit of one poor savage, if haply we may prevail to save him from the wrath to come, and in most cases his salvation is changed to backsliding as soon as our backs are turned." To the same general effect is the conclusion

* Since Colonel Clark's death the work has been ably carried on by Mrs. Clark.

reached by the religious workers of to-day, who say " these beings are in nowise fit subjects for a merely religious ministry."

I once told a young musician (a Scandinavian) at the Pacific Garden Mission that I was then in search of the very poor and miserable, the helplessly wretched, and asked him where they were to be found. He asked where I had been, and on telling him that I came fresh from "The Dive," "The Bad Lands," "Biler Avenue," "Niggertown," "Chinatown," etc., he asked if these were not poor enough. I said they were rather vicious, drunken, and depraved than poor; that I wanted to find the poverty that springs from misfortune rather than that from drink. To this he impulsively gave the pregnant answer:

"The Dive."

"There is none. You might find one or two others in five hundred, but it is drink in the case of all the rest."

And so it goes. Such is the evidence of the experts, the philanthropists, the missionaries, and the senses themselves. There are sixty saloons in two blocks of this dreadful Dismal Swamp. Each saloon pays $500 a year of city license alone ; pays its United

States Government license for selling spirits, beer, and tobacco; pays for all its stock in trade, its rent, its wages, and expenses—thrives like a Canada thistle on the barren soil of its environment. Five hundred dollars for license, $500 for rent, $1,000 for wages and expenses, and $1,500 for stock in trade makes $3,500. The sums paid by these "poor" must reach $4,000 a year, on the average, to each saloon; and sixty saloons gives $240,000 a year, all in one street, within a distance of two squares. Verily the savings of the rich are as nothing compared with the wastings of the poor. Beer is the alleviation and perpetuation of poverty.

I also asked the young musician about the condition of his fellow-Scandinavians, where their poor could best be studied. He replied that there were none. Individual helplessness was cared for by individual charities and the churches. That is what might be expected. The Scandinavian immigration has been, on the whole, the finest addition to the northwest. They are largely agriculturists, are temperate, industrious, strong, frugal, and hardy. Not seldom do great colonies of them go on cheap excursions back to visit the Fatherland. They pass through Chicago—men, women, and children—with bands playing and flags flying; they cross the sea and spend some time at the old home, spreading the news of Western freedom and plenty, and then return with many recruits and with fresh relish for the Greater Scandinavia they are building among us. Those who do remain in the cities are helpers worth having. The girls make the best house-servants—strong, intelligent, respectful, and self-respecting; and the men, though not blameless in the matter of drink, yet are not among the willing slaves to it. On the whole, they see the alternative presented to them—the two kinds of happiness already spoken of—and make what seems to us the wisest choice between them. The servants, as cooks and "second girls," earn from three to five or six dollars a week besides their board and lodging, and the demand for such as have anything like a fair knowledge of their business is always ahead of the supply.

GERMAN NIGHT AT HULL HOUSE.

They dress well, save money, and spend immense sums in helping their friends here and in the Fatherland.

In the "North Division," near the great gas-works, exists a large colony which of old earned the name of "Little Hell," and which presents features of deep shadow with gleams of growing light—a dark cloud with a silver lining. Many of the men are gas-work laborers, doing hard duty, earning large wages, and drinking deep draughts. They are of three races—Irish, German, and Scandinavian—the first-named the most able and the most turbulent. The wages earned since the works were started, if they had been wisely used, would have bought the entire plant; would have vested every dollar of the vast and profitable stock in the workers. The latter would now be the capitalists. But that is a mere truism. The wage-earners of the whole country would be the capitalists if it were not that they have preferred to take their joy drop by drop.

The bright lining of the dark cloud hovering about the gasworks is the Unity Church Industrial School and Boys' Club near by, and the Saint James's Church and Central Church Missions, not far away. The former (which I happen to know most about) was started in 1876 by the women of Robert Collyer's church, in an effort to do something for the poorest and most neglected children, the difficulty being that this class was soon supplanted by a better class, less in need of help—" people more anxious for what they could get than what they could learn." The others, children of the drunken and vicious, were always hardest to reach and to keep hold of.

From this grain of mustard-seed has grown a great tree. The excellent and benevolent Eli Bates bequeathed to the enterprise $20,000, which was used for the construction of a brick building having all the appliances for an industrial school, and there the worthy Unity Church people spend time and money to good purpose. There are classes in various branches, and a large and well-kept crèche.

A noticeable feature of this "lay mission" is the Boys' Club, where, for several months every year, meetings have been held on several evenings each week to give the youth of the neighborhood rational and wholesome fun with some incidental instruction. The boys range from eight to sixteen years old, and were at the start a "hard lot." Yet they always had some traits of good feeling. The young women teachers always found them easier to manage than did the men. And even when discipline had to be maintained by force, the majority was sure to be on the side of law and order. As far as possible, the boys are made to manage their own games and exercises, showing sometimes a good deal of ability. They number, on ordinary evenings, about sixty, the "picnic aggregate" reaching to a hundred and fifty. The older boys are workers during the daytime; the younger, attendants on public and parochial schools.

There is but little want among the families. Their houses are small and not crowded together; but the households occupy generally only two or three rooms each.

Whether influenced by the various missions near by, by the paving and improvement of streets, or by other causes, or partly by the one and partly by the others, the place is losing its old character, and even its ugly sobriquet is almost forgotten.

In Chicago the "fashion" and the larger part (though not by any means all) of the wealth of the city are on the "South Side" and "North Side," where also the deepest poverty and degradation are to be found. On the great "West Side" are the industrious and prosperous workers, with their tens of thousands of labor-bought homes. It may be a new idea to the denizens of older cities that laborers should, can, and do own their dwelling-places, both land and building. Far more than half the homes in Chicago are so owned and occupied. The chief part of real-estate speculation is the buying of suburban acres and subdividing and selling them in lots to thrifty workmen. Purchase for the sake of putting up houses to rent as dwellings (except in the case of flats) is now extremely rare. The chief agent in this homestead movement is to be found in the numerous "building societies," wherein the mechanic deposits his savings as they accrue, and then when be wishes to build his home he draws from the society whatever he may have laid up, and borrows from it what he may need in addition, paying a premium in addition to the usual interest. (This premium and interest inure to the benefit of the other depositors.) Membership in a building society, and the

Hull House Crèche, or Day Nursery.

hope of a bit of ground all his own, are wonderful incentives to temperance in the man and economy in the wife. And when the lot is selected, how he clings to it! Beer and whiskey are forgotten. Even schooling and some other good and proper cares are apt to be postponed. A city of such homes is safe from anarchy. As for any wielder of torch and dynamite, as soon as he steps forth into the light of the humble private fireside, and the "lamp in the window," he is in peril of his life.

On the West Side are also, especially in winter, the unemployed; some of whom could not find work if they would, some would not if they could, and some, when they can and do work, make the omnipresent saloon their savings-bank; a bank which takes in good money but pays out only false tokens.

I accompanied one of the "Volunteer County Visitors" on her walk in search of the people who should be helped by charity, public or private. We walked through a half-mile of street lined with the crowded habitations of the poor. At the farther end of it are visible the moving trains of the Fort Wayne Railway, and above and beyond these the masts and funnels of shipping. Being just outside the old "burnt district," its houses are of wood, ancient, squalid, dilapidated. There is not more than about one saloon to every street corner, therefore this is far from an "infested" region. It is chiefly occupied by Italians, who are not, as yet, the sots and terrors of the social system, and do not seem likely ever to become so. Groups of them are idling about, well enough dressed, but low-browed and ill-favored, looking with apparent surliness on visitors come to spy out the nakedness of the land. Within the houses we find the families crowded into two small rooms each, or thereabouts; and in those two rooms are all the operations of existence to be carried on in each case. Sleeping, eating, cooking, washing, ironing, sickness, child-bearing, nursing, living, dying, and burying—these considerations force themselves on the mind and suggest dismal pictures as one fancies a life so spent.

Yet as to mere room, warmth, shelter, dryness, and convenience, the inhabitants are better accommodated than is the campaigning soldier in his tent, having no furniture, clothing for night or day, or other appliances for comfort, except those he can carry with him from camp to camp in addition to his arms and accoutrements. But women and children are not soldiers. Camp miseries would kill them; one who has suffered such privation can scarcely feel the proper degree of pity for these creatures—warm, dry, fat, clothed, safe, at leisure and at liberty.

The poorest and most wretched household we found that day

was that of an old soldier, a gray-haired man of education and (at some time) of intelligence, once a lieutenant in a volunteer regiment. He was wounded at the battle of Fair Oaks. There he lies, grimy and vermin-infested, in a filthy bed, with a young grandchild beside him in like condition, and a drunken virago of a woman, ramping and scolding in the two rooms which constitute the family abode. She is quite the most repulsive being yet met with. A little inquiry develops the fact that this man was in the Soldiers' Home at Milwaukee (and could return there to remain, if he wished), well fed, clothed, and cared for, and that he left there because: "You see you can't stand it to be kept down all the time, and moved back and forth, and here and there, whether you like it or not." And he moved his black paws back and forth, and here and there, on the dingy bedclothes, to indicate how the Home deprived him of his freedom—his "liberty" to pass his time in the living death which his present condition seems to the onlooker.

Chicago's "Hull House" is already widely known as the "Toynbee Hall" of the West, though the parallelism between the two institutions is far from absolute and complete. In the first place, Hull House was started and is carried on by women, with only the occasional and exceptional help—welcome though it is—of the other sex. Then, too, the system is as different as are the conditions in which the two institutions are placed. Its best service in stimulating the intellectual life of the neighborhood has been in the establishment of its college-extension classes, which have grown into what is practically an evening college, with thirty courses weekly and a membership of one hundred and fifty to two hundred students of a high order.

In a widely different sphere is its strictly philanthropic work. Yet, even here, Hull House is not a mission, since no especial religion is inculcated and no particular social reform is announced as the object of its being. If people in the humbler classes of its visitors learn there to live good, clean, temperate lives, it is through

"Temperance Temple."
Built by the Woman's Christian Temperance Union.

the demonstration of the enduring beauty and gayety of such a life as contrasted with the lurid and fleeting joys of the other. Hull

House parlors, class-rooms, gymnasium, library, etc., are the rivals of the swarming grog-shops. Nobody, not even the ornaments of the college-extension classes, is more welcome than the poor fellow who has begun to feel that he can no longer struggle against poverty and drink, and nobody is less pointed at, preached at, or set upon than he. The choice is open to him, right hand or left hand as he sees fit, and it surely seems as if no sane human being could hesitate. At least the boy growing up with the choice before him, and the light shining on the parting of the ways, will take—is taking—the one those devoted young women are making so inviting to his footsteps.

It is not charity that Hull House offers, any more than it is precept. True, there are some cases which arise, outside the business of the House, where public or private beneficence is turned toward deserving helplessness. But that is not strictly Hull House work. The latter consists in bestowing friendship and sympathy, the sisterly heart, hand, and voice, on all who are willing to come within its sweet and pleasant influence.

With characteristic wisdom and good feeling the Board of the grand Chicago Public Library (free to all) has placed one of its sub-stations in the reading-room of Hull House; and in that large, handsome, well-lighted apartment applications for books are taken, and the books are delivered and returned, all quite without expense of any kind to the reader.

The building which contains the library and reading-room has been added to the Hull House structures by the liberality of Edward B. Butler. The same building contains a studio in which drawing-classes are held each evening, and an admirably fitted art-exhibit room in which some of the best pictures in Chicago are shown from time to time. The humanitarian side of the Hull House activity is maintained by the Nursery, the Kindergarten, the Diet Kitchen, the District Nursing, and the Industrial Classes. Its activities are multiform that they may meet the needs, not alone of the enterprising nor yet the poor, but of its neighborhood as a whole. That it has met such a need is shown by the fact that the weekly membership of its club and classes is nine hundred.

The Crèche, or Day Nursery, is surely as bright, sunny, and pretty a room as any ever devoted to that angelic purpose. Two little, low tables, two dozen little, low chairs, each holding a pathetic little figure, dear to some mother's heart, and a young lady as busy (and sometimes as puzzled) as a pullet with a brood of ducklings—these are the *dramatis personæ*. It is luncheon-time, and with much pains the babes have been brought to reasonable order, side by side, each restless pair of hands joined in a devotional attitude far from symbolic of the impatient being behind them. One small creature remains rebellious, and stands against the wall in tearful protest. The guardian angel explains that the small creature misses its mother, whereupon a visitor lifts it in his arms, and all is peace.

The Crèche has flourished greatly. The numbers vary from twenty-five to thirty, being governed by a curious law—the prevalence of house-cleaning! When many mothers can find jobs of scrubbing (which, by the way, earns a dollar and a half a day), then many babies are the helpless beneficiaries of the good offices of Hull House. But the benefit is not a gift; Hull House gives out no alms; every child is paid for at five cents a day.

The Sewing-Class is, if possible, a still more beautiful sight. Twenty or thirty little girls are gathered about low tables sewing away for dear life, and sitting among them are several young "society" women, guiding the immature hands and thoughts. It is proudly said that no social pleasures are allowed to stand in the way of this philanthropic duty.

From an admirable pamphlet entitled "Hull House: A Social Settlement," I condense the following sketch of labors and efforts:

Monday Evenings: Social Club, thirty girls. Debating Club, thirty young men. (The two clubs join later in the evening.)

Athletic Class. Drawing Class. Greek Art Class. Mathematics Class. English Composition Class.

Tuesday Evening : Working People's Social Science Club. (Addresses and discussions led by judges, lawyers, and business men.)

Russian Jews at "Shelter House."

Gymnasium. Drawing Class. Cooking Class. American History. Reading Party. Cæsar. Latin Grammar. Political Economy. Modern History.

And so on through the week. The noticeable varieties of interest include (besides the branches already named) Singing, Needlework, Diet Kitchen, Biology, Shakespeare, Lilies and Ferns, Victor Hugo, German Reception, Chemistry, Electricity, Clay Modelling,

English for Italians, Women's Gymnastics, etc. This vast curriculum is only for the evenings ; the mornings and afternoons and the Sundays have their own programmes ; and it may well be imagined that no business establishment goes far beyond this beehive of benevolence in orderly bustle and activity.

Hull House is fairly supplied with means. The use of the property it occupies was freely and generously bestowed upon it by Miss Helen Culver, to whom the property was devised by the late Charles J. Hull, whose old family residence it was. Then, too, the needs of the institution are wonderfully small compared with the ever-widening and deepening sphere of its influence.

Miss Jane Addams and Miss Ellen Gates Starr are the young women whose hearts conceived it, whose minds planned it, and whose small hands started it and have managed it thus far.

One of the young women had some private means of her own ; and such is the sway of their gentle influence among those who know them that when they are told that money must come, lo ! it appears. And, what is more, when they are forced to admit that their strength—unfortunately not superabundant—has reached its limit, other young helpers are at hand and the work never flags.

There exist in Chicago other benevolent institutions whose very number and variety preclude description. The City Directory contains the addresses of 57 asylums and hospitals, 28 infirmaries and dispensaries, 41 missions, 60 temperance societies, lodges, etc., and *thirty-seven columns* of secret benevolent associations, camps, lodges, circles, etc. The city is honeycombed with philanthropic associations in all magnitudes, shapes, and forms, from the ancient and honorable " Relief and Aid " (which won deathless fame after the Great Fire) down to the latest " Working-Girls' Luncheon Club," the Ursula, instituted by the graduates of an advanced school to provide and furnish, at cost, mid-day meals in the business districts for their toiling sisters. (There are several such clubs, and more are forming.) Everyone of the hundreds of churches is a centre of charitable effort. It becomes a net-work so all-pervading that one wonders that any should slip through, after all, and perish of want, as occasionally happens, nevertheless.

What is known as the " Poor Jews' Quarter " (as contra-distinguished from the splendid homes of their richer co-religionists) lies near the western end of Twelfth Street Bridge, and to the southward of the West Side Italian quarters already spoken of. Certainly it is not the abode of ease, luxury, and elegance ; its odors are not those of flowery meads, its architecture is not marked by either massiveness or ornamentation, its streets and alleys are not grassy (though they look as if they might be fertile under proper cultivation), and its denizens are more remarkable for number than for attractiveness. On the other hand, the region is still less suggestive of a " Ghetto," according to any prevailing tradition of those abodes. Children, ranging from infancy to adolescence, and from invalidism to rude health, throng the sidewalks. Many of these children have never seen a tree or a blade of grass. " In our summer country excursions," said a lady of Hull House, " we have much pleasure in watching them—they kneel down sometimes so as to study the grass and feel it with their hands." Yet the sidewalk seems to furnish a tolerable substitute for the grass-plat, and the passer-by has to edge close to street or fence to keep clear of the flying rope, turned by two girls, while a little string of others are awaiting their turn to jump, each one who " trips " taking the place of one of the turners—just as is done by their richer fellow-mortals, better fed and better dressed, but perhaps not more joyous and unregretful.

In the midst of this swarming colony rises—tall, large, handsome, and solid—the " Jewish Training School," under the management of a strong band of the solid Israelites of the city (representing, of course, solid millions of money) and the superintendency of Professor Gabriel Bamberger. Fifty thousand dollars a year is wisely and economically expended here, and eight hundred children and youths, of both sexes, *and all races and religions*, are taught and cared for. The classes in drawing and clay-modelling are especially notable.

Not far away is the "Shelter House" of the "Society in Aid of Russian Refugees." There the members of this unfortunate class

Another Group at "Shelter House."

find surcease of their woes and persecutions in a blessed harbor of temporary refuge, whence they are scattered to various employments and chances to earn an honest living, free from imperialism, officialism, priestcraft, and military service. They are a sturdy-looking set, and will not be long in learning that their greatest ill-treatment is turned to their greatest good luck when they arrive at the "Shelter House." They are "submerged" no longer.

When the back streets of Chicago are undergoing their spring cleaning, the mass of mud collected for removal in this quarter is incredible. The piles along the street-side are as high as they can be made to stand erect, and as close together as they can be. This is the accumulation of the months of December to March inclusive —the months when snow, frost, and short days impede the work so that a dollar laid out does perhaps not forty cents' worth of good. Then, too, the cold renders the vile deposit less hurtful to health, and the moisture and the frost keep it from flying about in the form of dust. The main streets are cleaned even when there is snow on the ground.*

One characteristic development of business-like philanthropy in Chicago is in the "Liberty Bell" and "Friendship" buildings for the accommodation of working-men. They are not germane to the subject of poverty, except to show its absence, prevention, or alleviation. The first-named was an experiment in the direction of furnishing to working-men good accommodations at rates almost nominal. A man is there offered a bath, a shave, and the use of a laundry (both provided with hot and cold water and soap), and a clean bed in a clean and ventilated room, all for ten cents. The whole main floor is devoted to a waiting-room with chairs and tables. In this room one sees from fifty to one hundred men, old and young, talking, smoking, reading newspapers, and the place is filled with the hum of conversation. In one corner is a group discussing work and wages; in another the younger fellows have made their newspapers into balls which they toss one to another. There is no drinking, no singing, and no boisterous mirth. "They take

---

* Even in well-swept London the streets are neglected in winter. "In one street is the body of a dead dog, and near by two dead cats, which lie as though they had slain each other; all three have been crushed flat by the traffic which has gone over them, and they, like everything else, are frozen and harmless."—Labor and Life of the People, vol. ii., p. 96, London, 1892.

their pleasure sadly, according to their wont," as Froissart remarks concerning their far-away ancestors.

From the profits earned by the "Liberty Bell" the "Friendship" has been built. There things are more handsomely done. Not only are there no beds in tiers, as at the other place; but each is entirely inclosed in a locked space, eight feet high, and protected by charged electric wires, so that the tenant and all his belongings are safe from intrusion or theft. The same accommodations (in more elegant form) are offered as in the former place, and the entire charge is fifteen cents. The originator of the pleasant and profitable scheme is now abroad, looking for further knowledge wherewith to provide further improvements.

At each place a good meal is served, in a restaurant attached, at an additional charge of ten cents. The savings of the men are accepted and cared for by the concern, and they amount to a very considerable sum. The men are largely dock-workers, sailors waiting for the opening of the lakes, mechanics out of a job, workers at light trades and callings about town, etc. All are comfortably clothed and quite free from any marks of want.

This is a pleasant aspect of the labor situation; but it is to be remembered that here we have only the able-bodied single men, the class which is last to feel the griping hand of poverty. Women and children, the difficult and distressing element in the social problem, are in all this left out of the account. The dock-laborers among these men—the largest class—earn from twenty to twenty-five cents an hour.

On the North Side (255 Indiana Street) is the "Home for Self-supporting Women," which, as its name implies, does a service for the other sex somewhat similar to that offered to men at the "Friendship." For obvious reasons the difficulties in dealing with the stronger sex are greatly magnified when the weaker is in question. Yet, great or small, those difficulties are braved, and, to a large extent, conquered. Better entertainment must be (and is) provided; larger charges must therefore be imposed, and that on individuals whose wages are smaller. Still the enterprise is nearly self-supporting, and when kindly fate shall inspire some rich and benevolent friend of woman to pay off a $10,000 mortgage on the realty of the Home, then its net income will overtake its outgo, and even in time exceed it, making its devoted ministers (all women)

A Waif at the Mission Dormitory.

able to extend its influence in an ever-increasing ratio. Meantime the annual reports are written in an admirable style of good-humored *naïveté* which shows that work and worry cannot daunt or sadden those whose hearts are in their business. It is a most worthy and successful effort at the best kind of help; but it still leaves untouched the problem of family helplessness—the soft, elastic, unbreakable bond which binds the hands and feet of mothers.

Near the centre of business are two institutions for the care of

15

homeless newsboys, bootblacks, and other young street workers, the "Waifs' Mission and Training School" and the "Newsboys' Home." The former has a school, a dining-room and kitchen, a dormitory with fifty beds, a bath-room, a gymnasium, a printing-office, etc., and its plan includes military drill (with a brass band formed among the boys themselves), instruction in the printing business, and the finding of places for boys old enough to enter steady employment. Its patrons and managers include judges of court, business men and capitalists, and a board of charitable women. The number of boys accommodated is limited to the number of beds.

An institution somewhat analogous to this is the "Illinois School of Agriculture and Manual Training for Boys," placed on three hundred acres of farming land at Glenwood, not far south of the city limits. Until this school was started (1887) there was absolutely no place to which a boy could be sent who was thrown upon the world by any of the lamentable casualties to which every community is subject—orphanage, desertion, forced separation from drunken or criminal parents. The courts of certain counties make use of this as a refuge for such boys, and allow a certain small monthly stipend for each; but this is necessarily far short of the absolute requirements of proper subsistence, clothing, and education, and more money than the school has yet received could be well used in it. The boys are provided with homes, chiefly with farmers, and the average outlay for each, up to the time when he is so provided for, is only about $60. The future life of the boy is kept in view and recorded; almost always with results that justify the efforts.

The Newsboys' and Bootblacks' Home is the oldest of the institutions of its class. It cares for some fifty or sixty boys, giving them decent sustenance and protection at lowest cost, and also providing for their amusement when circumstances permit. Some philanthropic persons object to these refuges of the human waifs and strays on the ground that they encourage boys to run away from their families. To this there seem to be two possible answers

—first, that every lodge, circle, hospital, asylum, and refuge runs to some extent against the family relation, not even excepting the fashionable club-houses; next, that the boys in the missions have perhaps found a better home than they left; that the change for them is a step upward, not downward. As far as one can see, it is a change from the gutter to the mission.

The *sweat-shop* is a place where, separate from the tailor-shop or clothing-warehouse, a "sweater" (middleman) assembles journeymen tailors and needle-women, to work under his supervision. He takes a cheap room outside the dear and crowded business centre, and within the neighborhood where the work-people live. Thus is rent saved to the employer, and time and travel to the employed. The men can and do work more hours than was possible under the centralized system, and their wives and children can help, especially when, as is often done, the garments are taken home to "finish." (Even the very young can pull out basting-threads.) This "finishing" is what remains undone after the machine has done its work, and consists in "felling" the waist and leg-ends of trousers (paid at one and one-half cent a pair), and, in short, all the "felling" necessary on every garment of any kind. For this service, at the prices paid, they cannot earn more than from twenty-five to forty cents a day, and the work is largely done by Italian, Polish, and Bohemian women and girls.

The entire number of persons employed in these vocations may be stated at 5,000 men (of whom 800 are Jews), and from 20,000 to 23,000 women and children. The wages are reckoned by "piecework," and (outside the "finishing") run about as follows:

Girls, hand-sewers, earn nothing for the first month, then as unskilled workers they get $1 to $1.50 a week, $3 a week, and (as skilled workers) $6 a week. The first-named class constitutes fifty per cent. of all, the second thirty per cent., and the last twenty per cent. In the general work men are only employed to do button-holing and pressing, and their earnings are as follows: "Pressers,"

$8 to $12 a week; "underpressers," $4 to $7. Cloak operators earn
$8 to $12 a week. Four-fifths of the sewing-machines are furnished
by the "sweaters" (middlemen); also needles, thread, and wax.

The "sweat-shop" day is ten hours; but many take work home

The "Bad Lands."

to get in overtime; and occasionally the shops themselves are kept
open for extra work, from which the hardest and ablest workers
sometimes make from $14 to $16 a week. On the other hand, the
regular work-season for cloakmaking is but seven months, and for
other branches nine months, in the year. The average weekly living expenses of a man and wife, with two children, as estimated by
a self-educated workman named Bisno, are as follows: Rent (three

or four small rooms), $2 ; food, fuel, and light, $4 ; clothing, $2, and beer and spirits, $1.

The first matter complained of is the wretchedness of the quarters. The proposed remedy for this is the establishment by clothiers of outlying workshops which shall be clean, light, and ventilated—in other words, not "sweat-shops." A city ordinance enacts that rooms provided for workmen shall contain space equal to five hundred cubic feet of air for each person employed ; but in the average "sweat-shop" only about a tenth of that quantity is to be found. In one such place there were fifteen men and women in one room, which contained also a pile of mattresses on which some of the men sleep at night. The closets were disgraceful. In an adjoining room were piles of clothing, made and unmade, on the same table with the food of the family. Two dirty little children were playing about the floor.

The second complaint regards the public good. It is averred, with apparent reason, that clothing should not be exposed to contamination and possible infection in rooms not set apart for working-rooms, especially in private houses, where members of the family, young and old, may quite possibly be ill of dangerously contagious fevers and other complaints. The danger of contagion from the hands of the workman himself is multiplied in proportion as the tenement is crowded where the garments are taken for work.

Another complaint, urged with much feeling, is that when the workers set up a "Union" shop of their own, where they did the very best work at prices as low as those charged at the "sweat-shops," but (by saving the profits of a middleman) were able to give more to the workers, they were deliberately and confessedly "frozen out" by the withholding of patronage by the clothing firms, and this after having been in prosperous and peaceable operation for two years. The "sweaters" could not force down wages as low as they wished, because the workers in the "Union" shops were doing so well. Therefore they got the employing firms to refuse work to the men's own establishment, and throw it all into the middleman's hands. A firm of employers for whom the association had worked two years were instrumental in this incredible cruelty. It is said by the workmen that they were driven to their action by others in the business, for when the little co-operative concern applied for work, they were referred to an association of the employing firms, and were there absolutely refused.

The "sweating system" has been in operation about twelve years, during which time some firms have failed, while others have increased their production tenfold. Meantime certain "sweaters" have grown rich; two having built from their gains tenement-houses for rent to the poor workers. The wholesale clothing business of Chicago is about $20,000,000 a year.

Mr. Bisno, the workman to whom I have alluded, has been led by his reading toward Socialism (very far from Anarchism), and he thinks that poverty and drink are parent and child—poverty the parent. A talk with him would be an enlightenment to any person who had not already adequate knowledge of the meaning of the short phrase "A good day's work." He would get a new idea of the unusual ability, mental and manual, the unflagging speed, the unwearied application which go to make the earning of a day's wages of the higher grades. He thinks that he could not maintain such speed without some liquid stimulus, in which other equally good workers think he is mistaken. (At the same time he is extremely moderate.) He says that beer is sold at five cents the measured pint (yielding two-and-a-half glasses), and that it is freely brought into the "sweat-shops," wherein, in fact, the workers are entirely independent of personal control, their work alone being subject to inspection and criticism. The inspection is close and constant, and failure entails the doing over of the job. Spoiling (such as tearing while ripping spoiled seams) leads to deductions from pay. The latter is very rare.

Division of labor is good; scattering of workers from great groups into smaller groups is good; employment of women in their own homes is good; prevention of theft is good, and cheapness of

IN A SWEAT-SHOP.

garments is good. Unwholesome atmosphere, moral and material, is bad; insufficient wages is bad; possibility of infection is bad, and child-labor is (usually) bad. How shall the good be preserved and the bad cured or alleviated?

At the head-quarters of the West Side police one is in the near neighborhood of the "Anarchist Riot" of 1886. In that building the police force was mustered and formed for its march out to the anarchist meeting-place, 500 feet distant; and there 67 of the police, killed and wounded, were laid when brought back a few minutes later. The messenger in attendance is one of the severely wounded, now too much shattered to do more than light tasks about the station. Conversation with some of the men at this station has led me to a new appreciation of the magnitude of the issues then and there fought out, and the finality of the settlement arrived at. A lieutenant of police recently said to me:

"The whole thing is played out. They will never make another experiment. There is no interest in anarchy or socialism any more, and no meetings to speak of. They do get together, some of them, at Twelfth Street Turner Hall, but you'd never know that they had ever planned a riot or loaded a bomb. No; they have no connection with hardship and poverty. They can always get their beer, and that's the main thing with them."

These quiet and unassuming officers of law and order know that they did their duty, and think that their success was a foregone conclusion. They do not know that though other "stronger" governments could have put down anarchy by force of arms, and hanged or shot the insurgents by martial law, yet this is perhaps the only government on earth which could have met such a movement by the ordinary police power, and then have given the guilty a long public trial before "a jury of their peers," and have relied on a verdict of conviction, a judgment of death, and the deliberate execution of that judgment.

Mr. Joseph Greenhut (himself a Socialist, somewhat out of sym-

Laundry and Bath at the Liberty Bell.

pathy with the alleviation of poverty, its absolute cure being, in his view, possible by changes in the constitution of society), furnishes many statistics showing the ruling rates of wages earned in some hundreds of trades and callings, from which the following are selected:

	Per diem.
Bricklayers, stone-cutters, and stone-masons	$4 00
Plasterers	3 50 to $4 00
Carpenters	2 50 to 2 80
Bridge-builders	2 50 to 3 25
Ship-carpenters and caulkers	2 00 to 3 50
Machinists, blacksmiths, and wagon-makers	2 00 to 2 50
Pattern-makers and horse-shoers	2 75 to 3 50
Engineers	2 00 to 5 00
Grain-trimmers	2 75 to 3 50
Lumber-shovers	3 00 to 6 00
Sewer-builders	2 00 to 3 00

Per diem.

Plumbers, gas-fitters, painters, photographers, printers, etc.....$2 00 to $3 50

Boot- and shoe-makers, cigar-makers, millers, stereotypers and electrotypers, copper, tin, and sheet-iron workers, brass finishers, upholsterers, etc................................... 1 75 to 3 00

Iron and steel mill-workers, japanners, etc..................... 1 50 to 6 00

Tailors and suit-makers.. 1 00 to 3 00

Type-founders, furriers, bookbinders, furniture-workers, distillers, brewers, etc....................................... 1 50 to 3 00

Sailors (with board) .... 1 50 to 2 00

Farmers... 1 50 to 3 00

Coopers, fish-packers, gravel-roofers, freight-house men, laundrymen, makers of iron and lead pipe, wire-goods, vault-lights, etc... 1 50 to 2 50

Brick-makers .... 1 00 to 3 00

Planing-mill hands .... 1 25 to 2 25

Harness-makers, musical instrument-makers .... 1 25 to 3 00

Market-men, ice-wagon men, etc............................... 1 50 to 2 75

Packing and slaughter-house men.............................. 1 25 to 4 00

Lumber-yard hands... 1 25 to 1 50

Dock laborers.. 1 00 to 2 00

Confectioners, millinery and straw-goods makers, hair-workers, etc... 1 00 to 3 00

Female clerks... 1 00 to 2 75

Glove and mitten-makers...................................... 60 cents to 3 00

By the week.

Drug clerks ....$12 00 to $25 00

Telegraph and telephone operators............................ 10 00 to 20 00

Bakers and barbers... 10 00 to 14 00

Stablemen.. 9 00 to 15 00

Teamsters .... 9 00 to 12 00

Dressmakers.. 6 00 to 15 00

Office stenographers and typewriters......................... 6 00 to 20 00

Mr. Greenhut estimates the immigrant nationalities (including their children) composing Chicago as follows: Germans, 400,000; Irish, 210,000; Sclavonians, 100,000; Scandinavians, 110,000; English, Scotch, and Welsh, 80,000; French Canadians, 15,000; Italians, 15,000; French, 5,000; Colored, 13,000; and Chinese, 2,000.

No one doubts but that the drink-bill of Chicago—estimated at $1,000,000 a week, of which three-fourths comes from the pockets of the poor—would change into prosperity, practically, all the adversity of the unfortunate classes, just as the drink-bill of Russia—$1,000,000 a day—would supplant famine by abundance. Much poverty comes from drink that does not come from drunkenness.

"Liberty Bell."

A man may spend in drink the total profit on his earnings, the total surplus above necessary outgoes, and it may—usually does—amount to an insurance fund which, well invested, would form a respectable fortune during his prosperous years. Then, when old age, sickness, or accident befalls, he is penniless. His poverty springs from drink ; no matter if he never was drunk in his life. The man who drinks up what he might save is as short-sighted as the husbandman who should needlessly eat up his seed-wheat.

"Paying off" is often done in saloons, in which the paymaster may or may not be interested. It is a vile and hurtful practice. A late article in a Chicago paper contains the following words on this theme :

Contractor Piatkiewicz said some of his workmen habitually spent for liquor half their earnings, and that on one pay-night, several years ago, he recollected that out of a total of $480 due his men, the chips in the basket gave to the saloon-keeper $200. To add to this, he said that as many " treats all around " were made as there were men in the saloon. From a large number of sources it was learned that it is the custom with the Polish laborers—the violation of which means disgrace—for each man on pay-night to treat all his fellows, the bartender and contractor included, and for the two latter, when it comes their turn, to treat the men. It is needless to say that the contractor and bartender rarely have to pay for what they " set up " to the crowd.

The possible remedy for this state of things—if there be any remedy—is outside the province of the present essay. Suffice it to say here, that the non-expert observer, however sympathetic, is prone to feel that any effort at relief of the " chosen miseries " which does not strike at the cause of the choice, is futile.

A late issue of the Chicago *Tribune* had the following suggestive paragraph :

WORK WAITING FOR UNEMPLOYED.

THE STATEMENT ABOUT CHICAGO'S ARMY OF IDLE MEN REFUTED.

" The statement that there are 30,000 to 50,000 laboring men out of employment to-day in Chicago is false," said Oscar Kuehne yesterday. Mr. Kuehne is the General Agent of the German Benevolent Society and is in a position to know. " I could have furnished," he continued, " during the month of March, employment to 300 or 400 more men than I did, if I had had the men to fill the applications that came into my office. Farmers from within a radius of thirty miles of Chicago come to me to supply them with farm-laborers, and when I tell them that I haven't men for them, and can't get the sort of men they want, they ask in surprise where these 50,000 unemployed in Chicago are. At one o'clock this afternoon there were thirty farmers in my office after laborers. They would have employed fifty men, but I had to disappoint them. The truth of the matter is that there is no excuse for the idleness of an energetic young man who is not married. He can get work if he wants it. For a married man there is more excuse. He is not free to move about as the unmarried man is, and is more limited in his choice of occupations. We find it more difficult to get work for men of families."

There is some chosen poverty which is not necessarily connected with drink. Many instances arise in the minds of men and women who are trying to do their philanthropic duty.

The pitiable man is he who cannot get work to do, and in so far as this article on poverty in the West does not present the harrowing pictures of want elsewhere, it must be accounted for in the same way as was the shortness of the celebrated chapter on " Snakes in Iceland." Work and wages, seed-time and harvest, have not yet failed in the land. And the art of making the wise choice of possible joys, though not yet fully learned, is gaining ground.

The overwhelming tendency of modern life is toward the cities. It almost seems as if they would have to be walled about in order to keep in the country the proportions—four-fifths at least—which must remain there in order to provide food for all. Everything done " to alleviate the condition of the poor in great cities " works in the direction of bringing more into them ; and no argument or persuasion, or more solid consideration of betterment, prevails to get them out after once immersed in the pleasurable excitement of gregarious existence ; they would rather starve in a crowd than grow fat in quietude—especially if the " crowd " is sprinkled with aromatic " charity."

Humanity, like other semifluids, moves in the line of least resistance and most propulsion. Idleness drifts toward where commiseration and alms-giving are most generous and unquestioning ; love of drink toward where beer and liquor are most plentiful. The free soup-kitchen is a profitable neighbor for the saloon. Labor is a blessing—in disguise ; and a free gift is often a disguised curse.

Then is a part of the prevalent philanthropic feeling, though coming from the noblest part of our nature, tainted with sentimentality and sensationalism ? Is it, to a certain extent, the vagary of good men and women who, consciously or unconsciously, regard physical labor as only a necessary evil ? Is it part of the new creed which sees in drink not the cause but the consequence of want and misery ? *Quien sabe?* At any rate, if any statement should be made of the Western aspect of the matter, as it appears to men who regard duly paid toil as the condition of well-being, which statement did not present this possibility as at least an obtruding suspicion, it would be false and defective.

" In the sweat of thy face shalt thou eat bread " was not a curse but a blessing, and so shall be until a dreary Utopia prevail, competition giving place to combination, mankind being beaten up into an omelet, and excelling and excellence no more.

** Major Joseph Kirkland, the writer of this paper, was born in Geneva, N. Y., on January 7, 1830, and died in Chicago, May 4, 1894. He was a well-known lawyer who had been for a number of years prominently identified with Chicago. His first studies of social questions were made while engaged in coal mining in Illinois and Indiana. Two novels by him, " Zury, the Meanest Man in Spring County," and "The McVeys," attracted wide attention for their truth to the life depicted and strong powers of characterization.

The Riverside. St James's Ratcliff
with Limehouse Church

A RIVERSIDE PARISH

By WALTER BESANT

AUTHOR OF "ALL SORTS AND CONDITIONS OF MEN"

ALONG THE BANKS OF THE THAMES—THE PORT OF LONDON—THE SAILOR POPU-
LATION—PAST LAWLESSNESS OF THE RIVERSIDE PARISHES—ROTHERHITHE—
SHIPWRIGHTS' AND OTHER STRIKES—THE PARISH OF ST. JAMES'S, RATCLIFF
—ITS SOCIAL HISTORY—CHARITABLE UNDERTAKINGS—CLUBS AND LARGER
WORK—SOME DEVOTED LIVES.

THERE are several riverside parishes east of London Bridge,
not counting the ancient towns of Deptford and Greenwich,
which formerly lay beyond London, and could not be reckoned as suburbs. The history of all these parishes, till the present century, is the same. Once, southeast and west of London,
there stretched a broad marsh covered with water at every spring-
tide; here and there rose islets overgrown with brambles, the
haunt of wild fowl innumerable. In course of time, the city having grown and stretched out long arms along the bank, people
began to build a broad and strong river-wall to keep out the floods.
This river-wall, which still remains, was gradually extended until it
reached the mouth of the river and ran quite round the low coast
of Essex. To the marshes succeeded a vast level, low-lying, fertile

region affording good pasture, excellent dairy farms, and gardens of fruit and vegetables. The only inhabitants of this district were the farmers and the farm-hands. So things continued for a thousand years, while the ships went up the river with wind and tide, and down the river with wind and tide, and were moored below the

A Sketch in the Docks.

Bridge, and discharged their cargoes into lighters, which landed them on the quays of London Port, between the Tower and the Bridge. As for the people who did the work of the Port—the loading and the unloading—those whom now we call the stevedores, coalers, dockers, lightermen, and watermen, they lived in the narrow lanes and crowded courts above and about Thames Street.

When the trade of London Port increased, these courts became more crowded; some of them overflowed, and a colony outside the walls was established in St. Katherine's Precinct beyond the

16

Tower. Next to St. Katherine's lay the fields called by Stow
"Wappin in the Wose," or Wash, where there were broken places
in the wall, and the water poured in so that it was as much a marsh
as when there was no dyke at all. Then the Commissioners of
Sewers thought it would be a good plan to encourage people to
build along the wall, so that they would be personally interested
in its preservation. Thus arose the Hamlet of Wapping, which,
till far into the eighteenth century, consisted of little more than a
single long street, with a few cross lanes, inhabited by sailor-folk.
At this time—it was toward the end of the sixteenth century—began that great and wonderful development of London trade which
has continued without any cessation of growth. Gresham began it.
He taught the citizens how to unite for the common weal; he gave
them a Bourse; he transferred the foreign trade of Antwerp to the
Thames. Then the service of the river grew apace; where one
lighter had sufficed there were now wanted ten; "Wappin in the
Wose" became crowded Wapping; the long street stretched farther and farther along the river beyond Shad's Well; beyond Ratcliff Cross, where the "red cliff" came down nearly to the river
bank; beyond the "Lime-house;" beyond the "Poplar" Grove.
The whole of that great city of a million souls, now called East
London, consisted, until the end of the last century, of Whitechapel
and Bethnal Green, still preserving something of the old rusticity;
of Mile End, Stepney and Bow, and West Ham, hamlets set among
fields, and market-gardens, and of that long fringe of riverside
streets and houses. In these rural hamlets great merchants had
their country-houses; the place was fertile; the air was wholesome; nowhere could one see finer flowers or finer plants; the
merchant-captains — both those at sea and those retired — had
houses with garden-bowers and masts at Mile End Old Town.
Captain Cook left his wife and children there when he went sailing
round the world; here, because ground was cheap and plentiful,
were long rope-walks and tenter-grounds; here were roadside tav-
erns and gardens for the thirsty Londoner on a summer evening;

H. Thomson March 92.
The Pool from Ratcliff Stairs

THE POOL FROM RATCLIFF STAIRS,

here were placed many almshouses, dotted about among the gardens, where the poor old folks lengthened their days in peace and fresh air.

But Riverside London was a far different place; here lived none but sailors, watermen, lightermen, and all those who had to do with ships and shipping, with the wants and the pleasures of the sailors. Boat-builders had their yards along the bank; mast-makers, sail-makers, rope-makers, block-makers; there were repairing docks dotted about all down the river, each able to hold one ship at a time, like one or two still remaining at Rotherhithe; there were ship - building yards of considerable. importance; all these places employed a vast number of workmen—carpenters, caulkers, painters, riggers, carvers of figure-heads, block-makers, stevedores, lightermen, watermen, victuallers, tavern-keepers, and all the roguery and *ribauderie* that always gather round mercantile Jack ashore. A crowded suburb indeed it was, and for the most part with no gentle-folk to give the people an example of conduct, temperance, and religion. At best the master-mariners, a decorous people, and the better class of tradesmen, to lead the way to church. And as time went on the better class vanished, until the riverside parishes became abandoned entirely to mercantile Jack, and to those who live by loading and unloading, repairing and building the ships, and by showing Jack ashore how fastest and best to spend his money. There were churches—Wapping, St. George in the East, Shadwell, and Limehouse they are there to this day; but Jack and his friends enter not their portals. Moreover, when they were built the function of the clergyman was to perform with dignity and reverence the services of the church; if people chose not to come, and the law of attendance could not be enforced, so much the worse for them. Though Jack kept out of church, there was some religious life in the place, as is shown not only by the presence of the church, but also by that of the chapel. Now, wherever there is a chapel it indicates thought, independence, and a sensible elevation above the reckless, senseless rabble. Some kinds of

Nonconformity also indicate a first step toward education and culture.

He who now stands on London Bridge and looks down the river, will see a large number of steamers lying off the quays; there are barges, river-steamers, and boats; there are great ocean-steamers working up or down the river; but there is little to give the stranger even a suspicion of the enormous trade that is carried on at the Port of London. That Port is now hidden behind the dock gates; the trade is invisible unless one enters the docks and reckons up the ships and their tonnage, the warehouses and their

"Their first yearning is for finery."

contents. But a hundred years ago this trade was visible to any who chose to look at it, and the ships in which the trade was carried on were visible as well.

Below the Bridge, the river, for more than a mile, pursues a straight course with a uniform breadth. It then bends in a north-easterly direction for a mile or so, when it turns southward, passing Deptford and Greenwich. Now, a hundred years ago, for two miles and more below the bridge, the ships lay moored side by side in double lines, with a narrow channel between. There were no docks; all the loading and the unloading had to be done by means of barges and lighters in the stream. One can hardly realize this vast concourse of boats and barges and ships; the thousands of men at work; the passage to and fro of the barges laden to the water's edge, or returning empty to the ship's side; the yeo-heave-oh! of the sailors hoisting up the casks and bales and cases; the shouting, the turmoil, the quarrelling, the fighting, the tumult upon the river, now so peaceful. But when we talk of a riverside parish we must remember this great concourse, because it was the cause of practices from which we suffer to the present day.

Of these things we may be perfectly certain: First, that without the presence among a people of some higher life, some nobler standard, than that of the senses, this people will sink rapidly and surely. Next, that no class of persons, whether in the better or the worser rank, can ever be trusted to be a law unto themselves. For which reason we may continue to be grateful to our ancestors who caused to be written in large letters of gold, for all the world to see once a week, " THUS SAITH THE LORD, Thou shalt not steal," and the rest: the lack of which reminder sometimes causeth, in Nonconformist circles, it is whispered, a deplorable separation of faith and works. The third maxim, axiom, or self-evident proposition is, that when people can steal without fear of consequences they will steal. All through the last century, and indeed far into this, the only influence brought to bear upon the common people was that of authority. The master ruled his servants; he watched over them; when they were young he had them catechised and taught the sentiments proper to their station; he also flogged them soundly; when they grew up he gave them wages and work; he made them go to church regularly; he rewarded them for industry by fraternal care; he sent them to the almshouse when they were old. At church the sermons were not for the servants but for the masters; yet the former were reminded every week of the Ten Commandments, which were not only written out large for all to

A Mother's Meeting.

see, but were read out for their instruction every Sunday morning. The decay of authority is one of the distinguishing features of the present century.

But in Riverside London there were no masters, and there was no authority for the great mass of the people. The sailor ashore had no master; the men who worked on the lighters and on the ships had no master except for the day ; the ignoble horde of those who supplied the coarse pleasures of the sailors had no masters; they were not made to do anything but what they pleased ; the church was not for them ; their children were not sent to school ; their only masters were the fear of the gallows, constantly dangled before their eyes at Execution Dock and on the shores of the Isle of Dogs, and their profound respect for the cat-o'-nine-tails. They knew no morality ; they had no oth-er restraint ; they all together slid, ran, fell, leaped, danced, and rolled swiftly and easily adown the Prim-rose Path ; they fell into a savagery the like of which has never been known among English-folk since the days of their conversion to the

Children at Prayer in the Chapel, Heckford House.

Christian faith. It is only by searching and poking among un-known pamphlets and forgotten books that one finds out the act-ual depths of the English savagery of the last century. And it is not too much to say that for drunkenness, brutality, and igno-rance, the Englishman of the baser kind touched about the lowest depth ever reached by civilized man during the last century. What he was in Riverside London has been disclosed by Colqu-houn, the Police Magistrate. Here he was not only a drunkard, a brawler, a torturer of dumb beasts, a wife-beater, a profligate—he was also, with his fellows, engaged every day, and all day long, in a vast systematic organized depredation. The people of the river-

side were all, to a man, river pirates; by day and by night they
stole from the ships.   There were often as many as a thousand vessels lying in the river; there were many hundreds of boats,
barges, and lighters engaged upon their cargoes.   They practised
their robberies in a thousand ingenious ways; they weighed the
anchors and stole them; they cut adrift lighters when they were
loaded, and when they had floated down the river they pillaged
what they could carry and left the rest to sink or swim; they
waited till night and then rowed off to half-laden lighters and
helped themselves.   Sometimes they went on board the ships as
stevedores and tossed bales overboard to a confederate in a boat
below; or they were coopers who carried under their aprons bags
which they filled with sugar from the casks; or they took with
them bladders for stealing the rum.   Some waded about in the
mud at low tide to catch anything that was thrown to them from
the ships.   Some obtained admission to the ship as rat-catchers,
and in that capacity were able to carry away plunder previously
concealed by their friends; some, called *scuffle-hunters*, stood on the
quays as porters, carrying bags under their long aprons in which
to hide whatever they could pilfer.   It was estimated that, taking
one year with another, the depredations from the shipping in the
Port of London amounted to nearly a quarter of a million sterling
every year.   All this was carried on by the riverside people.   But,
to make robbery successful, there must be accomplices, receiving-
houses, fences, a way to dispose of the goods.   In this case the
thieves had as their accomplices the whole of the population of the
quarter where they lived.   All the public-houses were secret markets attended by grocers and other tradesmen where the booty was
sold by auction, and, to escape detection fictitious bills and accounts were given and received.   The thieves were known among
themselves by fancy names, which at once indicated the special
line of each and showed the popularity of the calling; they were
bold pirates, night plunderers, light horsemen, heavy horsemen,
mud-larks, game lightermen, scuffle-hunters and gangsmen.   Their

"Her bowsprit and her figurehead stick out over the street."

thefts enabled them to live in the coarse profusion of meat and drink, which was all they wanted; yet they were always poor because their plunder was knocked down for so little; they saved

nothing ; and they were always egged on to new robberies by the
men who sold them drinks, the women who took their money from
them, and the honest merchants who attended the secret markets.

I dwell upon the past because the present is its natural legacy.
When you read of the efforts now being made to raise the living,
or at least to prevent them from sinking any lower, remember that
they are what the dead made them. We inherit more than the
wealth of our ancestors ; we inherit the consequences of their mis-
deeds. It is a most expensive thing to suffer the people to drop
and sink ; it is a burden which we lay upon posterity if we do not
continually spend and be spent in lifting them up. Why, we have
been the best part of two thousand years in recovering the civilization which fell to pieces when the Roman Empire decayed. We
have not been fifty years in dragging up the very poor whom we
neglected and left to themselves, the gallows, the cat, and the
press-gang only a hundred years ago. And how slow, how slow
and sometimes hopeless, is the work !

The establishment of river police and the construction of docks
have cleared the river of all this gentry. Ships now enter the
docks ; there discharge and receive ; the laborers can carry away
nothing through the dock-gates. No apron allows a bag to be
hidden ; policemen stand at the gates to search the men ; the old
game is gone—what is left is a surviving spirit of lawlessness ; the
herding together ; the hand-to-mouth life ; the love of drink is the
chief attainable pleasure ; the absence of conscience and responsibility ; and the old brutality.

What the riverside then was may be learned by a small piece of
Rotherhithe in which the old things still linger. Small repairing-
docks, each capable of holding one vessel, are dotted along the
street ; to each are its great dock-gates keeping out the high tide,
and the quays and the shops and the care-taker's lodge ; the ship
lies in the dock shored up by timbers on either side, and the workmen are hammering, caulking, painting, and scraping the wooden
hull ; her bowsprit and her figurehead stick out over the street.

Between the docks are small two-storied houses, half of them little shops trying to sell something ; the public-house is frequent, but the " Humors " of Ratcliff Highway are absent ; mercantile Jack at Rotherhithe is mostly Norwegian and has morals of his own. Such, however, as this little village of Rotherhithe is, so were " Wappin in the Wose," Shadwell, Ratcliff, and the "Lime-house" a hundred years ago, with the addition of streetfighting and brawling all day long ; the perpetual adoration of rum ; quarrels over stolen goods ; quarrels over drunken drabs ; quarrels over all fours ; the scraping of fiddles from every public-

A Little Dance at the Girls' Institute.

house, the noise of singing, feasting, and dancing, and a never-ending, still-beginning debauch, all hushed and quiet—as birds cower in the hedge at sight of the kestrel—when the press-gang swept down the narrow streets and carried off the lads, unwilling to leave the girls and the grog, and put them aboard His Majesty's tender to meet what fate might bring.

The construction of the great docks has completely changed this quarter. The Precinct of St. Katherine's by the Tower has almost entirely disappeared, being covered by St. Katherine's Dock; the London Dock has reduced Wapping to a strip covered with warehouses. But the church remains, so frankly proclaiming itself of the eighteenth century, with its great churchyard. The new Dock Basin, Limehouse Basin, and the West India Docks, have sliced huge cantles out of Shadwell, Limehouse, and Poplar; the little private docks and boat-building yards have disappeared; here and there the dock remains, with its river-gates gone, an ancient barge reposing in its black mud; here and there may be found a great building which was formerly a warehouse when ship-building was still carried on. That branch of industry was abandoned after 1868, when the shipwrights struck for higher wages. Their action transferred the ship-building of the country to the Clyde, and threw out of work thousands of men who had been earning large wages in the yards. Before this unlucky event Riverside London had been rough and squalid, but there were in it plenty of people earning good wages—skilled artisans, good craftsmen. Since then it has been next door to starving. The effect of the shipwrights' strike may be illustrated in the history of one couple.

The man, of Irish parentage, though born in Stepney, was a painter or decorator of the saloons and cabins of ships: he was a highly skilled workman of taste and dexterity: he could not only paint but he could carve: he made about three pounds a week and lived in comfort. The wife, a decent Yorkshire woman whose manners were very much above those of the Riverside folk, was a few years older than her husband: they had no children. During the years of fatness they saved nothing; the husband was not a drunkard, but, like most workmen, he liked to cut a figure and to make a show. So he saved little or nothing. When the yard was finally closed he had to cadge about for work. Fifteen years later he was found in a single room of the meanest tenement-house: his furniture was reduced to a bed, a table, and a chair: all that they had was a little tea and no money—no money at all. He was weak and

Searching the men at the Dock Gates.

SEARCHING THE MEN AT THE DOCK GATES.

ill with trudging about in search of work : he was lying exhausted on the bed while his wife sat crouched over the little bit of fire. This was how they had lived for fifteen years—the whole time on the verge of starvation. Well, they were taken away; they were persuaded to leave their quarters and to try another place where odd jobs were found for the man, and where the woman made friends in private families for whom she did a little sewing. But it was too late for the man; his privations had destroyed his sleight of hand, though he knew it not; the fine workman was gone ; he took painters' paralysis, and very often when work was offered his hand would drop before he could begin it ; then the long years of tramping about had made him restless ; from time to time he was fain to borrow a few shillings and to go on the tramp again, pretending that he was in search of work ; he would stay away for a fortnight, marching about from place to place, heartily enjoying the change and the social evening at the public-houses where he put up. For, though no drunkard, he loved to sit in a warm bar and to talk over the splendors of the past. Then he died. No one, now looking at the neat old lady in the clean white cap and apron who sits all day in the nursery crooning over her work, would believe that she has gone through this ordeal by famine, and served her fifteen years' term of starvation for the sins of others.

The Parish of St. James's, Ratcliff, is the least known of Riverside London. There is nothing about this parish in the Guidebooks; nobody goes to see it. Why should they? There is nothing to see. Yet it is not without its romantic touches. Once there was here a cross — the Ratcliff Cross — but nobody knows what it was, when it was erected, why it was erected, or when it was pulled down. The oldest inhabitant now at Ratcliff remembers that there was a cross here — the name survived until the other day, attached to a little street, but that is now gone. It is mentioned in Dryden. And on the Queen's accession, in 1837, she was proclaimed, among other places, at Ratcliff Cross — but why, no one knows. Once the

The Quaker Meeting-House.

Shipwrights' Company had their ball here; it stood among gardens
where the scent of the gillyflower and the stock mingled with the
scent of the tar from the neighboring rope-yard and boat-building

yard; in the old days, many were the feasts which the jolly ship-wrights held in their hall after service at St. Dunstan's, Stepney. The hall is now pulled down, and the Company, which is one of the smallest, worth an income of less than a thousand, has never built another. Then there are the Ratcliff Stairs—rather dirty and di-lapidated to look at, but, at half-tide, affording the best view one can get any where of the Pool and the shipping. In the good old days of the scuffle-hunters and the heavy horsemen, the view of the thousand ships moored in their long lines with the narrow passage between was splendid. History has deigned to speak of Ratcliff Stairs. 'Twas by these steps that the gallant Willoughby embarked for his fatal voyage; with flags flying and the discharge of guns he sailed past Greenwich, hoping that the king would come forth to see him pass. Alas! the young king lay a-dying, and Willoughby himself was sailing off to meet his death.

The parish contains four good houses, all of which, I believe, are marked in Roque's map of 1745.

One of these is now the vicarage of the new church; it is a large, solid, and substantial house, built early in the last century, when as yet the light horsemen and lumpers were no nearer than Wapping. The walls of the dining-room are painted with Italian landscapes to which belongs a romance. The paintings were executed by a young Italian artist. For the sake of convenience he was allowed by the merchant who then lived here, and employed him, to stay in the house. Now the merchant had a daughter, and she was fair; the artist was a goodly youth, and inflammable; as the poet says, their eyes met; presently, as the poet goes on, their lips met; then the merchant found out what was going on, and ordered the young man, with good old British determination, out of the house; the young man retired to his room, presumably to pack up his things. But he did not go out of the house; instead of that, he hanged him-self in his room. His ghost, naturally, continued to remain in the house, and has been seen by many. Why he has not long ago joined the ghost of the young lady is not clear, unless that, like many ghosts, his chief pleasure is in keeping as miserable as he possibly can.

The second large house of the parish is apparently of the same date, but the broad garden in which it formerly stood has been built over by mean tenement-houses; nothing is known about it; at present certain Roman Catholic sisters live in it and carry on some kind of work.

The third great house is one of the few surviving specimens of the merchant's warehouse and residence in one. It is now an old and tumble-down place. Its ancient history I know not. What rich and costly bales were hoisted into this warehouse; what goods lay here waiting to be carried down the Stairs, and so on board ship in the Pool; what fortunes were made and lost here one knows not. Its ancient history is gone and lost, but it has a modern history. Here a certain man began, in a small way, a work which has grown to be great; here he spent and was spent; here he gave his life for the work, which was for the children of the poor. He was a young physician; he saw in this squalid and crowded neighborhood the lives of the children needlessly sacrificed by the thousand for the want of a hospital; to be taken ill in the wretched room where the whole family lived was to die; the nearest hospital was two miles away. The young physician had but slender means, but he had a stout heart. He found this house empty, its rent a song. He took it, put in half a dozen beds, constituted himself the physician and his wife the nurse, and opened the Children's Hospital. Very soon the rooms became wards; the wards became crowded with children; the one nurse was multiplied by twenty; the one physician by six. Very soon, too, the physician lay upon his death-bed, killed by the work. But the Children's Hospital was founded, and now it stands, not far off, a stately building with one of its wards—the Heckford Ward—named after the physician who gave his own life to save the children. When the house ceased to be a hospital it was taken by a Mr. Dawson, who was first to start here a club for the very rough lads. He, too, gave his life for the cause, for the illness which killed him was due to overwork and neglect. Devotion and death are therefore associated with this old house.

The fourth large house is now degraded to a common lodging-house. But it has still its fine old staircase.

The Parish of St. James's, Ratcliff, consists of an irregular patch of ground having the river on the south, and the Commercial Road,

Boys Playing Bagatelle in Heckford House.

one of the great arteries of London, on the north. It contains about seven thousand people, of whom some three thousand are Irish Catholics. It includes a number of small, mean, and squalid streets; there is not anywhere in the great city a collection of streets smaller or meaner. The people live in tenement-houses, very often one family for every room—in one street, for instance, of fifty houses, there are one hundred and thirty families. The men are nearly all dock-laborers—the descendants of the scuffle-hunters, whose traditions still survive, perhaps, in an unconquerable hatred of government. The women and girls are shirt-makers, tailoresses, jam-makers, biscuit-makers, match-makers, and rope-makers.

In this parish the only gentle-folk are the clergy and the ladies working in the parish for the Church; there are no substantial shopkeepers, no private residents, no lawyer, no doctor, no professional people of any kind; there are thirty-six public-houses, or one to every hundred adults, so that if each spends on an average only two shillings a week, the weekly takings of each are ten pounds. Till lately there were forty-six, but ten have been suppressed; there are no places of public entertainment, there are no books, there are hardly any papers except some of those Irish papers whose continued sufferance gives the lie to their own everlasting charges of English tyranny. Most significant of all, there are no Dissenting chapels, with one remarkable exception. Fifteen chapels in the three parishes of Ratcliff, Shadwell, and St. George's have been closed during the past twenty years. Does this mean conversion to the Anglican Church? Not exactly; it means, first, that the people have become too poor to maintain a chapel, and next, that they have become too poor to think of religion. So long as an Englishman's head is above the grinding misery, he exercises, as he should, a free and independent choice of creeds, thereby vindicating and asserting his liberties. Here there is no chapel, therefore no one thinks; they lie like sheep; of death and its possibilities no one heeds; they live from day to day; when they are young they believe they will be always young; when they are old, so far as they know, they have been always old.

The people being such as they are—so poor, so helpless, so ignorant—what is done for them? How are they helped upward? How are they driven, pushed, shoved, pulled, to prevent them from sinking still lower? For they are not at the lowest depths; they are not criminals; up to their lights they are honest; that poor fellow who stands with his hands ready—all he has got in the wide world—only his hands—no trade, no craft, no skill—will give you a good day's work if you engage him ; he will not steal things ; he will drink more than he should with the money you give him; he will knock his wife down if she angers him ; but he is not a criminal. That step has yet to be taken ; he will not take it ; but his children may, and unless they are pre-vented they cer-tainly will. For the London-born child very soon learns the meaning of the Easy Way and the Primrose Path. We have to do with the people ignorant, drunken, helpless, always at the point of destitution, their whole thoughts as much concentrated upon the difficulty of the daily bread as ever were those of their ancestor

Brushmaker, St. James's, Ratcliff.

who roamed about the Middlesex Forest and hunted the bear with a club, and shot the wild-goose with a flint-headed arrow.

First there is the Church work ; that is to say, the various agencies and machinery directed by the vicar. Perhaps it may be a new thing to some American readers to learn how much of the time and thoughts of our Anglican beneficed clergymen are wanted for things not directly religious. The church, a plain and unpretending edifice, built in the year 1838, is served by the vicar and two curates. There are daily services, and on Sundays an early celebration. The average attendance at the regular Sunday midday service is about one hundred; in the evening it is generally double that number. They are all adults. For the children another service is held in the Mission Room. The average attendance of the Sunday-schools and Bible classes is about three hundred and fifty, and would be more if the vicar had a larger staff of teachers, of whom, however, there are forty-two. The whole number of men and women engaged in organized work connected with the Church is about one hundred and twenty-six. Some of them are ladies from the other end of London, but most belong to the parish itself; in the choir, for instance, are found a barber, a postman, a care-taker, and one or two small shopkeepers, all living in the parish. When we remember that Ratcliff is not what is called a "show" parish, that the newspapers never talk about it, and that rich people never hear of it, this indicates a very considerable support to Church work.

In addition to the church proper there is the "Mission Chapel," where other services are held. One day in the week there is a sale of clothes at very small prices. They are sold rather than given, because if the women have paid a few pence for them they are less willing to pawn them than if they had received them for nothing. In the Mission Chapel are held classes for young girls and services for children.

The churchyard, like so many of the London churchyards, has been converted into a recreation-ground, where there are trees and flower-beds, and benches for old and young.

Outside the Church, but yet connected with it, there is, first, the Girls' Club. The girls of Ratcliff are all working-girls; as might be expected, a rough and wild company, as untrained as colts, yet open to kindly and considerate treatment. Their first yearning is for finery ; give them a high hat with a flaring ostrich feather, a plush jacket, and a "fringe," and they are happy. There are seventy-five of these girls ; they use their club every evening, and

The Choir of the Parish Church.

they have various classes, though it cannot be said that they are desirous of learning anything. Needlework, especially, they dislike ; they dance, sing, have musical drill, and read a little. Five ladies who work for the church and for the club, live in the clubhouse, and other ladies come to lend assistance. When we consider what the homes and the companions of these girls are, what kind of men will be their husbands, and that they are to become mothers of the next generation, it seems as if one could not possibly attempt a more useful achievement than their civilization. Above all, this club stands in the way of the greatest curse of East London—the boy and girl marriage. For the elder women there are Mothers' Meetings, at which two hundred attend every week; and there are branches of the Societies for Nursing and Helping Married Women.

For general purposes there is a Parish Sick and Distress Fund; a fund for giving dinners to poor children; there is a frequent distribution of fruit, vegetables, and flowers, sent up by people from the country. And for the children there is a large room which they can use as a play-room from four o'clock till half-past seven. Here they are at least warm; were it not for this room they would have to run about the cold streets; here they have games and pictures and toys. In connection with the work for the girls, help is given by the Metropolitan Association for Befriending Young Servants, which takes charge of a good many of the girls.

For the men there is one of the institutions called a Tee-to-tum Club, which has a grand *café* open to everybody all day long; the members manage the club themselves; they have a concert once a week, a dramatic performance once a week, a gymnastic display once a week; on Sunday they have a lecture or an address, with a discussion after it; and they have smaller clubs attached for football, cricket, rowing, and swimming.

For the younger lads there is another club, of one hundred and sixty members; they also have their gymnasium, their foot-ball, cricket, and swimming clubs; their classes for carpentry, wood-carving, singing, and shorthand; their savings' bank, their sick club, and their library.

Only the better class of lads belong to this club. But there is a lower set, those who lounge about the streets at night, and take to gambling and betting. For these boys the children's play-room is opened in the evening; here they read, talk, box, and play bagatelle, draughts, and dominos. These lads are as rough as can be found, yet on the whole they give very little trouble.

Another important institution is the Country Holiday ; this is

Smoking Concert at the Tee-to-tum, St. James's, Ratcliff.

accomplished by saving. It means, while it lasts, an expenditure of five shillings a week ; sometimes the lads are taken to the sea-side and live in a barn ; sometimes the girls are sent to a village and placed about in cottages. A great number of the girls and lads go off every year a hopping in Kent.

Add to these the temperance societies, and we seem to complete the organized work of the Church. It must, however, be remembered that this work is not confined to those who attend the services or are Anglican in name. The clergy and the ladies who help them go about the whole parish from house to house; they know all the people in every house, to whatever creed they belong; their visits are looked for as a kind of right; they are not insulted even by the roughest; they are trusted by all; as they go along the streets the children run after them and hang upon their dress; if a strange man is walking with one of these ladies they catch at his hands and pull at his coat-tails—we judge of a man, you see, by his companions. All this machinery seems costly. It is, of course, far beyond the slender resources of the parish. It demands, however, no more than £850 a year, of which £310 is found by different societies, and the sum of £500 has to be raised somehow.

There are, it has been stated, no more than seven thousand people in this parish, of whom nearly half belong to the Church of Rome. It would, therefore, almost seem as if every man, woman, and child in the place must be brought under the influence of all this work. In a sense all the people do feel the influence of the Church, whether they are Anglicans or not. The parish system, as you have seen, provides everything; for the men, clubs; for the women, nursing in sickness, friendly counsel always, help in trouble; the girls are brought together and kept out of mischief and encouraged in self-respect by ladies who understand what they want and how they look at things; the grown lads are taken from the streets, and, with the younger boys, are taught arts and crafts, and are trained in manly exercises just as if they were boys of Eton and Harrow. The Church services, which used to be everything, are now only a part of the parish work. The clergy are at once servants of the altar, preachers, teachers, almoners, leaders in all kinds of societies and clubs, and providers of amusements and recreation. The people look on, hold out their hands, receive, at first indifferently—but presently, one by one, awaken to a new sense. As they receive they cannot choose but to discover that these ladies have given up

The Sewing Class, Girl's Institute.

their luxurious homes and the life of ease in order to work among them. They also discover that these young gentlemen who "run" the clubs, teach the boys gymnastics, boxing, drawing, carving, and the rest, give up for this all their evenings—the flower of the day in the flower of life. What for? What do they get for it? Not in this parish only, but in every parish the same kind of thing goes on and spreads daily. This—observe—is the last step *but one* of charity. For the progress of charity is as follows: First, there is the pitiful dole to the beggar; then the bequest to monk and monastery; then the founding of the almshouse and the parish charity; then the Easter and the Christmas offerings; then the gift to the almoner; then the cheque to a society; next—latest and best —personal service among the poor. This is both flower and fruit of charity. One thing only remains. And before long this thing also shall come to pass as well.

Those who live in the dens and witness these things done daily must be stocks and stones if they were not moved by them. They are not stocks and stones; they are actually, though slowly, moved by them; the old hatred of the Church—you may find it expressed in the workingman's papers of fifty years ago—is dying out rapidly in our great towns; the brawling is better; even the drinking is diminishing. And there is another—perhaps an unexpected—result. Not only are the poor turning to the Church which befriends them, the Church which they used to deride, but the clergy are turning to the poor; there are many for whom the condition of the people is above all other earthly considerations. If that great conflict—long predicted—of capital and labor ever takes place, it is safe to prophecy that the Church will not desert the poor.

Apart from the Church what machinery is at work? First, because there are so many Catholics in the place, one must think of them. It is, however, difficult to ascertain the Catholic agencies at work among these people. The people are told that they must go to mass; Roman Catholic sisters give dinners to children; there is the Roman League of the Cross—a temperance association; I think that the Catholics are in great measure left to the charities of the Anglicans, so long as these do not try to convert the Romans.

The Salvation Army people attempt nothing—absolutely nothing in this parish. There are at present neither Baptist, nor Wes-

Lightermen putting off to work

Hugh Thomson
c March 1892

LIGHTERMEN AFTER DINNER PUTTING OFF TO WORK FROM RATCLIFF STAIRS.

leyan, nor Independent chapels in the place. A few years ago, on the appearance of the book called the " Bitter Cry of Outcast London," an attempt was made by the last-named body ; they found an old chapel belonging to the Congregationalists, with an endowment of £80 a year, which they turned into a mission hall, and carried on with spirit, for two years mission work in the place ; they soon obtained large funds, which they seem to have lavished with more zeal than discretion. Presently their money was all gone and they could get no more ; then the chapel was turned into a night-shelter. Next it was burned to the ground. It is now rebuilt and is again a night-shelter. There is, however, an historic monument in the parish with which remains a survival of former activity. It is a Quaker meeting-house which dates back to 1667. It stands within its walls, quiet and decorous ; there are the chapel, the ante-room, and the burial-ground. The congregation still meet, reduced to fifty ; they still hold their Sunday-school ; and not far off one of the fraternity carries on a Crêche which takes care of seventy or eighty babies, and is blessed every day by as many mothers.

Considering all these agencies—how they are at work day after day, never resting, never ceasing, never relaxing their hold, always compelling the people more and more within the circle of their influence ; how they incline the hearts of the children to better things and show them how to win these better things—one wonders that the whole parish is not already clad in white robes and sitting with harp and crown. On the other hand, walking down London Street, Ratcliff, looking at the foul houses, hearing the foul language, seeing the poor women with black eyes, watching the multitudinous children in the mud ; one wonders whether even these agencies are enough to stem the tide and to prevent this mass of people from falling lower and lower still into the hell of savagery. This parish is one of the poorest in London ; it is one of the least known ; it is one of the least visited. Explorers of slums seldom come here ; it is not fashionably miserable. Yet all these fine things are done here, and as in this parish so in every other. It is continually stated

18

as a mere commonplace—one may see the thing advanced everywhere, in " thoughtful " papers, in leading articles—that the Church
of Rome alone can produce its self-sacrificing martyrs, its lives of
pure devotion.   Then what of these parish-workers of the Church
of England?   What of that young physician who worked himself
to death for the children ?   What of the young men—not one here
and there—but in dozens—who give up all that young men mostly
love for the sake of laborious nights among rough and rude lads ?
What of the gentlewomen who pass long years—give up their
youth, their beauty, and their strength—among girls and women
whose language is at first like a blow to them ?   What of the clergy
themselves, always, all day long, living in the midst of the very
poor—hardly paid, always giving out of their poverty, forgotten in
their obscurity, far from any chance of promotion, too hard-worked
to read or study, dropped out of all the old scholarly circles ?   Nay,
my brothers, we cannot allow to the Church of Rome all the unselfish men and women.   Father Damien is one of us as well.   I have
met him—I know him by sight—he lives, and has long lived, in
Riverside London.

A SCHOOL FOR STREET ARABS

By EDMUND R. SPEARMAN,

AUTHOR OF ARTICLES AND REPORTS ON EDUCATION IN FRANCE

THE MUNICIPAL COUNCIL OF PARIS AND THE " MORALLY ABANDONED "—STREET
CHILDREN WITHOUT CARE—PLANS OF M. BRUEYRE—DR. THULIÉ—D'ALEM-
BERT SCHOOL FOR PARIS STREET BOYS—MONTÉVRAIN—OCCUPATIONS OF THE
BOYS — PRINTING, THE TURNING-SHOP, CABINET-MAKING — VALUE OF THE
BOYS' WORK — THE DAILY ROUTINE — THE DRILL — THE VETERANS — THE
SCHOOL TABLE—HEALTH STATISTICS—FUTURE OF THE PUPILS.

STREET Arabs are often picturesque to look at, especially on
the canvases of the fair bride of an African explorer. They
are also amusing in their "cheek" and their "lingo" especially in the pages of Dickens. But they are also highly dangerous
to the public peace if allowed to "run to seed," the seed being often
robbery, outrage, and even murder. The street Arab battalions of
London during recent years have kept whole districts under a
reign of terror, and one notorious murder in Marylebone, connected
with the wild excesses of the London urchins, a few years ago set
all tongues to wagging over the necessity of some sweeping reform.
The street Arab grows into the "larrikin" and "hoodlum," the
"rough" and "plug ugly," and becomes less picturesque and more
obnoxious.

While London has been talking, Paris has been acting. The
philosophic guardians of the French capital have, during the last
decade, taken the street Arab in hand to some purpose, and have
dealt with him in a manner to serve as a model to the other great
capitals of the world, where the same questions are sure to present
themselves for solution.

The Municipal Council of Paris has invented a new theory in legislation regarding the young. The street Arab is, according to them, to be known henceforth in jurisprudence as the " morally abandoned." Other cities and other lands have taken to task the juvenile convicted vagrant and criminal, and devised schemes for their reclamation ; but the Parisian authorities apply the axiom that the " ounce of prevention is worth more than a pound of cure," and take the children before they have become either misdemeanants or criminals. The juvenile criminal and juvenile vagabond, in nine cases out of ten, is the child of certain classes of parents who are unfit to have the care of children. Such are the older criminals themselves, the notoriously vicious, and the notoriously debauched or dissipated. By a new French law (July 24, 1889), all this special class of parents are denied all rights over their children. This law is the result of the Paris lever, which, in this as in so many other matters, raised the whole of France.

Previous to 1889 there was no legal authority in France to hand over non-convicted children above twelve years of age to the public charge. Moreover there was no authority to take into state charge any children below twelve not convicted of offence who had not been cast adrift by their parents, although the said parents might be worse than none. This great lack in the French legislation especially struck the attention of M. Loys Brueyre, who, in his capacity as head of the children's bureau in the office of poor relief in the Department of the Seine, had peculiar facilities for knowing the shortcomings of the system. M. Brueyre felt that a large number of children were wandering the streets under no proper parental care, or, worse still, highly improper care, who would make better citizens than those already in charge under the orphan, foundling, and common laws. At present these children were plunging into certain careers of ignorance, vice, and crime.

There is nothing like "teaching by example," and, before moving the unwieldy and stolid fabric of national legislation, the authorities of the capital were first appealed to, and asked to put the idea into practice, showing the practicability of reclaiming these juvenile vagabonds, then get the country to adopt it, after it saw "how the thing worked." M. Brueyre found an able backer in the work in M. Michel Moring, director of the department of the Paris poor relief, who induced the Council of the Seine to take up the matter. The Council consists of the well-known Municipal Council of Paris, with the deputies from the *banlieue* or communes in the suburbs outside the fortifications. All matters relating to the police and poor relief are treated as departmental affairs. The Seine Council debated several schemes, such as the establishment of a departmental orphan asylum, and the care of all children where the mother was "*seule et misérable*," or where the father was "*veuf ou abandonné par sa femme.*" All these propositions being set aside as impracticable, the Council finally came around to M. Brueyre's idea. This idea was first developed before a special committee of the Council, consisting of M. Moring, Dr. Thulié (ex-president of the Council and also of the Anthropological Society), and M. Charles Lafont (one of the representatives for Paris in the Chamber of Deputies). In December, 1879, this commission reported most favorably, and, although the premature death of M. Moring, in May, 1880, deprived the scheme of its ablest supporter, a good substitute was found in M. Moring's successor, M. Charles Quentin, who gave the new protégés that great requisite in successful movements of reform and legislation—a name. M. Quentin dubbed the children proposed to be taken in state keeping the "morally abandoned," a most happy appellation.

To Dr. Thulié we owe the careful fostering of the idea in the channels of legislation. His painstaking reports on the progress of the matter have been summarized in his elaborate work on the Paris foundlings,* a perfect triumph of typography achieved by the children for whom the author did so much to give an opportunity to gain their present position. From the first all the foster-parents of the new scheme were active in their several directions.

* Enfants Assistés de la Seine. Paris, 1887.

M. Quentin, as head of the Paris branch of that curious compound of public and private charity, the French poor relief, used every available occasion to give facilities for launching the venture. Among other opportunities he was enabled to purchase, for forty thousand francs, a beautifully located farm in the Department of the Seine-et-Marne, for the installation of some hospitalary or hygienic establishment. M. Quentin induced the Council to devote this purchase to the use of one of the new schools. It is now the location I am about to describe. Meanwhile M. Lafont had interested his powerful fellow-legislator, the distinguished M. Theophile Roussel (then a fellow-deputy, but since elected a senator), who has divided his life between chemistry for adults and philanthropy for juveniles, to broach the legal reform. M. Roussel (who is the author of the standard law for the protection of nursing children, known as the Roussel Act) formulated still another important law for child protection, the one which became at length enacted in 1889. Dr. Thulié collected all the accumulated wisdom of past experience on the subject, including the advice of the prison reform societies, and especially the noble Pastor Robin, the Protestant philanthropist of Belleville, and of M. Charles Lucas, of the Institute, the accomplished architect and resolute advocate for the abolition of death penalties, and of other prison reforms. Most important of all was the mission of M. Brueyre himself, who happened to be blessed with a store of rich friends and the knack of interesting them in helping forward good works. Funds were the chief requisite ; for the Council could not or would not vote much money for the venture, as it hardly had the power. The donations obtained by M. Brueyre were mostly from the kings of the *haute finance*, including several of the Rothschilds. Some of these donations were for the service generally, and some for particular undertakings. Several schools were thus inaugurated. A school of horticulture at Villepreux, not far from Versailles, was one of the first ventures. This was at first a great success, being especially under the benevolent eye of M. Roussel himself. The Minister of Agriculture gave an annual donation, and two scholarships at the Barres School of Forestry, near Montargis, were also created for the benefit of the Villepreux scholars. This last is a great honor, for in Loiret the picked guardians of the national forests are trained. Villepreux has languished of late, from various causes, but may yet recover its early vigor. Another school has been placed at Alençon, principally of typography, the young printers being trained and their labor used by a local printer. To this school a shoemaking department has been added. Still another school for girls, of weaving and housekeeping, was started

The D'Alembert School Buildings at Montévrain.

at Yseure, a little commune in central France, but the pupils were so few that it was soon closed. The most important of all the ventures, however, was the school of cabinet-making, with a minor printing annex, which, in 1881, was, as before mentioned, authorized by the Municipal Council to be placed at Montévrain in the Seine-et-Marne. In honor of the co-founder of the Encyclopædia, the Municipal Council (which holds as gospel that all good dates from the Revolution, and that, the Revolution being the sum of all wisdom, the Encyclopædia was its prophet) named the new venture the D'Alembert School.* The immediate inauguration of the vent-

---

* Some of the more orthodox revolutionists insist on calling it the Alembert School, considering the aristocratic prefix as rank heresy.

ure was provided for by the munificent gift of fifty thousand francs by the Baron de Sarter. This sum was afterward supplemented by a like amount from Madame Dagnan. Still another of M. Brueyre's financial friends, M. Edouard Kohn, has given nine thousand five hundred francs at various times and Madame S. Emden three thousand francs. These various benefactions are duly acknowledged in letters of gold on a tablet at the school to-day. This rich supply of funds has encouraged the Municipal Council to devote an increasing amount of attention to the plan, and to allow considerable subsidies from the general fund. The school was opened in August, 1882, and has had an increasingly prosperous history. It has had the devotion of two thoroughly enthusiastic directors, M. May, the first, being replaced a year or two since by M. Dehesden, and both of them have evidently had their whole hearts in the undertaking. No more agreeable day can be passed in the country around Paris than by a visit to the D'Alembert School, for anyone who has the "open sesame" of an order from the Place de Grève.

Fifteen miles to the eastward of Paris, on the Strasbourg line, is the quaint old town of Lagny, lying on the south bank of the wide and sleepy Marne, having a twin town (Thorigny) on the north bank. The fine old bridges and the lazily moving canal-boats give a notion of the easy-going life of other days. The bustle and modern innovations of the great steam highway are hidden from the river-side. The crooked old streets of Lagny seem only made for palfreys and cavaliers. Taking the eastern highway out of the town, we soon find ourselves climbing to high ground, whence we look across the river valley to the flourishing settlement of Dampmart. The Marne valley is sweet to the eye and refreshing to the lungs. No choicer spot could be found to escape the close confinement of town life at such short distance from Notre Dame and the Hôtel de Ville. Here, just east of Lagny, in the sparsely settled commune of Montévrain—the home of the D'Alembert School—at a spot where the painstaking road-builders of the "king's highway," in the days when kings were rife in France, have spanned the sudden fall of a deep hollow by a fine viaduct of solid earth. Close under the high land to the right, a steep slope is left toward the still deeper falling ground on the left. Thus, quite below the roadway, and reached by a flight of steps and inclined paths, are hidden the buildings of the farm. These buildings are not now attached to their former domain, but will be added most likely in a short while for increased accommodation. Covering the former fields toward the roadway, the new structures and new dispositions of the ground for the school might themselves be unnoticed by a careless passer-by, being all below the road-level. The official who was inspired with the notion of placing an asylum on the spot was certainly endowed with the gift of "happy thoughts." The situation is simply ideal; on one side it nestles against the hill-side, protected from the bleakness of a too exposed position, while toward the river the broad expanse of valley below gives air and sunshine in abundance. Here the D'Alembert School lodges, feeds, and instructs a constant succession of Parisian street Arabs, giving them indeed an industrial paradise.

The grounds are ample, and include trim-kept gardens and lawns to the road-side, with high shrubberies hiding most of the place. To the rear the two chief workshops are placed high up at either extremity of a long parade, this latter being the exercise ground and gymnasium. The parade is the rear and much the larger of the two open courts, the one nearer the road being separated by a large building used in three floors as a dormitory, the upper story being under a pitched roof with dormer windows. To the right of this front court is the directors' office and residence, while to the left is the mess-room and storage-house. At the rear of the great court or parade is a fourth dormitory in a low building, while to its right is the "police cell" for bad boys (a structure whose office is almost a sinecure), and to the left is an engine-house with a third workshop devoted to turning. The majority of the young workers are however employed in the two large brick pavilions which face each other from the high banks that bound the premises. In the river end of the left-hand or western pavilion is installed the school of printing. The lower story is devoted to the presses, hand and foot, while above is the composing-room. Two large machine presses are placed in the adjoining end of the rear building, next to the turners, and thus, like the latter, have the use of the power from the engine-room.

The printing occupies about thirty of the boys, and, like all the other departments, is under the direction of a master of the craft. Judging by the results, the teaching printer must be a born genius at the task : the work turned out by these young aspirants to "the Art preservative of Art" will bear comparison with the best in any land, and is of the most varied and difficult description, including a great variety of ornamental and "table work." Of course, excellent method and ample materials, in the shape of a full assortment of type and other necessaries for a great printing-office go a long way to help the young printers. But their tutor and the aptitude and interest taken by the pupils are the chief factors. On my visiting rounds I encountered one bright little lad who had only been four days in the school, yet had set up a short galley of type, the proof of which was better than some I have seen come from old printers. Of course he must have been exceptionally clever and have been carefully coached ; but all the pupils seem to be able to perform somewhat similar prodigies. An older pupil, of eighteen months' standing, was setting up a railway time-table, which not one compositor in five hundred would dare to undertake at first sight. The street Arab as a printer is evidently a success. No printing-office in the world can show such a galaxy of choice and capable apprentices as can the D'Alembert School.

The work in the press-room below is of as great excellence as the type-setting above, and, although there are no "long runs" (as printers call taking a great many impressions of the same work) to keep the two large machines of the latest improved patterns in two adjoining buildings always in motion, the young printers are as adept in this branch of the trade as in the others. Doubtless, when the capabilities of this printing-office get fully into the general administrative craniums, the imprint of Montévrain will be as familiar in French official documents as "Eyre & Spottiswoode, Printers to the Queen," on the English archives, or "Government Printing Office, Washington," on those of the United States. This

The Printing Office.

was not originally intended for the chief printing school of the service, that at Alençon having printing as its special feature, while at Montévrain only a handful of boys were originally set to the composing-stick and ink-roller. The easy access to Paris, however, soon occasioned the printing of the overseeing bureau to drift to Montévrain, which soon outstripped the more distant rival, now still engaged on private work. At present Alençon is becoming more and more an apprenticeship of its alternated trade, the trade of the twin Saints Crispin-Crispanus. The shoemakers can as well be five hundred miles away as fifty.

The handiness of the printers to Paris has not caused them to oust the other trade of Montévrain, however, for the very good reason that all the other young apprentices are engaged in manufacture which is even more important as an adjunct to the administrative bureau than the printing. They, in fact, make a large proportion of the furniture for the hospital service of Paris.

I have mentioned the turning-shop adjoining the press-room on one side, and the engine-room on the other, in the rear buildings. There are only a few boys here, because the ornamental work is a minor factor in ordinary cabinet-making. The product is nevertheless worthy of comparison with the most beautiful furniture in the matter of artistic finish, although simple as a rule. The sawing is mostly done by the master turner, a circular saw being the last thing intrusted to a workman, and especially dangerous to novices, however careful and clever. The work in the turning-room is the most dangerous on the premises, and liable to take odd fingers and thumbs as a toll on the highway to knowledge. The boys when I visited them seemed to have thus far escaped with only a bandaged forefinger on the eldest of their number, due doubtless to the momentary forgetfulness of some recent day. For, although not trusted with the circular saw itself, all turning is done at rapidly oscillating engine-driven instruments, and the least carelessness occasions injury either to the work or to the workman. The youths here were producing various ornamental designs with the confident dexterity of a master of the craft, although the chips, from gouges, chisels, grooving-planes, and bevelling-knives, showered like driven snow over the chucks and mandrels of the turning-lathes and moulding-gear, and the loud crunching of the sharp iron on the hard fibre was quite enough to frighten the nervous observer.

Leaving the clever young turners to their sanctuary of sawdust,

I next visited the lower floor of the opposite end of the chief workshops, beyond the printing-room. Here the first elements of the cabinet-making trade were being instilled into the heads of some fifteen of the younger pupils, planing and polishing the large smooth surfaces of furniture being here the special feature. The great bulk of the articles in hand seemed to be washstands and tables. At the time of my visit a great stock of new furniture was being made for the Bichat Hospital at Paris, large alterations and renovations there requiring a new supply. The superintendent at the polishing-up workshop seemed to have a more mischievous crew than any other: probably the less steady attention required for the work allows animal spirits more scope. Hence the rebukes of the schoolmaster were rife here—the only specimens I noticed on my visit.

On the floor above, the work was chiefly fitting and finishing, putting on ornaments, locks to drawers and doors, etc., the fire and glue-pot being ever at hand. Here the work was of special nicety, and the ingenuity shown by the young workmen in mortising, pinning, clamping, etc., being very wonderful. In a room of twenty boys, of course, a single overseer has to trust almost entirely to each one's talent and faithfulness of detail. If the work were solely matter of practice, to be thrown aside when done, the after-examination and correction of faults would be all necessary. As a fact, the work is all disposed of for important use, and will not only bear comparison with the furniture sold in the fashionable salesroom, but is superior to most modern work, which is generally made to sell and not to use.

The truth is, the cabinet-making trade is one which has suffered more than any other by the modern mania for hurry-skurry, shoddy manufacture, and mere show in place of substance. The so-called " craze " for old furniture, rife during the last thirty or forty years, has this solid basis of reason that the furniture of our ancestors is an altogether different product, outside all considerations of fashion, from that of the modern cabinet-maker, who knows not his trade, but is a mere particle in a great machine of cheap and slovenly production. This school at Montévrain was partly started as a protest against this bad tendency in the cabinet trade, by one of the leading and most enlightened cabinet firms of Paris, that of Damon-Kreiger, in Saint-Antoine. The Municipal Council would scarcely have been able to launch their novel scheme without the assistance of this far-sighted house. The cabinet-making of Paris is famous the world over, but, like that elsewhere, has been going rapidly to the bad. A genuine cabinet-maker, master of his trade, below middle age, has almost ceased to exist in the French capital. The firm of Damon-Kreiger keenly felt this lack. The extreme division of labor and a machine-like production is profitable enough to master and men, if fashions never changed. But fashions do change, and fashions in furniture as well. It was found that the machine workman of divided labor was incapable of producing good work in another direction, when his own special feature became obsolete and a new one was wanted. It is only the master of all branches of the art who can thus easily shift about. The process of extreme division of labor has been built up in all trades by a sort of process of living on brain capital. The old race of workmen, with their all-round capacity, could easily develop special features in various directions. But gradually this breeds but mere human machines. When these human machines are asked to work another way they cannot respond. The streets of our great capitals are swarming with helpless, worthless, beggared workmen, thrown out of employment by mere violent shifts of fashion and their own inability to adapt themselves to altered conditions. With the streets of Paris full of unemployed workmen, such a firm as these Saint-Antoine cabinet-makers cried in vain for competent artisans. They evidently had some of the old-fashioned love for faithful apprenticeship. But the workman no longer apprentices his son, the son no longer submits to apprenticeship. The father wants his son to support himself from the day he sets to work; the son thinks he has the right to assume an independent position thenceforth. But here was a chance for the firm of Saint-Antoine. The city of Paris had a stock of boys, intelligent, and yet amenable to discipline, and only too glad to take sufficient time to learn a thorough trade. In fact, the longer the better ; for it meant good living and a pleasant home meanwhile — things hitherto unknown — and therefore to be all the more appreciated. So the firm of Damon-Kreiger not only furnished a picked band of working instructors in the trade and abundant material for the work, but also agreed to take the work even at a cost far above that in their own workshops ; for it was stipulated by the city that the boys must be paid from the very start for such work as they did. In this way a valuable beginning was obtained.* In course of years, when a thoroughly efficient staff of apprentices was generated, including a good proportion of boys of two and three years' training, practically capable journeymen, the products, of course, became very much more valuable, and the school was able to be almost self-supporting.

The solid character of the product of the school to-day I well appreciated when I crossed the extensive exercise yard and mounted the high bank to the opposite workshop. Here but a small number of boys are employed, the chief portion of the pavilion, the larger of the two, and having three stories, being devoted to storage of the work and of specimens of special results or trophies of industry. Some of these were exhibited at the great exhibition of 1889, and included most beautiful examples of not only plain but ornamental work, in ebony and rosewood. There was a state bed

---

* For the clew to this interesting episode in the early history of the D'Alembert School, I am indebted to the report of a conversation between an intelligent foreman in the Damon-Kreiger employ (M. Lepine) and M. Francisque Sarcey (the famous dramatic critic), in the *Gagne-Petit* newspaper. This daily journalistic refulgence of all the talents (which was really "too good to last," and like "the good, died young") printed, at the end of April, 1885 (and near the close of its own career), an account of the visit of M. Sarcey with the publisher and certain officials to Montévrain. The articles (like most French journalism) are rather erroneous if not erratic, but, as their source would indicate, naturally most entertaining.

which Louis Quinze himself might have envied, while some of the
inlayings of tables and sideboards were simply exquisite. To the
professional eye, however, the triumph of all the exhibits was a
large hard-wood cylinder, perfect in its smooth circle, the most difficult of all turning processes. It is far more important that the

The Carpenter Shop.

young workmen are apt in the plain, honest work they are chiefly
engaged in.

In this pavilion the workers are principally employed in the
carpentry and joinery features of the cabinet trade. Doors and
sashes and all the specialties of the joiner are here manipulated,
and the young workmen show that at a pinch they could build a
house as well as furnish it.

The upper floor of this right-hand (or eastern) pavilion is devoted to two school-rooms, one for general study, and the other for drawing and design. Each room is fitted with all the accessories of not only elementary but higher instruction. Maps and charts adorn the walls, while implements of example and experiment in the rudiments of the sciences are visible in the cabinets. The benches look neat, and little injured by the proverbial jack-knives of the village urchin in the country school-rooms. The drawing-school is, of course, a most important feature, and the scholars can not only show their ingenuity on the blackboard and paper sheets, but can carry out the ideas here developed by speedy application in the workshop. The trade of the cabinet-maker is specially fertile in opportunities for the ingenious designer, while even the printers, in their artistic ornamental work, have some field also for application of the instruction.

The hours of schooling are somewhat peculiar, but perhaps best adapted to the circumstances. The young learners take their lessons just after rising from, and just before going to, their beds. This gives a solid day in the more active employment. The following is the daily routine at Montévrain :

5 A.M. Rising, morning toilet, and arrangement of dormitories.

5.45 A.M. School.

7 A.M. Soup.

7.30 A.M. Workshop.

11 A.M. Gymnastics.

12 M. Luncheon.

2 P.M. Workshop.

6.30 P.M. Dinner.

7 P.M. School.

8.30 P.M. Bed.

On four days in the week there is one extra hour of school (8.30 to 9.30), for the pupils in music and drawing, two evenings for each. The regular schoolmaster is replaced in these lessons by special instructors.

The gymnastics are a great pride of the school, the grand parade

19

between the two banks bounded by the workshops offering exceptional facilities for various manœuvres. Besides the cross-bars,
swings, etc., such as are characteristic of every French barrack yard,
the boys here make a special feature of fireman's exercise; they
have not only a fire-engine, but an experienced instructor from the
corps of *sapeurs-pompiers ;* for all the French firemen are either soldiers in the service of the state or organized as local military battalions. The school has also had the advantage of a special instructor from the famous military gymnastic school at Joinville-le-
Pont, just east of Paris. From these advantages they have been
enabled to compete with marked success in the athletic competitions so rife in France of recent years, the mania for athletics being
the feature of the age. The D'Alembert School boasts a great collection of wreaths, medals, and other trophies, from gymnastic and
fire exercise competitions, even as far away as the historic old town
of Provins, in Champagne, whence the D'Alembert School carried
away in triumph a pretty little statuette of Joseph Viola, the Avig-
non boy hero of the Revolution (killed by the Royalist insurgents
of '93 while cutting the cables on the Rhône), offered by President
Carnot himself. All these prizes are displayed in great state in the
directors' office. Perhaps some of the snobbish spirits (found even
among school-boys) of more fashionable establishments may feel
shocked at seeing the street Arabs of Paris prove themselves best
in the tug of war, but the D'Alembert boys never allow their illustrious name to be backward in the race, and the supercilious critics
(if any such exist) may be reminded that the great D'Alembert himself, not a physical, but an intellectual, giant, was not only a Paris
street Arab, but a Parisian foundling.*

* As D'Alembert is the most illustrious name on the roll of the juvenile outcasts
of Paris, a few recently disclosed facts regarding his earliest experiences in life will
be interesting. D'Alembert was the product of one of the many amours of Cardinal
de Tencin's erratic sister, the famous authoress of the *Princesse de Clèves*, escaped nun,
and Parisian leader of literary fashion. D'Alembert's father was the Chevalier Destouches, another illustrious literary connection, the chevalier being of the family of
Philippe Destouches, the poet. Several biographical errors being generally repeated

As every able-bodied Frenchman is a soldier, of course military exercise is a portion of the athletic instruction—a full supply of guns

regarding D'Alembert's birth, M. Léon Lallemand produced the following authenticated facts on June 8, 1885, in an address before the Academy of Sciences, and has included them in his excellent *Histoire des Enfants abandonnés:*

" In the Biographie Universelle of Michaud (new edition, tome i., page 385) will be found the following information concerning the origin of D'Alembert :

" ' Alembert (Jean le Rond d'), born at Paris, November 16, 1717, was exposed on the steps of St. Jean le Rond—a church near Notre Dame, now destroyed. The existence of this child appeared so frail that the Commissaire of Police who received it, instead of sending it to the Enfants Trouvés, thought it necessary to give it special care, and with this view confided it to the wife of a poor glazier. Perhaps he had received some instructions to act in this manner, for although the parents never made themselves known, a few days after its birth they retook the abandoned one from where they had left it.' Same details in the *Nouveau Dictionnaire de la Conversation et de la Lecture* (2me Ed., Didot, 1873, tome vii., p. 104).

" These recitals, extracts from the eulogy on D'Alembert delivered before the Academy of Sciences by Condorcet, contain, side by side with the truth, some points which are not exact and which it is important to correct.

" D'Alembert was really abandoned on the steps of the church of St. Jean le Rond, and the procès-verbal of the exposure, published above, shows that special precautions had been taken, for the poor forsaken ones were never placed in wooden boxes. People were generally quite content to deposit them on the earth or on a bench. The story of the commissaire who did not dare to have the child taken to the Maison de la Couche on account of its weakness, is absolutely false, as is proved by the register of admissions for the year 1717, where, on folio 513, under the register No. 1584, we find :

" ' Jean le Rond, newly born—on the procès-verbal of Commissaire Delamere of 16th November, 1717, given in nurse to Anne Freyon, wife of Louis Lemaire, living at Crémery.

" ' First month, 5 livres for the first month, ended 17 December, 1718.

" ' 5 January, 1718, 2 livres, 5 francs to 1 January, 1718, when the child was returned to its parents. This child was given up to Sieur Molin, doctor in ordinary to the King, who charged himself with it by deed before Beussel, notary, on January 1, 1718.'

" It is thus established, 1st, That D'Alembert was *deposited at the Maison de Couche, and placed at nurse in Picardy for six months.* 2d. That his parents, not wishing to betray their incognito, chose M. Jacques Molin, known as Dumoulin, one of the most celebrated practitioners of his time."

It is worth noting that D'Alembert chose to remain a foundling. When he had become monarch of the mind of France, greater than the king, his erratic mother wished to claim him. It was too late. He refused the offer.

of small pattern (not the famous new Lebel, but breech-loaders of another species) enable the D'Alembert battalion to forestall the time when each youth will have to serve his three years in the active army. For, though the trades here learned are for life, the young artisans, each and all, have to have their first experience of manhood, the same as other citizens, in the calling of war.

The Drum Major.

The guns are a noticeable feature in the dormitories, standing in racks at either end of each sleeping-apartment. In fact these dormitories have somewhat the look of barrack life. There are about thirty beds in each of the principal ones, each bed with a small locker at its head, in which, in military order, are found the dress-suits, brushes, etc., of the youth appertaining thereto. The boys work ordinarily in blue jeans and bareheaded, but the "Sunday suits" are quite gala affairs, with spruce naval caps and gold-lettered ribbon, a handsome white flannel shirt with rolling collar and corded throat, a double-breasted blue tunic with brass buttons and ornaments in the lapels, a pair of blue trousers, and a pair of flannel pantaloons and white gaiters. This supply makes two full rig-outs, for both military and gymnastic exercises, the waist for the latter in great galas being adorned with dazzling red and sky-blue sashes, a store of which are kept in the school wardrobe. This wardrobe is the only portion of the premises where the boys are not their own servants. Two seamstresses and a wardrobe mistress keep the whole of the stock of clothes in excellent repair, and also have charge of all spare garments, issuing such as are needed. The washing is not done at Montévrain, but sent to Paris, to the Hospital Lariboissière, which, being near the Strasbourg station, can accommodate the school in the course of its own great labors without any inconvenience.

Sunday is a general holiday at Montévrain. The Municipal Council, being rampantly secular, there is no chapel or chaplain on the premises. As the boys are all given leave on Sunday, those over sixteen can attend church if so inclined. Probably few of them thus spend the Sunday, boys not being much given to that idea of their own accord. Those under sixteen have their Sunday leave in charge of an attendant. The hours of the leave are from

The Trumpeter.

2 to 7 P.M. Each boy is given five sous for pocket-money on Sundays, to lay out in "cakes and ale." During the four years' apprenticeship a certain sum is put by to give them at the end of their apprenticeship, as a start. Besides this, a boy away from his apprenticeship can stay and work until eighteen years of age, when he departs for the army. If he comes at the minimum age of twelve (as the majority do), this means two years, from sixteen to

eighteen. These boys are called the "veterans," and are paid three francs a day, one franc being however charged for keep. The "veterans" are paid each three months, but are allowed advances of fifteen francs a month. They have full liberty on Sunday, to go to Paris and return when they please. These "veterans" occupy a portion of the fourth dormitory (the rest not being used as yet), and are barred off from the room, having trunks instead of lockers, and altogether begin to blossom out a bit. As the jolly director said, rattling on in his description : "*Voici la canne, le paraluie, et quelquefois le parasol aussi,*" and a merry twinkle came into his eye. These "veterans" are quite free to go to any other employment, with the consent (which is never refused) of the officials at Paris, as the Poor Relief Bureau stands *in loco parentis* in every respect, even to consent to marriage, until twenty-five years of age, a Frenchman's legal majority ; but the good living and secure employment at Montévrain are better than an uncertainty. One of them went away with eight hundred francs and then enlisted to work at his trade in the artillery for six years, where he would get extra pay, and not get out of practice ; he has already been promoted.

M. Dehesdin related an interesting tale, illustrating the far-reaching benefits of such institutions as the D'Alembert School. In Paris, a poor working painter, with five children, three boys and two girls, died suddenly, and his death was followed soon by that of his widow. The children would have been helpless, being beyond the limit of twelve years, at which the law for the help of abandoned children and orphans draws the line, had not the boys been allowed to come, all three, to Montévrain, where one became a printer and two became cabinet-makers. The two girls had to shift for themselves, but one went to service, while the other, the eldest, had just obtained a place as book-keeper before the family catastrophe. In course of time the boys got their trades and places in Paris, the eldest being allowed the short one year's military service as support of a family, for a family they have again become. The eldest sister, having hired apartments, recalled the younger from service to set up as the housekeeper, and then gathered the three brothers together. Thus, by the help of the timely intervention of the D'Alembert institution, a family was saved which would otherwise have been scattered in hopeless misery.

Such a return to home life must have been a sweet variety for these brothers, for, after all, good living, beautiful surroundings, and healthy employment as have our street Arabs at Montévrain, there is an eternal barrack huddling and drill, which even young humanity must wish occasional relief from. Perhaps it would not do to allow these lads of untried propensities to live away from an inspecting eye. Still, it seems as if tiny apartments of their own might make them more responsible and civilized citizens, teaching them self-respect and self-dependence. They could do the household duties as now, although separately. At present two boys each day are detailed to act as the mess servants of the establishment, assisting the cook and waiting on the tables. The boys cannot do their own cooking, however, a woman cook, with the women of the wardrobe, being the only female element connected with the school. Besides the instructing staff, there are three attendants who have charge of the discipline. One of these is the fire inspector before mentioned, and another is the accomplished gymnast.

The diet of the school is a very formal affair, the bill of fare for each meal for a month being printed. The morning meal consists of various kinds of soup—herb soup, meat soup, rice soup, onion soup, leek soup, julienne soup, and panade being scattered through the thirty-one days. In like manner the noon meal is varied with veal, hashed beef, mutton, fresh pork, sausages, black-puddings, and beef in various fashions, and all with a variety of vegetables. The evening meal is a sort of compromise between dinner and supper, being soup and vegetables—potatoes, beans, lentils, macaroni, on part of the days, and on others soup and meats, including roasted veal. The diet also includes wine from the city's own wine-cellar, and a moderate allowance of fruits, dessert, etc., in season. Altogether, the living is not bad at Montévrain.

The behavior of the boys at table, a sure index of boarding-school life (even in a Squeers academy), is remarkably pleasant. My first insight into the routine, on my visit (as I arrived at high noon), was to see the lads marshalled on the parade by their drill-master, marched to the tables and seated in the dining-hall to the left of the front court. They ate with relish and satisfaction as well as decorum, and when, at two o'clock, I saw them again summoned by trumpet-call to the parade-ground, to march to the two work-shops, a large detail to the left and a little one to the right, there was a cheerfulness and a promptitude which told, more than words, of good living and happy existence.

On the diet above, the street Arabs thrive most wonderfully. The health of the school is generally perfect, the doctor's bill being lower than at almost any similar collection of juveniles gathered haphazard from anything but healthy surroundings. There has been but one death in the ten years since the establishment of the school, that of a boy, in 1889, from a pulmonary consumption. A great hygienic advantage of the establishment is the proximity of the limpid Marne, in the waters of which the boys take regular baths in the summer months, nearly all of them becoming accomplished swimmers. In winter they have to content themselves with the ample bath-rooms of the establishment, where they are given three baths a week.

The accommodations of the school could easily be made quite equal to three or four hundred pupils, and in course of time that number may be reached, when the idea gets generally accepted in the official brain. This will largely increase the value of the establishment, for the product will increase in proportion to the workers, while the expenses will not rise in quite the same proportion, a school of one hundred being relatively much more costly than one of fourfold the number. At present the cost, though on a liberal scale, is recouped to a considerable degree. In 1889, for instance, the credits to the school actually exceeded the debits by over forty thousand francs, because a large arrear of products of former years were then brought in. The actual product for that year was over one hundred thousand francs to one hundred and sixty thousand francs of cost, not a bad showing for a great public " charity." As the number of older and skilled pupils becomes greater, the value of the products increases. The product of 1890 included thirty thousand francs for printing alone, and two or three times as much in the cabinet-making line.

The school is by far the most successful of the new " morally abandoned " ventures, and its fame gets already noised about. In fact, parents and guardians have offered large sums to be allowed to have their children given the beneficial physical and industrial training at Montévrain—a strange turn of fortune's wheel when the well-to-do citizen envies for his own cherished offspring the lot of the poor street Arab! Of course such offers are refused. The Municipal Council have not yet summoned up courage to take up the mournful inheritance of 1848, and the "national workshops." All these fond parents can easily get their offspring admitted at Montévrain by simply becoming bad citizens themselves and throwing their children into the streets.

In initiating Montévrain and its mates, the French officials made a careful study of the legislation and establishments in Great Britain and the United States. The interesting story of the development of reformatory and industrial schools is a record of the generous rivalry and emulation between different states of western Europe and their transatlantic neighbors, in private and public efforts, for over a century past. The French reformers combined the best features of the whole field, and, moreover, made a distinct advance on all. The English law allowed the removal of the children found in certain associations. The Massachusetts law annuls all parental right over its reformatory protégés. The New York plan included apprenticeship at various trades. In Scotland, Sheriff Watson first gave technical instruction to young vagrants in association. The Council of the Seine decided to initiate a wholesale crusade for the removal of all children in obviously improper hands, to assume the annulling of parental rights, to educate their children with all the advantages of those in the care of careful guardians, and to do this by large boarding-schools with a variety of teachers. Until the strict legal sanction of the legislature could be had, the Council acted upon its own assumption. There were frequent cases of drunken, brutal, and criminal parents coming with effrontery and bluster to reclaim their offspring, generally to advance their own selfish schemes. All such were promptly kicked out of doors. Of course the courts were open to them; it was well known that they would never dare to appeal to the law, an appeal almost certainly liable to end in a damaging exposé of their own characters, perhaps bringing them into the clutches of the very law itself, and most certainly confirming the denial of rights over their children, rights which the children themselves invariably repudiated. At length the law of 1889 settled the matter for once and all. The distinctive character of Montévrain and the other new schools is the "weeding" process. These schools cannot be a success without it. The weakness of previous ambitious industrial refuges is the necessity of using only the often poor human material—and using *all* this material—which comes for treatment.

In their Redhill enterprise the London Philanthropic Society was taunted by a *Quarterly* reviewer with its little chance when it lacked the enthusiasm and exceptional care of Mr. Turner, the founder. The reform school for western New York, in Rochester, which imitated Montévrain on a large scale in 1884, will find a difficult task if it hopes to bring all the young outcasts into the necessary limited curriculum of highly technical trades. No such impossibility is attempted at Montévrain. The stupid, incompetent, and refractory youths are carefully sifted out and sent elsewhere. The widely-spread network of agricultural colonies, and other aids for the ill-provided juvenile in France, enables this to be done. Thus the *élite* of the street Arabs can always be provided for at Montévrain. Thus is this special school almost sure of success.

The banished boys are sometimes allowed to return. Of course the incompetent have little care to renew their failures, but in cases of mere childish waywardness of really bright youths they often beg to go back to such a cheerful home, where their talents find such gratifying scope. In case of genuine amendment these prayers are answered. Thus the Montévrain school is a very model of good conduct. The Parisian street Arabs take pride in their eminent privileges, and the graduates of Montévrain are as liable to achieve praiseworthy social distinction as the graduates of any learned university in the world.

THE POOR IN NAPLES

By JESSIE WHITE VA. MARIO,

AUTHOR OF GOVERNMENT REPORTS ON THE ITALIAN POOR

HORRIBLE CONDITION OF THE NAPLES POOR A QUARTER OF A CENTURY AGO—
PASQUALE VILLARI'S INVESTIGATIONS—THE DWELLINGS—EFFORTS AT IM-
PROVEMENT—THE RAMPA DI BRANCACCIO—THE CEMETERY FOR THE POOR—
THE CHOLERA OF 1884—VOLUNTEER NURSES—KING HUMBERT'S VISIT AND
REFORMS—THE SANITARY CONDITIONS—"NAPLES MUST BE DISEMBOWELLED"
—EFFORTS OF THE MUNICIPALITY—THE EVICTED POOR—THE NEW BUILD-
INGS—NEEDS OF THE CITY—THE HOSPITALS—EMIGRATION.

THE old saying *Vedi Napoli poi morir* may be translated "See
misery in Naples to learn what misery means"—to realize
what amount of hunger, nakedness, vice, ignorance, supersti-
tion, and oppression can be condensed in the caves, dens, and ken-
nels, unfit for beasts, inhabited by the poor of Naples. In 1871 it
was affirmed by the "authorities" that, of the entire population of
the city, two-thirds had no recognized means of livelihood; no one
knew how more than a quarter of a million human beings lived,
still less where they passed their lives of privation, pain, and
wretchedness; or how, when death ended all, their bodies were
flung down to rot together in foul charnel holes, far away and apart
from the holy ground where the upper third were laid to rest that—

> "From their ashes may be made
> The violets of their native land."

Five years later, in 1876, when misery, gaunt and stark, reared
its head for the first time defiantly in every city, town, and village

of Italy—the grinding tax, proving the proverbial feather on the too patient camel's back, "inquiries into distress, its causes and possible remedies," were proposed by some of the old makers of Italy, who maintained that the aim of the revolution had been to create a country for all the Italians and not for a privileged few. The government sanctioned the proposal, and the agricultural inquiry was set on foot and carried out in every province by special commissioners. It revealed such depths of misery in the rural districts as could never be imagined or believed in by those who still apostrophize:

> " Thou Italy, whose ever golden fields,
> Ploughed by the sunbeams only, would suffice
> For the world's granary. "

In Lombardy, Mantua, and Venetia, all fertile wheat-producing provinces, it was found that the patient, toiling, abstemious peasant, fed upon maize exclusively, tasting white bread only at gleaning time, rarely touching wine, washing down his unsavory *polenta* with impure, fetid water, was affected with *pellagra*. This awful disease—now, alas, become endemic and hereditary—after wasting the body by slow degrees, affects the brain and lands the victims raving maniacs in the male and female mad asylums of Venice and of Milan. It is now being successfully grappled with in the first stages, by the parish doctors who, in many communes, are authorized to administer white bread, wine,.and even meat; in the second, by special establishments where patients are received and treated, *i.e.*, well fed until they recover *pro tem.;* while for the poor wretches who have reached the third stage, there is no help but in the grave, no hope save in a speedy release.

But a worse state of things was revealed in Naples by private studies and researches set on foot by Pasquale Villari * and the re-

---

* The present writer was among the recruits, but for a long time declined to write of misery in Naples for the Italian press, believing that the state of the poor in London was even worse than in Naples. Professor Villari, the well-known author of the lives of Savonarola and Machiavelli, Minister of Public Instruction, undertook

cruits he pressed into the service of his native city. The facts and figures set down in unvarnished prose in his "Southern Letters," convinced the authorities "that something must be done if only to protect the 'upper third' from the possible upheaval of the seething masses below, increasing ever in numbers, terribly disproportioned to the means of accommodation provided for them."

Heart-rending as were the descriptions given of the misery of the masses by Villari, Fucino Renato, Fortunato Sonnino, and others, they by no means prepared me for the actual state of things which I heard, saw, and touched in Naples, accompanied alternately by priests, policemen, and parish doctors, and always by old friends and comrades of the campaigning days when all believed that the overthrow of despots, the ousting of the foreigner, the abolition of the temporal power, when Italy should be one in Rome, would find bread and work for all as the result of liberty and the ballot.

I spent hours and days, later, weeks and months, in the lower quarters of Porto, Pendino, Mercato, and Vicaria, in the *fondaci*, the cellars, caves, grottos, brothels, and *locande* (penny-a-night

to go to London and see for himself, and on his return we received a long letter, from which the following is an extract:

"I assure you, on my honor, that the poor in Naples are infinitely worse off than the poor in London. Furnished with an order from the chief of police in London, I have visited, with detectives in plain clothes, the worst quarters of the city—the Docks, the East End, saying always: 'Show me all that is most horrible in London. I want to see the dwellings of the most wretched and miserable inhabitants.'

"Great and widespread is misery in London; but I do not hesitate to declare, with profound conviction, that those who say that the conditions of the poor in London are worse than those of the poor in Naples, have either never seen the poor in London or have never visited the poor in Naples. If it happens that cases of death from starvation are more frequent in London than in Naples, the cause lies in the climate of London. If in Naples we had the climate of London a very large number of our poor would find peace in the grave and cease to live a life that is worse than death.

"Pasquale Villari.

"Florence, March 30, 1876."

After the receipt of this letter we published, in 1877, a book entitled La Miseria di Napoli.

AN EVICTED FAMILY OF NEAPOLITANS.

lodging-houses) where the *miserables* congregate. Sickening were the sights by day, still sadder the scenes by night as you passed church steps, serving as the only bed for hundreds ; under porches where you stumbled over, without awakening the sleepers, who also occupied the benches of the vendors of fish and other comestibles in Basso Porto, while in fish-baskets and empty orange-boxes, curled up like cats but without the cat's fur coat, were hundreds of children of both sexes who had never known a father and rarely knew their mother's name or their own. It was a farce to talk of statistics of births and deaths in these quarters. "The existence of the boys is known to the authorities," writes an eminent physician, now (Assessore d'igiene) Sanitary Officer in the Municipality of Naples, "when they are taken up for theft or a *piccola mancanza ;* of the girls when they come on the brothel registers " (abolished, humanity be praised! in 1889). Of what use was it to take stock of vice, disease, and crime, save to hold it up as the legitimate outgrowth of the foul dens in which the "masses" herd? In the first report made by the corporation it was shown that 130,000 lived in the *bassi e sotterranei*, in cellars, caves, and grottos. No mention was then made of the *fondaci*, which the Swedish physician, Axel Munthe,* stigmatizes as "the most ghastly human dwellings on the face of the earth."

Let the American reader take that wonderful book, "How the Other Half Lives," and look at the photograph of Hell's Kitchen and Sebastopol (page 6). Imagine such a building, but with blank walls all round, no windows in any, entered by a dark alley leading to a court where the common cesspool fraternizes with the drinking-water well, where, round the court, are stables for cows, mules, donkeys, and goats—while in the corners of the same court, tripe, liver and lights vendors prepare their edibles, or stale fish-mongers keep their deposits—and they will have the framework and exterior of a *fondaco*. Then let them construct in their mind's eye one single brick or stone staircase leading up to inner balconies—up,

---

* See Letters from a Mourning City.

up, three, four, or five stories.   Fifteen or twenty rooms are entered
from each balcony, which serves for door and window, there being
no other aperture ; each corner room on each story being absolutely
dark even at mid-day, as each balcony is covered with the pavement
of the upper one.   Put a hole between each two rooms for the pub-
lic performance of all private offices ; shut out from the top story such light as might gleam from the sky, by dint of poles, strings, ropes, and cords laden with filthy rags — and you have a more or less accurate idea of the interior of the *fondaco* at Naples.

A Girl of the People.

All of these I have visited at in-
tervals during the last seventeen years, finding their numbers diminished at each visit, but never until lately have I found a new tenement inhabited by
the evicted *funnachère* for whom they were ostensibly built.

In 1877 the municipality made a grant of land to a co-operative
society for the purpose of building houses for the poor.   As soon
as these were finished, small shop-keepers, civil servants, etc., secured all the apartments ; then irritated by the taunts that they
were living in houses built for the poor, inscribed on the front of

the block, "The houses of the Co-operative Society are not poor-houses!" Again, in 1879, a loan was raised for demolishing the worst *fondaci* and grottos, cellars, and caves, and for the erection of airy, healthy tenements for the people, and in 1880 the writer was invited by the mayor to inspect these. Capital houses they were! built on the spot where last I had seen the *fondaci*—Arcella, Castiglione, Conventino, San Camillo, Cento Piatti, Piscavino S. Felice, Miroballo—and after due admiration of the spacious court, wide street, decent ingress, outer balconies, etc., I ventured to ask: "Where are the *funnachère?* These clean, well-dressed people, with their pianos and excellent furniture, are not the poor creatures we used to visit here."

"Of course they are not," said the contractor, "what are they to us?" while a vice-syndic said: "This is my section; I know that my *rione* is redeemed, that we have got rid of the plebs: what care we where they are gone? Let them burst, it would be better for them. *Crepino pure, che sarà meglio!*" *

As I was turning from the spot in silent despair, an old man came up and said: "I can tell you where some of the poor creatures are gone. They were turned out into the streets, many of them went into the *fondaci* that remain, two families, and even three in a room; the price of these has been raised as the numbers grow less, and many of them are in the grotto at the Rampa di Brancaccio." With a newspaper man, sceptical of "the misery of the poor in Naples," and an English and a German lady, I walked along the splendid Corso Vittorio Emanuele, whence you have the finest view of Naples, of Vesuvius and the sea, and suddenly

> "Out of the sunlit glory
> Into the dark we trod—"

literally dropping down into the grotto del Brancaccio, where, at first, absolute darkness seemed to reign.

It was a cavern with mud for pavement, rock for walls, while the

* I quote from a letter printed in the *Pungolo*, of Naples, on the day of the visit.

water dripped from the ceiling, and one sink in the centre served for the " wants of all." Here were lodged more than two hundred human beings, some forty families ; their apartments being divided by a string where they hung their wretched rags. The families who had the " apartments " by the grating that served for window, paid ten, nine, eight, seven lire per month each. These poor creatures subscribed among themselves two lire so that a poor old man should not be turned out, but allowed to sleep on straw by the common sink, and they fed a poor woman who was dying, with scraps from their scant repasts. This grotto yielded its owner a monthly rent, always paid up, far exceeding that paid by the inhabitants of the new tenements and decent houses, and he continued to so " grind the faces of the poor " until 1884, when King Cholera carried off his tenants, and the grotto was closed, as was the charnel-house to which the inmates were carried to their last abode.

In order to convince the sceptic still further that there was no exaggeration in the accounts of the horrors, we invited him to accompany us to what was then the only cemetery for the poor of Naples. It is an immense square with three hundred and sixty-five holes, each covered with a huge stone, with a ring in each for uplifting. On the first of January, hole No. 1 was opened and all the poor who died on that day were brought up in great pomp of funeral car and trappings, with priests and tapers, etc. The first to be thrown in was a corpse with shirt and trousers. " He is a private," said La Raffaella, the poor woman who used to take charge of the child corpses, kiss each of them so that they might take the kiss to "limbo." " He died at home and his people had dressed him." He was placed in the zinc coffin, the crank swung this over the hole, you heard a fall, then the coffin came up *empty ;* next were flung down the naked corpses of the inhabitants of the poorhouses and charitable institutions, then the little children. Last came up the car of the Hospital Degli Incurabili, with the scattered members swept from the dissecting-table. Then the hole

An Old Street in the Poor Quarter being Metamorphosed.

No. 1 was closed not to be reopened until next year. On the mor-
row, over hole No. 2 the same horrors were re-enacted. The victims of King Cholera in 1884 were the last buried in these charnel-

holes; the cemetery was closed when he was dethroned, and a new cemetery for the poor opened just opposite the monumental cemetery of the rich at Foria.

It was in the summer of that year that the cholera reappeared and its swift and sudden ravages compelled attention to the "where" and "how" its numerous victims lived and died. In these same quarters of Porto Pendino, Mercato, and Vicaria, 20,000 died of cholera in 1836–37; an equal number in 1854–65, 1866, and 1873, while the higher quarters of Naples were comparatively free from the scourge. In 1884, from the 17th of August to the 31st, the cases were not more than three every twenty-four hours. On the 1st of September 143 were attacked, 72 succumbed on the 10th of the same month; 966 cases, 474 deaths, are given as the official statistics; the sum total of deaths is variously stated at eight, nine, and ten thousand. But official bulletins are never trustworthy in these cases, the authorities strive to abate panic, and it is a well-known fact that numbers of cases were never reported to the municipality, the dead being carried off in carts and omnibuses to the special cholera cemetery and charnel-house, without any possible register. Dr. Axel Munthe, who lived and worked among the poor during the entire time, gives it as his belief, supported by others, that during "not one but four or five days there were about one thousand cases per diem." So markedly was the disease confined to the poor quarters that for many days it was impossible for the municipal authorities to do anything to alleviate its ravages; the poor, ignorant, superstitious plebs being firmly convinced that the cholera had been introduced among them for the express purpose of diminishing their numbers.

Hence the refusal to go to the hospital, to take the medicines sent, to allow disinfectants to be used, to abstain from fruit, vegetables, and stale fish, even when good soup and meat were offered instead. Then it was that King Humbert went to Naples and visited in person the stricken patients in their *fondaci* and cellars, in the caves and slums, and this, his first experience of actual misery,

GOSSIP IN PENDINO STREET, NAPLES.

save as the result of war or a sudden catastrophe, made such a profound impression on his mind that he promised the poor people there and then that they should have decent houses built expressly for them. Even now they will tell you that *Oo Re* kept his word, but that the *Signori* have taken the *palaces* all for themselves.

The royal example was speedily followed; bands of students and workingmen under the white cross proffered their services, and the Neapolitan citizens who had not all fled, enlisted under the doctors, who are ever brave and devoted in Italy, and worked as nurses, cooks, helpers of the living, even as porters of the dead. The poor people, ever grateful, gentle, docile, yielded to these "kind strangers," and allowed themselves to be taken to the hospitals or tended in their own dens where, by the White Cross band alone, assistance was furnished to 7,015 cases. Of the volunteer nurses, Lombards, Tuscans, Romans, some ninety in all, several were attacked but only three succumbed, all adhering strictly to the rules laid down as to diet and the specifics to be used in case of seizure. The cholera, at its height between the 10th and 18th of September, abated gradually from that day until the 9th of October, when suddenly, on the 10th and 11th, 122 were attacked and 37 succumbed. This 10th of October is the first of the famous *ottobrate*, when the poorest of the poor managed to get a taste of the new wine which is still fermenting, and that year it is very probable that they toasted with unwonted zeal the disappearance of the cholera, which on the 9th had not made a single victim. The luscious blue figs, the bread and watermelons which could in that cholera year be had for a song, were also unusually abundant. The regulations at last enforced by the authorities had been relaxed; the sale of rags recommenced, and to all these causes may doubtless be owing in part the reappearance of the foe supposed to be vanquished.

But fortunately for poor Naples, the cholera found in King Humbert an adversary determined to resist its intrusion for the future; and men of science, doctors, students, were encouraged to study the causes of the disease even more diligently than the cure for it, when in possession. When the sudden reappearance filled the city with fresh alarm, and the poor, wretched people were soundly abused in the newspapers for their "orgies," more than one professor affirmed that the real cause must be traced to the sudden change of temperature, to the southwest wind, sirocco, which prevents the sewers from discharging their contents into the sea and drives the refuse back to the streets and shores, which, in the quarters of Pendino and Porto, are almost on a level with the sea; and to the condition of the water under ground which, swelled by the tremendous rainfalls, carried more putrid matter than usual into the drinking-wells and streams. Certain it is that as soon as the *tramontana* (north wind) began to blow, and the low tides allowed the impurities to put out to sea, the cholera diminished and for three years returned no more. Then came the narrations in the newspapers of the actual state of the habitations of the poor—how human beings and beasts were crowded together, how the stables were never cleaned, how the sinks filtered into the wells —twelve hundred and fourteen of these being foul but "possibly cleansible," while sixty-three were ordered to be filled up and closed. It was shown that these quarters were more densely populated than any other portion of Europe, London included; while the insalubrious trades were carried on in the most populous portions of the overcrowded quarters, there being no less than two hundred and thirty-five large and small rag and bone stores in the midst, while decayed vegetables, the entrails of beasts, and stale fish were left where flung, scavengers and dustmen confining their labors to the quarters of the "upper third."

All these accounts King Humbert read attentively, and to old Depretis, then prime minister, said: "Italy must redeem Naples at any cost." And the old statesman answered: "Yes, Naples must be disembowelled." *Bisogna sventrare Napoli.* A bill was presented to the Chamber for the gift of fifty millions of lire, and the loan of other fifty millions for the sanitation of the unhealthy quarters of the city, and for the decent housing of the poor, and the sums were voted without a murmur, so great was the sympathy felt for the victims of the cholera and their survivors, whose misery was portrayed with heart - rending eloquence. The senate approved, and the king set his zeal to the decree on January 15, 1885.

As studies for the amelioration of the poor quarters and the sanitation of Naples had been carried on, and paid for, and the authors of plans decorated during the last ten years, it was supposed that (the financial question solved) the work would be commenced there and then, but two more years were wasted in finding out " how not to do it."

Until 1850 Naples had always been reckoned one of the healthiest cities in Italy. Typhus and diphtheria were rare ; no one had ever heard of a Neapolitan fever.

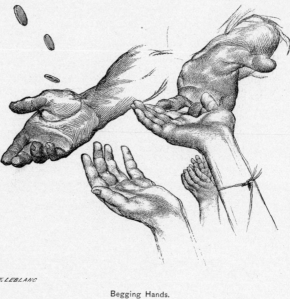

F. LEBLANC

Begging Hands.

True, when the rains were heavy the city in many parts was inundated with flowing streams called *lave*, and wooden bridges were erected over several streets, otherwise traffic would have been impossible. Once the so-called *lava dei vergini* carried away a horse and carriage in its impetuous course. To remedy this state of things the government of King Bomba ordered a system of sewers which, either owing to the ignorance of the engineers or the jobbery of the contractors, rendered the last state of Naples worse than the first.

Into these sewers, which had insufficient slope, not only the rainwater, but the water from sinks, all the contents of the cesspools, were supposed to flow. But in seasons of drought nothing flowed ; all remained in the sewers. Often the sewers were so badly constructed that instead of carrying off the contents of the cesspools they carried their own contents into the drinking-wells. Hence the stench often noticed in some of the best streets of Naples. Some of the conduits are almost on a level with the street ; many of them have burst. One of the best modern engineers of Naples writes : "If you uncover the streets of our city, ditches of putrid matter most baneful to health will reveal themselves to the eye of the indiscreet observer." He quotes one special spot, *Vicolo del Sole*, "where cholera, typhus, every sort of lung disease had reigned supreme." This "Sun alley," where the sun never shines, was closed, and the health of the neighborhood became normal. But when a number of people were ousted from their houses for the excavation of the *corso reale*, the Vicolo was again inhabited, and out of seventy-two inhabitants, the cholera carried off sixty. Every time that excavations were made in any part of the low quarters of Naples, typhus, diphtheria, or the newly invented Neapolitan fever broke out—and, to quote official statements, "If one case of fever broke out in a house where the cesspool communicated with the drinking-well, all the families who drew water from that well were laid low with the same fever. Again, these horrible sewers when they succeeded in emptying themselves, did so in the most populous quarters of the city, so that the Riviera became a putrid lake, and in the best quarters of Chiaja the stench at eventide was so horrible that the people used to call it the *malora di* Chiaja (bad hour of). When the southwest wind blew the high tide prevented the sewerage from going out to sea, so all the matter brought down remained strewed along the shore. The best hotels were closed owing to the fever that prevailed, and are now nearly all replaced by others built in the higher quarters, the Rione Amadeo, Corso Vittorio Emanuele, etc.

Hence the first thing to be thought of for the sanitation of Naples was the renovation and purification of the drains. The fewest possible excavations, the greatest possible extent of *colmate* (raising the level), was clearly indicated ; and as this " silting up " the lower quarters has to be done, not as in Lincolnshire fens by allowing water to leave its own sediments, but by material imported, it was and is a very costly proceeding.

Alas! that the lessons taught by the former attempts at redeeming the slums should have been forgotten, or rather deliberately neglected. " Don't begin at the end instead of at the beginning," said G. Florenzano, in 1885. " Don't begin by pulling down the old houses until you have built new ones for the evicted tenants of the *fondaci*, grottos, etc. If you go on the old system the poor creatures who now have a roof over their heads will have to crowd the remaining *fondaci* even as did those of Porto when you beautified the Via del Duomo, or they will crowd into the cloisters of S. Tom-

"Hunger," a Sketch in the Poor Quarter.

maso di Aquino, where the cholera mowed down so many victims.
You can pull down houses in a week, but it takes a year to build
them, and another year must elapse before they are habitable."
The discussions and commissions went on for two years and a half.
There was the question of whether the municipality should expro-
priate, demolish, and rebuild on its own account. The majority
were against this, urging that public bodies are the worst of all
workers. Then should the whole contract be given to one society
or to several? And here the war of the "one lot" or "lot of lots"
raged fiercely. "Whoever gets the contract, however few or many
be the contractors," said Villari, from his seat in the Senate, and
other sentimentalists, "let them be bound over to build healthy
houses for the poor who will be evicted from the slums, on a site
not so far from their old homes as to prevent them from carrying
on their daily employments, and at rents certainly not higher than
those they pay at present."

To this, practical people answered that: "No building society
would build at a loss, and that healthy houses in healthy sites in
the populous quarters of Naples could not be erected for the letting
price of five lire per room."

"Then let the municipality first deduct from the hundred millions given for the poor of Naples such sums as *are* necessary for
building these houses without profit," retorted the sentimentalists;
"in the long run they will be found to pay, but in any case they
must be built."

As usual the *vox clamante* resounded in the desert only. In
1888, the municipality entered into a contract with a building society of Milan for the entire work of expropriation, demolition of old
houses, the construction of new ones, and the all-important work
of laying down the sewers and paving the streets above. The laying down of gas and the canalization of the water of the Serino in
the new quarters was alone retained in the hands of the municipality and separately contracted for. The contract itself, to use the
words of the minority of the "communal councillors," represented

CHEAP BATHING.

a direct violation of the spirit of the law passed by the Italian parliament in the interests of the community and for the sanitation of Naples, while the commission of inquiry delegated by the council to examine and report on the works, affirmed that " Private speculation, substituted for the superintendence of the commune and the State, naturally ignored the philanthropic impulse of the law, allowing industrial calculation and bankers' rings to boss the enterprise especially planned for the benefit of the poorest classes and to sanify the lowest quarters of the city." So much for the spirit of the contract.

Coming to its execution, the municipality neither armed itself with sufficient powers for compelling the contractors to perform their work properly, nor did it put such powers as were reserved into execution. Consequently expropriations which, by the terms of the contract, ought to have allowed three months to elapse between the notice to quit and the actual departure, were often carried out within a week of the notice given. Availing themselves of the law which sanctions expropriations at a fixed price for public benefit, the society bore hard on many small proprietors, whose houses they took without any immediate need, and these, until the time comes for their demolition, are underlet to the worst class of usurers, who have evicted the tenants and doubled the rent. Then the first houses were jerry built. One fell while building and killed several workmen. Again, the contract bound the society to build houses only three stories high, to avoid the overcrowding so complained of in the old quarters. They built them of four stories. The courtyards were to occupy one-sixth of the whole area of each tenement—they were found to occupy barely one-seventh or even one-eighth. Finally (and this raised a popular outcry at last), in no single tenement built by the society could the evicted poor find a room, because they were all about twice the price of their former ones, and so far removed from the scene of their daily labors that it was very doubtful whether they could inhabit them at all. It is neither edifying

12

nor interesting to seek out who were the chief culprits ; certainly
the municipal authorities, who took no thought for the poor for
whom the money was voted, were the original sinners.   But when
the hue and cry was raised the money was spent and it was no use
crying over spilt milk.   The municipality was bankrupt.   Besides
inheriting the debts and deficits of its predecessors, it had squandered vast sums on useless works, given three millions to the society which built the King Humbert Gallery—a capital building
for the cold and uncertain climate of Milan ; quite a superfluity in
sunny Naples, where everybody lives in the open air, and where
you can hardly yet get sellers and buyers to use the new covered
market-place instead of the street pavements.

So the municipality was dissolved by the government and a
Royal Commissioner sent to take the affairs of the commune in
hand.   When I came here affairs seemed past praying for, the
state of overcrowding in the poorest quarters was worse than ever.
I found houses condemned as unsafe and propped up with shores,
without a window-pane or door on hinges, crowded to excess—the
fondaci left standing with double their old numbers of inhabitants ;
the cellars full, and at night the streets turned into public dormitories.   True, the water from the Serino had been brought into
Naples, and this is a priceless boon which can only be appreciated
by those who remember the bad old days when even at the best
hotels you dared not drink a glass of unboiled water ; when the
poor people had to purchase water at one or two sous per litre,
those who could not do so going athirst.   Then the old charnel-
house is actually closed, and the new cemetery is as beautiful as a
cemetery need be.   Though it has only been open five years it is
already nearly full.   The poor have the graves and a parish coffin
gratis, but after eighteen months the " bones are exhumed to make
room for the fresh corpses."   The families who can afford to do so
pay for a niche in which to deposit the " bones," while the remains
of those who have no friends able to do so are placed in a huge *cis-
tern* outside the cemetery.   At any rate the poorest have now for a

time a grave to themselves and need not say with envy as they used to do when accompanying some *signore* to the monumental cemetery, "*O Mamma mia, vurria murì pe staccà!*" "Mother mine, I would die to stop here."

Then Naples as a city is undoubtedly renovated and beautified; always *bella*, ever *dolce*, it is now one of the most commodious cities in the world. Trams take you from Posilipo to the royal palace, from the Via Tasso to the *Reclusoria*. New palaces, new houses rise up to the east and west of the city.

Besides the demolitions and reconstructions of the famous Società di Risanimento, another society has

On the Stairs of Santa Lucia.

built largely at the *Rione Vasto* at *Capuana, case economiche* and *edifizi civili* which we should call workmen's houses and houses for well-to-do people. Even so in the *Rione Arenaccia Orientale,* in the

Rione S. Efrem Vecchio Ottocalli Ponti Rossi.   In the *Rione Vomero-Arenella* the Banca Tiberina has built enormously; constructed two *funicolari* (cable railways), and in two years the population of that quarter has increased from 751 to 3,991; but there are no *funnachère* among them.

In the favorite quarter of foreign artists, Santa Lucia, where the oyster and " fruits of the sea" mongers and their wives, the sulphur-water vendors, fryers of *polipi* and *peperoni*, congregate, these *luciani* also inhabit *fondaci* not quite as filthy as those of Porto and Pendino, nor are they nearly as docile.   They strongly objected to the tramway as an invasion of their rights, and laughed to scorn the builders of the new houses on the shore of the Castello Dell' Uovo and of the new *loggie* for the shell-fish vendors.   "The first high wind," they say, would carry stalls and fish into the sea, and as for the new houses, they *pizzicano* (are too dear), *non jamme 'n terra* (they shall not demolish our houses), they tell you, and as yet no one has dared to tackle them.   The new houses are divided into charming little apartments with a kitchen and convenience in each, but the kitchen and one room cost 15 lire, others 20, 30, even 35 lire.

With a budget of thirty million lire and a huge deficit, little margin was left to the Royal Commissary, who had to cut down estimates, retrench in every department, " economize to the bone," but as winter approached, the cry of the people became audible in high places.   It was one thing to camp out in the summer, but quite another to use the streets for bed and the sky for roof in the months of December, January, and February, while the new commission of engineers and medical men pronounced many of the hovels still inhabited to be " dangerous to life and limb," and ordered the society to repair or close them at once.   The society chose the latter alternative, thus reducing still further the scant accommodation—but the Royal Commissary was not a " corporation." He had a soul, or at least a heart.   "For six months," he writes, in his report to the government at the close of his mission, "a famished mob, *turba famelica*, have thronged the stairs of the municipality; children of both sexes, utterly destitute, who must of necessity go to the bad; mothers clasping dying babies to their milkless breasts; widows followed by a tribe of almost naked children; aged and infirm of both sexes, hungry and in tatters—and this spectacle, which has wrung my heart, reveals but a small portion of the prevalent destitution. One can but marvel at the docile nature of the lower orders of Neapolitans, who bear with such resignation and patience their unutterable sufferings. One cannot think without shuddering of this winter, which overtook whole families without a roof over their heads, without a rag to cover them, without the slightest provision for their maintenance."

To remedy this awful state of things in some degree, this royal extraordinary commissary, in Naples for six months only (Senator Giuseppe Saredo), gave it to be understood that the society *must* find means of lodging the evicted poor in some of the new tenements at the old prices. He even consented to a compromise, by which, leaving all the work of laying down drains and filling up low places intact, he consented to the delay in certain buildings which ought to have been completed in the third *biennio*, on the conditions that the society should cede tenements capable of housing fifteen hundred people, no single room to cost more than five lire per month. The first great exodus took place in December, 1891; unfortunately, the housing schedules were not all given to people who could not afford to pay more than five lire; and when I visited the tenements the brass bedsteads and mahogany chests of drawers told tales of past homes in quite other places than in the slums. But in many rooms we did find our *funacchère;* the thin end of the wedge was inserted, and when the Royal Commissary's term of office came to an end the new Syndic repeated the experiment, and arranged with the society for other tenements capable of housing other two thousand of the poorest. This time the vice-syndics have had a warning that if they give schedules to any but the houseless poor their offices and honors will be transferred. At first the idea of removing the poor costermongers, porters, coal-

heavers, fish, snail, and tripe venders so far from their old slums
and haunts seemed unpractical and even cruel; but having revisited
those haunts and the slummers in their new homes, seen the shops
opened on the ground floors of the new dwellings, turned on the
water-tap which is in each room or apartment, inspected the closets
which are perfectly scentless, I can only express a feeling of thank-
fulness that the axe has been laid at the root of the tree at last.

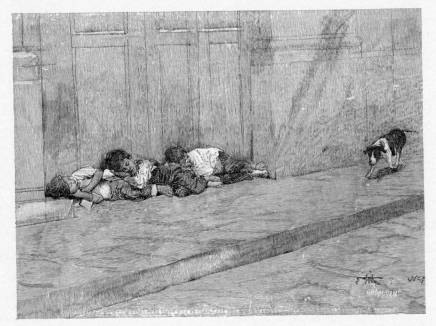

Where Street Arabs Sleep.

It is not only a question of health and longevity—the poor people in the *fondaci* cellars and underground dens were entirely at
the mercy of the *camorra* which, however the police and the authorities may flatter themselves, has never been killed and very
slightly scotched. These poor creatures, crowded in one spot, are
the terrified victims of the *camorrist*, that "unclean beast of dishonest idleness" of yore, who now has cleaned himself up a bit, but is

as bestial, dishonest, and idle as ever. With the dispersion of the slummers and the allotment to each of a room or rooms with doors that lock, and windows that open, the *camorrists'* reign is over, especially as the society, though compelled to charge only five lire per room, has no help from the municipality in collecting rents, and therefore selects for porters (concierge) men who attend to their interests and not to those of the *camorra*.

What is now wanted in the new quarters are infant schools, elementary and industrial schools, of all of which Naples possesses some of the most perfect that I have ever seen in Italy or in England. Naples, a city of contrasts in all respects, is especially so in the management of her public and private institutions.

Of charitable institutions belonging to the poor by right, Naples has enough and to spare, with two hundred edifices and over eight or ten millions of annual income. But these edifices and this income serve every interest save that of the poor. Administrators, priests, governors, electors, deputies, councillors and their clients get thus the lion's share. The Albergo dei Poveri, with an income of over a million and a half, maintains a family of employees exceeding seven hundred, while the poor, many of whom are merely protégés of the rich, have dwindled down to two thousand. The children have scarcely a shirt to change; the school for deaf and dumb boys has been so neglected for years that only of late has the new director been able to form a class. The girls in charge of the *figlie della carità*, French nuns, are kept so hard at work at embroidery and flower making that their health is ruined, and the agglomeration of old men and women, young boys and girls under one roof is by no means conducive to order, discipline, or morality. One "governor" succeeds another. One sells 5,000 square metres of land to a building society for eleven lire per metre, at a time when in certain portions of the city land is worth three and four hundred lire. His successor brings an action against the purchaser and the costs are enormous. Another has farmed out the rents to some collector at far too low a price; another action is

brought. The chemist is proved to have substituted flour for qui-
nine, Dover's powders without opium, and is suspended. But the
corpo delicto, *i.e.*, the analyzed medicines, have disappeared ; the
chemist will come off triumphant and the Albergo dei Poveri will
have to pay costs and damages, and possibly to meet an action for
libel. Of course there is a deficit in the budget ; and this will continue to increase, whoever may be governor, as long as the system
remains and as long as places are created for protégés of Senator
A, Deputy B, or Counsellor C.

The enormous hospital of the *Incurabili*, where also a royal com-
missionary presides, was found to be in a most deplorable state.
The number of patients reduced from one thousand to seven hundred ; the meat of inferior quality to that prescribed. Despite the
25,000 lire which appear in the budget for linen, there were not
sufficient sheets to change the beds of the sick, yet there was an accumulated deficit of 869,030 lire, and for last year alone 200,000 lire.
As the present special commissioners have really reduced the expenditure, while increasing the number of patients admitted, diminished the enormous number of servants, and by supplying food to
those on guard deprived them of the temptation to steal the rations
of the sick ; as they have thoroughly cleansed the hospital from
garret to cellar, constructed water-closets, etc., we hope they will
be allowed to remain in office sufficient time to render a return to
former abuses impossible.

Some improvement there is, we notice, in the Foundling Hospital, which was in a wretched state, the mortality among infants
amounting to ninety-five and even one hundred per cent. The system adopted of giving them out to be nursed by poor families in
the city and country round Naples, answers admirably, as the poor
people here regard them as the " Virgin's children "—*figlie della
Madonna*. Still there are over three hundred big, lazy girls in the
establishment who ought to have been put out to earn their living
long ago.

The *Casa di Maternita*, added to the establishment, is admirably conducted, and the secrets of the poor girls or women who demand admission are religiously kept.

The famous convent of the *Sepolte Vive* of Suor Orsola Benincasa, which created such a sensation in the newspapers a year since, is now completely reformed; the few surviving nuns are pensioned off and allotted a residence in some distant portion of the enormous edifice, while the income of 100,000 lire is applied to the education of poor children. There are also classes for the children of parents who can pay, a normal school, and a kindergarten.

As the reformed law of charitable institutions is only two years old, and the government and municipal authorities are

Interior of a Poor Quarter.

doing their best to apply it in spite of the clergy and the vested interests of innumerable loafers, we may hope that in time to come the poor and the poor alone may profit by this their own and only wealth. How such wealth may be profitably applied is shown by the numerous establishments founded and maintained by private charity.   The children's hospital, *Ospitale Lina*, founded and maintained by the well-known philanthropist, Duchessa Ravaschiera, is a perfect gem.   There are eighty beds, each occupied by a poor child for whom a surgical operation is necessary.   All the first surgeons and doctors of Naples give their services.   The Duchess herself, who founded the hospital in memory of her only daughter, Lina, superintends it in person, often living and sleeping there, and the delight of the children when " *Mamma Duchessa* " enters the wards is very touching.

The asylum for girls orphaned during the cholera of 1884 is another example of how much can be done, with comparatively small sums, under personal supervision.   Here 285 boarders and 250 day scholars are maintained at a cost of little over 100,000 francs, subscribed by individuals, the Bank of Naples, the Chamber of Commerce, etc.   All the children frequent the elementary schools, and are each taught a trade, dressmaking, plain needlework, making and mending—*maglieria* (machine-knitted vests), stockings, petticoats, etc., artificial flowers, embroidery, and lace making.   At the Exposition of Palermo there was a beautiful collection of the work done by the girls of this school ; we could wish that they were not compelled to toil so many hours a day, but necessity knows no law, and the administration of the superintendent, Baron Tosti, is above all praise.   There are two educational and industrial schools for boys in Naples which may serve as models to the other provinces of Italy and to other nations.

The *Instituto Casanovas,** for boys who have attended the infant schools, was founded in 1862 by Alfonzo della Valle di Casanova. Elementary schools and workshops were opened under the same roof and carried on privately with great success until 1880; then

---

* An American lady, well known in Boston for her work in prison reform, said to us, as we were taking her over these schools : " We have nothing so good as this in America."

recognized as a *Corpo Morale* by the government, which assigned a large building with open spaces for gymnastics and recreation, surrounded by eleven new workshops. Industrial schools generally are a failure, owing to the expense incurred by the payment of directors of workshops, the purchase of machines, tools, instruments, and raw material. In this establishment the workshop alone is given rent free to the master — blacksmiths, carpenters, tailors, boot-makers, brass-workers, cameo, lava workers, workers in bronze, sculptors, ebonists, wood-carvers, and printers—with whom a regular contract is signed, for a certain number of years, by which, on "November 1st, directors A, B, and C shall open a workshop, furnishing it with all such machines and instruments as are necessary for carrying on and teaching his trade to a fixed number of pupils." In case of bankruptcy the master must at once quit the workshop. The boys for the first two years, that is until they are nine, attend the elementary schools exclusively ; then they or their parents choose their trade, and as soon as their work becomes profitable, they are paid a certain sum fixed by the master-workman and the director of the establishment, who receives the pay of the boys weekly and gives half to them, half to the establishment. At first the boys were compelled to place all their portion in postal savings banks, but as all are day scholars and are housed and fed by their parents, it was found that these, being too poor to maintain them, removed them from the school before they were proficient in their respective trades. From the report up to March 6, 1892, we find 559 "present," 104 pupils who had quitted the establishment as skilled workmen, all of whom are eagerly sought by the directors of workshops in this city. The income of the institute does not exceed 72,000 francs, of which 22,000 is paid to school-masters and servants ; the remainder goes in buildings, prizes to the pupils, etc. The *Casanova* opera also has a beautiful department at the Exposition at Palermo, where albums and pamphlets show its whole history from the beginning.

A similar institution, much rougher, but even more meritorious, is the working school in the ex-convent of S. Antonio a Tarsia. The boys collected here are the real waifs and strays taken from the streets—gutter-sparrows, literally. The founder is Giovanni Florenzano, ex-member of parliament and (*assessore*) officer of public instruction in the municipality of Naples. It is conducted on the same principles as that of Casanova, but, alas! not with equal funds.

One of the New Blocks of Tenements in Naples.

There is a workshop for carpenters, ebony-workers, wood-carvers, and gilders, for blacksmiths, workers in bronze, for the manufacture of iron and steel instruments, and a large printing-office. The boys gathered there number from two hundred and fifty to three hundred. Unfortunately the impecuniosity of the municipality has deprived this school of four thousand francs annually.

Signor Florenzano, who has done much for popular instruction in Naples, in 1883 opened a Sunday-school for recreation in a large hall with a pretty garden in the Vico Cupa a Chiara, where seven hundred children, all under separate patronage of benevolent men and women, were clothed, and on every Sunday taught choral singing, gymnastics, and military exercises. Alas! both the hall and garden have been demolished by the pickaxe of a building society, and the children are dispersed. This idea of placing every boy in the working school under the protection of some well-to-do person is excellent. A few more such industrial schools as these of Casanova and Tarsia would be the making of the next generation of Neapolitan boys. These private institutions also form a striking contrast with the so-called reformatories, penitentiaries, and correctional establishments with which Italy, and especially Naples, abounds. In three of these which we visited we may say, without fear of contradiction, that there are no reforms, and no penitents in any of them. In one of these, where each boy costs three francs per day, *discoli*, merely naughty boys and boys sent by their own parents to be disciplined, are mixed up with culprits who have been condemned once, twice, and thrice, for whom " paternal discipline " is a derision, who break down the doors of their cells, kick the jailors, and yet are fed on coffee and milk in the morning, meat at mid-day, soup at night, and wine three times a week.

We have not space for even a brief reference to prison discipline in Italy, but we may say as a general rule that delinquents and criminals alone are housed, fed, clothed, and cared for by the State ; that the greater the crime, the more hardened the criminal, the better does he lodge, dress, and, till yesterday, fare !

We must not close this story of the poor in Naples without a reference to two other institutions dedicated to the poor alone. The one is the school for the blind at Caravaggio, which, with the boarding-house and school founded by Lady Strachen, offer a pleasant contrast to the blind institute at S. Giuseppe, dependent on the *Albergo dei Poveri*. The blind institute, now called Prince of Naples, founded by the brothers Martucelli, is admirable. The blind boys and girls read, write, print, and play various instruments, are shoe-makers, carpenters, basket and Venetian blind-makers. The correspondent of the London *Times*, on seeing the department of this school at the Palermo Exhibition, could hardly believe that the work was done by blind children.

The Froebel Institute, now called the Victor Emanuel International Institute, was founded by Julia Salis Schwabe, an enthusiastic admirer of Garibaldi, who, in 1860, appealed to women to open popular schools for the education of the poor in the southern provinces. Professor Villari took it under his especial protection, and the old medical college at S. Aniello was assigned for the purpose, so that poor girls taken from the streets could be housed, fed, and educated. At present the boarding-school has been much reduced, but the day, infant, and elementary schools are simply perfect. Side by side with the classes for poor children, are paying classes for the well-to-do, who are taught to find pleasure in bringing clothes and boots for their poorer companions. The " haves " pay seven lire a month, which suffices to give a capital soup every day to about four hundred children of the " have nots." The establishment serves also as a training-school for teachers of this Froebelian, or as it ought to be called, Pestalozzian system, certainly the most admirable yet invented for keeping children bright, happy, and active, and while placing no undue strain on their intellectual faculties, disciplining and preparing them for the age when these can be exercised. It is a school such as this which I long to see opened in the new quarters where the children taken from the *fondaci* cellars and slums in general are now housed. Very dismal they look, shut up in the respective rooms, seated upon the window-sills, longing for the open street, of *basso porto*, the filthy court-yards, where there were goats and rats to play with, any amount of dirt for the " makin' o' mud pies," and the chance of a stray *pizza* or *frazaglia*, the gift of kindly foodmongers. Now, of course the porters forbid the leaving open the doors of the " apartments," the squatting on staircases, the congregating in the courtyards where

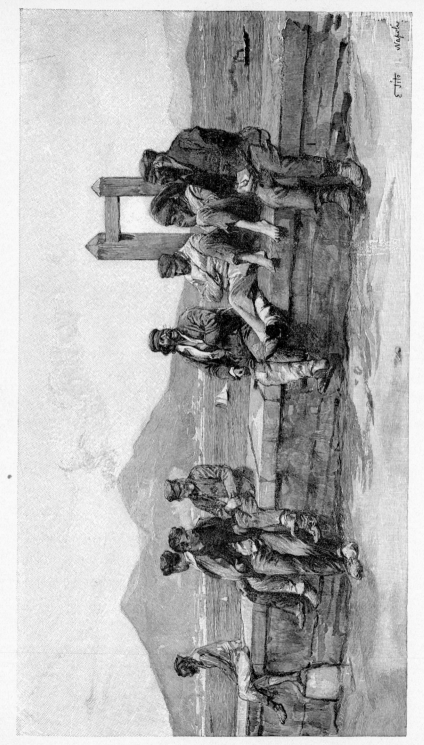

THE PLEASURES OF IDLENESS.

no "washpools" have been erected, "expressly to prevent the slummers from reducing the new tenements to the state of the old *fondaci.*" All this is highly proper, but very forlorn for the little ones.

By degrees it is to be hoped that the inhabitants of Naples, rich and poor, will be induced to go and live in the suburbs. At present there is a population which has increased from a little over four hundred thousand to nearly six hundred thousand, crowded over eight square kilometres; deduct the space occupied by churches and public buildings, and there is little more than seven square kilometres. And this is the first greatest misfortune for the poor in Naples. The problem of housing them solved, it will be, after all, but the alpha of the business. There is neither "bread nor work" for the masses, who increase and multiply like rabbits in a warren. On this point they are extremely sensitive. Finding a lad of eighteen, for whom we were trying to get work, just married to a girl of sixteen, we ventured to remonstrate, asking how they were to keep their children? "*Volete anche spegnere la razza dei pezzenti*"—"Do you want even to extinguish the race of miserables?" the husband asked, indignantly.

Hitherto the surplus population of the provinces has swarmed off to Brazil and the United States. From the former country many of them return with sad tales of whole families swept away by yellow fever, of hard labor hoeing coffee with insufficient remuneration, and the impossibility of obtaining proper nourishment. And now comes the natural but sad report, from the United States accentuated by Mr. Chandler, in the *Forum,* that republican citizens are tired of the poor, meek, feckless, unclean offshoots of royal courts and aristocratic institutions who extract a livelihood from New York's ash-barrels; who contract for the right to trim the *ash-scows* before they are sent out to sea, whereas a few years ago men were paid a dollar and a half a day for the said "trimming;" who keep the stale beer dives and pig together in the "Bend;" who used at home to receive but five cents per day and "wittals" that dogs

22

refuse, undersell their labor abroad, and thus lower the wages of the natives.

We cannot wonder that the cry is: "Send them back—here they are encumbrances."

But when this safety-valve is closed some new outlet will have to be found to prevent an explosion, and the "upper third" will do well to devise the ways and means while yet there is time.

AGENCIES FOR THE PREVENTION OF PAUPERISM

By OSCAR CRAIG,*

LATE PRESIDENT OF THE NEW YORK STATE BOARD OF CHARITIES.

POVERTY AND PAUPERISM—THE FOUR CLASSES OF OUR POPULATION—PROCESSES
WHICH TEND TO INCREASE PAUPERISM—PAUPER IMMIGRATION—LAWS TO
CONTROL IT—THE HEAD MONEYS—THE RETURN OF ALIEN PAUPERS—THE
BIG SYSTEM OF OUT RELIEF—ORGANIZED CHARITY—AS AN AGENT IN THE
PREVENTION OF PAUPERISM—THE CHARITY ORGANIZATION SOCIETY OF NEW
YORK—OTHER AGENCIES OF BENEVOLENCE—CHURCH CHARITIES—THE JEWS
—TREATMENT OF THE INSANE POOR—MANAGEMENT OF THE COUNTY POOR-
HOUSES—THE CARE OF DEPENDENT CHILDREN—REFORMATORIES—THE DIS-
CIPLINE OF CONVICTS—THE QUESTION OF HEREDITY—MR. BRACE'S TESTI-
MONY—THE STATE CHARITIES AID ASSOCIATION—THE FACTORY LAW.

POVERTY and pauperism are words which should not be used
as equivalents, or even as synonyms. The terms stand for
things or thoughts which in some respects are antithesis.
An individual may be both a poor person and a pauper; but the
majority of the poor, when not demoralized by unwise interference
or neglect, are neither purposely nor actually in the attitude of
pauperism, which is that of dependence on public or private char-

* The Hon. Oscar Craig, President of the New York State Board of Charities
(whose persistent and sacrificing efforts for the poor by scientific, as well as humanitarian, methods, have been increasingly acknowledged since his untimely death in
January, 1894), wrote the chapter herewith published in the spring of 1892. A part
of it, very much condensed, was published in *Scribner's Magazine* for July, 1893, but
the present is the first publication in its entirety of one of the last and most mature
expressions of the views of a man who spoke with the highest authority by reason
of his extensive experience and knowledge, as well as by his remarkable clarity of
judgment. Mr. Craig intended further to revise this paper for book publication.

ity in the form of either indoor or out-relief; while a large minority, if not a major part, of paupers misrepresent or suppress either infrequently their accumulations of property, or more often their ability to work, which is their capital, and so pass as poor persons only by their false pretences or concealments.

Another distinction must be made. The productive classes should not be identified with even "the poor." The worker who toils continuously and effectually, such as the parish priest or minister of the gospel or teacher in the rural district, the farmer, the artisan, or the humble laborer, may be in destitute circumstances, or in distress of desire to supply the higher wants of his family with the small means at his command; but such workers make the world rich in spiritual worth and material wealth, and accumulate the potential forces, moral and physical, which, being liberated from time to time, lead to the progress of the world. They are, in such points, differentiated from the simply indigent or worthy poor, who, though patient, enduring, suffering uncomplainingly, striving to avoid the dependence of pauperism, and if defeated renewing the struggle for an honest living, are handicapped in the race by some incumbrance or inefficiency, proceeding from incomplete correspondence with their environment, or imperfect organism, or defective energy or vitality; and who (while deserving the favors of the strong to "help them to help themselves," and perhaps more the favorites of heaven than many who succeed better in the struggle for existence on earth) are nevertheless not energetic factors in industrial activities or in the performance of duties to society.

A distinct set remains to be mentioned, viz.: the opulent who are not rich by the results of their own industry for the moral or material ends of society, and who, neglecting their social obligations, suffer atrophy of virile and moral powers, and, like paupers, live on the world's surplus without adding to it or giving any fair equivalent for their maintenance.

These four categories may thus be arranged in two divisions: first—*the poor* and *working classes*, both of which are entitled to our respect for different sorts of praiseworthy qualities ; and, second— *the idle rich* and *the pauper*, neither of which is worthy of our praise. Eliminating from consideration the affluent who lead useless lives, as of no account, we have the remaining unprofitable class of the second division contrasted with the two estimable classes of the first division.

Observing these distinctions, it is obvious that any principle or policy which leads toward the prevention of pauperism, conduces *pro tanto* to the protection of both the poor and the producing classes. To defend the workers, as members of the social organism most entitled to honor, is to shield them from unjust taxes levied to support persons who are able but unwilling to work, or to maintain in comfort and comparative luxury, to a degree relatively higher than the average families of tax-payers can enjoy, even those who are willing but unable to work. To preserve the poor from injury is to guard not merely their physical welfare but also their moral well-being, and to ward off the forces that break down their manhood and thus tend to disintegrate society.

To *prevent pauperism* is to go before the processes which lead to it, and to anticipate the causes which, if not counteracted, tend, by successive steps, to make the productive and independent worker lapse into indigence, and the indigent to descend into dependence. Preventive measures are therefore better than any and all means that are merely repressive or remedial.

The work of prevention is so imperfect in most communities, while the processes for the propagation of pauperism are so successful in many countries of Europe, that there is imposed on public authorities in the United States the duty of exclusion or expulsion of all immigrants who may be infected with this vice or disease. This proscriptive duty devolves on charity administration in the State of New York more than elsewhere in America, for the reason that its territory includes the principal port of entry, and therefore naturally returns the worst elements, while most of the able-bodied and the right-minded pass into the interior States, where they become worthy and valuable citizens of the Republic.

It may be suggested that the return of such immigrants, who have effected a landing by eluding the agencies of the Federal Government, does not go to the true end of the prevention of this disease, or even its reduction or relief in the world at large. But this view is not so broad as at first sight it seems to be, in subordinating patriotism to philanthropy, and is not so comprehensive as that which justifies the necessary means for the preservation of the social organisms and life of America, with their potential advantages and benefits to the whole world. *There is no room for doubt that immigration, if unrestricted, would soon change from what now is mostly good, to that which would be mainly bad, if not in actual ratio of numbers, at least in real proportion of power.*

It is difficult for Americans, in their magnanimity, to realize or fully believe, however realistic may be the story, that government and other agencies in Europe have deliberately and successfully conducted their diseased, filthy, vicious, and criminal dregs of society, by ocean steamers, as sewers, into cesspools made of the ports and towns of the United States. But such is the fact established by evidence convincing and cumulative. The late Dr. Anderson, President of the Rochester University, and member of the State Board of Charities for the Seventh Judicial District, submitted to the board a paper dated January 12, 1875, which cites admissions made by publicists and other authorities abroad, showing this fact. And it has been confirmed by proofs annually gathered since the year 1873, by the Secretary of the State Board of Charities, and by the findings of the Board made in its annual reports to the Legislature.

The State of New York has sought relief in various enactments. Chapter 277 of the laws of 1831, and chapter 230 of the laws of 1833, were practically inoperative, on account of the difficulty of proving the intent or knowledge of the master of the vessel, or other person, introducing the convict or the pauper into the State. The act passed May 15, 1847, entitled "An Act Concerning Passengers in Vessels Coming to the United States," and the amendatory and supplementary acts, created commissioners of immigration, and among other things made the consignees, masters, agents, and owners of vessels liable for the support of immigrants who were "lunatic, idiot, deaf, dumb, blind, infirm, maimed, over sixty years old, widows having families, or for any cause unable to support themselves," provided that such liability might be discharged by paying a commutation tax of two dollars and fifty cents *per capita* on all immigrants within twenty-four hours after leaving the vessel. The result, of course, was that the commutation money was always assessed on the immigrant at his place of departure. The law directed the commissioners to pay, from such money, the cost of maintaining such immigrants as became a public charge within the State, but not beyond the period of five years from landing. This statutory indemnity was inadequate, on account of the short term of maintenance and of the small sum of "head money," by reason of which the commissioners, though restricted by the five years' clause, incurred debts which their resources would not cancel. While about nine thousand foreigners were thus maintained from such commutation money, between the years 1868 and 1873 inclusive—a period just prior to the first subsequent legislation hereafter mentioned—there were foreign-born inmates of county poor-houses and city alms-houses in the State, during the same six years, to an annual average of thirty-five thousand to forty thousand, being about two-thirds of the total population of these houses, though foreign-born persons were only about one-third of the total census of the State. Another inevitable limitation in the law was that it could cover only the ports of entry within its jurisdiction, while the classes of defective and dependent persons provided against were in large numbers shipped to Canadian ports, and thence forwarded over the border, with their destinations practically fixed, as if ticketed, to the poor-houses and almshouses of the counties and cities of the State.

This statute provoked comments from jurists on the question of its validity. Finally, the Supreme Court of the United States (in the case of Henderson *et al. v.* Mayor of New York *et al.*, decided in October, 1875) declared that the provisions in the law for levying the tax on immigrants, and the penalties leading to it, were in regulation of commerce, and therefore in violation of the Federal Constitution.

After this decision, cutting off the inflow of the "head money," the unnaturalized paupers who had floated on the currents of immigration and had become moored by our charity cables under the five years' clause, were supported by the Commissioners of Immigration on Ward's Island, from appropriations by the Legislature of the State in the years 1876 to 1883, amounting to $1,140,500, and on credit in county poor-houses, city almshouses, incorporated hospitals, orphan asylums, and other charitable institutions, in the further amount of $105,008.96, which is a debt against the State to be paid from the proceeds of the sale of its property on Ward's Island ; and also from a loan of $200,000 made in 1875 by The Emigrants' Industrial Savings Bank of New York, secured by a mortgage on the Ward's Island property, which mortgage was, in 1882, assigned to the Comptroller of the State as an investment for the United States Deposit Fund, thus making the funny combination of a mortgage held by the State on its own property, and as security for trust funds.

But these various sums represent only a small part of the deficiency of the "head moneys," as already shown by reference to the ordinary statistics of alien pauperism, which was a public charge, not on the State at large, but on counties and cities. The proofs demonstrate that the Supreme Court, in cutting off the commutation contracts, released the people of New York State from a most destructive and deplorable policy of inviting foreign convicts, lunatics, and paupers to come, with the implied covenant of maintenance for five years and probably for life.

At the time of this decision (1875), there was no National statute on the subject. Subsequently Federal Legislation was repeatedly invoked by the State Board of Charities of New York, in correspondence with the State Department and Senators and Representatives at Washington, and with the National Conference of Charities and Correction, and the boards and authorities of other States. The result of the agitation was the act of Congress to regulate immigration, passed in 1882, by which it was provided, among other things, that if there shall be found among immigrants on vessels, "any convict, lunatic, idiot, or any person unable to take care of himself or herself without becoming a public charge, . . . such person shall not be permitted to land." This law was at first executed by State authorities, but is now enforced by Federal officers, under regulations of the Secretary of the Treasury of the United States. Assuming, for argument's sake, that its administration has been reasonably diligent, the fact remains that great numbers of alien paupers annually elude the Federal examinations and obtain a footing on our shores, perhaps the majority of whom infest the city and the State of New York.

The Legislature of the State has provided for the return of such foreign and unnaturalized paupers as are assisted by cities, charitable societies, and other agencies to emigrate, after the expiration of one year from their immigation (which is the period limiting such action by officers under the Federal statute). Under the Alien Pauper Law of New York, enacted in 1880, and enforced by the Chief Secretary of its State Board of Charities, seventeen hundred and twenty-nine of these assisted immigrants, most of them being remnants of the imperfect execution of the law of Congress, have been sent to their homes or places of settlement, by through tickets to those places in foreign countries. Such returns have been accomplished in humane ways, at an expense of less than twenty-two dollars *per capita*, or about one-fifth of the cost of maintenance for one year, computed at two dollars per week, and about one seventy-fifth of their support for life, on an estimate of expectation of fifteen years, which is verified by experience. Thus, at a total expenditure of $37,238.46, the expulsion of these organized invaders of the soil of New York has saved to the taxpayers of the State over $2,700,000.

These general statistics are taken from the annual reports of the State Board of Charities to the Legislature of New York; and the data for the fiscal year closing September 30, 1891, are as follows:

The number of alien paupers removed by the Board from the poor-houses, almshouses, hospitals, asylums, and other charitable institutions of this State, and sent to their homes in different countries of Europe, during the fiscal year ending September 30, 1891, pursuant to chapter 549 of the laws of 1880, was as follows: To England, 38; to Ireland, 37; to Italy, 32; to Austria-Hungary, 15; to Germany, 22; to Scotland, 13; to Sweden and Switzerland, each, 5; to Russia, 4; and to Denmark, 2—total, 173.

The examination showed that they were deported from their several European homes to this country by the following agencies, viz.: By cities and other municipalities, 34; by their relatives, guardians, and friends, 67; by various European immigration and benevolent societies, 49; by individuals under contract to labor, 23—total, 173.

Preceding the Alien Pauper Law was the State Pauper Law, enacted June 7, 1873, and amended in 1874 and 1875, which is still in full force and effect. Under its provisions, the Secretary of the State Board of Charities returns to their homes or friends in other States of the Union and other countries, State paupers, that is to say, dependent persons having no legal settlement by sixty days' residence in any of the counties of the State, and found by the Secretary in the State almshouses, which are certain county poor-houses selected and designated by the State Board as receptacles of these classes.

The report of the State Board of Charities, transmitted to the Legislature February 17, 1892, shows that the whole number of persons committed as State paupers under this act since it went into effect, October 22, 1873, has been 24,153, viz.: males, 18,813; females, 5,340. Of these 15,071 have been furnished transportation to their homes or places of legal settlement in other States and countries, and this State thus released of the burden and expense of their support and care through life. To have maintained these paupers in the poor-houses and almshouses of the State, at the low rate of $100 each per annum, would have involved an annual outlay of $1,507,100 ; and, calculating the average duration of their lives at fifteen years, they would, in the end, have entailed the enormous expenditure of $22,606,500, by the various cities and counties of the State. The average annual expense since the law went into effect, for maintenance, supervision, and care, and for the removal of 15,071 helpless paupers to their homes or places of legal settlement, has been less than $40,000, or about $25 per person.

Every invasion of the delinquent, diseased, and destitute classes which is finally turned back by the State government, if not at first repelled by the Federal authorities, deters unnumbered irruptions of similar sorts ; by making such experiments of vagrant mendicants from sister States uncertain, or rather rendering it almost certain that their ventures will prove unprofitable and unpleasant to themselves ; and by discouraging benevolent societies, municipalities, and government agencies in Europe, from their bolder attempts to organize such immoral incursions into our territory. Thus, the State Pauper Law and the Alien Pauper Law have not only immediately effected an actual saving of perhaps $25,000,000 as already computed, but on a fair estimate of probabilities, have resulted in sparing the resources of the State the useless expenditure of larger sums of money, as well as its social and moral economies, much disorder, and the blood and life of its people, the contagion and infection of disease and vice.

The public system of out-relief, as organized and administered in many places, is a prolific propagator of pauperism. Until our departments and bureaus of local, as well as State and National, governments shall be regulated by a reformed civil-service divorced from partisan politics, the dispensation of alms in money or food or other things, by public officials, to recipients in their homes, will continue to be a source of corruption. The taint affects the body politic directly, as does all venality in public life. The fraud upon the service is of no account, in comparison with the wrong done in converting whole families and circles of people, who are actually or potentially self-supporting, into the most shameful mendicants and dependants. The offspring of households so "helped" soon become helpless parasites upon the public.

Organized charity, administered by voluntary societies, is the remedy for such evils. The first association of this sort in the United States was formed in the year 1877, in the city of Buffalo, N. Y. Similar societies now exist in Philadelphia, Boston, Brooklyn, and about one hundred other American cities, the forms and plans of which differ in certain respects, some of them more than others resembling the pioneer organization of London, but the best of them providing no financial aid except through outside agencies or in emergencies.

The Charity Organization Society of the City of New York, formed January 26, 1882, is destined to do a great work in the metropolis. Its "New York Charities Directory" contains over four hundred pages of valuable notes of more than three hundred benevolent, and more than five hundred congregational, agencies, omitting only those which are reported adversely by the State Board of Charities, or otherwise known to be unworthy.

The following extracts from the Constitution show the principles of the society :

Every department of its work shall be completely severed from all questions of religious belief, politics, and nationality.

No person representing the society in any capacity whatsoever shall use his or her position for the purpose of proselytism.

The society shall not directly dispense alms in any form.

The chief objects of the society are :

To be a centre of intercommunication between the various churches and charitable agencies in the city. To foster harmonious co-operation between them, and to check the evils of the overlapping of relief.

To investigate thoroughly, and without charge, the cases of all applicants for relief which are referred to the society for inquiry, and to send the persons having a legitimate interest in such cases full reports of the results of investigation.

To obtain from the proper charities and charitable individuals suitable and adequate relief for deserving cases.

To procure work for poor persons who are capable of being wholly or partially self-supporting.

To repress mendicity by the above means and by the prosecution of impostors.

To promote the general welfare of the poor by social and sanitary reforms, and by the inculcation of habits of providence and self-dependence.

Its tender of services has been accepted by nearly all the religious and relief associations; and its references of cases receive the immediate attention of the Department of Public Charities and Correction. It is to the credit of the city government that its administration of out-relief has been reduced to the annual sum of about $20,000. The writer being a citizen of no mean city in the same State, which has less than one hundred and fifty thousand inhabitants, regrets that its annual outlay in the old ways for the old objects of out-relief, is relatively larger, being about $33,500, or nearly double that of the metropolis, for less than one-tenth of the population. In the matter of places where spirituous and fermented liquors are sold to be drunk at the bar or on the premises, the two cities are in comparison as follows: In Rochester, exclusive of drug-stores, about twelve hundred, of which about nine hundred and fifty are licensed; in New York, about nine thousand licensed and unlicensed saloons and places, according to the writer's estimate from data given by Mr. Robert Graham, the Secretary of the Church Temperance Society, confirmed by advices published in the New York *Sun*, on the alleged authority of Superintendent Byrnes. That the provincial city has needs to be met by the direct agency and the indirect influence of its infant society for the organization of charity, is clear in the light of the facts cited.

The popular apprehension should embrace one prominent fact, found from general statistics, viz.: that public indoor relief is not increased by diminishing public out-relief, which shows that cases requiring out-relief are supplied by private societies or persons, and that other cases applying for it do not, when refused, come upon the public in any way, the exceptions, if any, proving the rules governing each class of cases. It is to be remembered always that the good ministry of charity (though by the older maxims confined in theory to the relief of only the industrious or the virtuous) is by the better precepts and practices under modern methods extended to the worthy and the unworthy, by moral measures as well as material means adapted to reach each individual case for the preservation or restoration of the person directly involved, and the consequent protection of society. This is the work of charity organization. It is to be understood also that the aim to organize the powers for good against the organized forces of evil, in communities where the citizens have not time to investigate or to co-operate in works of mercy, does not relieve the constituent or the corresponding members of charity organization from the duty, or deprive them of the blessedness, of beneficence. The design is to inform the conscience of benevolent people with the proofs in each case; and not to discharge them from, but to charge them with, the obligations of humanity.

Other forms of charity organization are found in older types. The Society of St. Vincent de Paul, in the city of New York, organized in 1835 and incorporated in 1872; the New York Association for Improving the Condition of the Poor, organized in 1843 and incorporated in 1848; the Society for the Relief of Poor Widows with Small Children, in New York, organized in 1798 and incorporated in 1802; the Children's Aid Society of the City of New York, organized in 1853 and incorporated in 1855, and numerous other associations in the metropolis; with the Rochester Female Charitable Society for the Relief of the Sick Poor, organized in 1822 and incorporated in 1855, now operating in eighty-four defined districts, to which are assigned about one hundred visitors under eighteen active directresses—one and all represent associations in the State of New York which were precursors in the evolution of charity organizations, and proceeded on the underlying principles of the dispensation of moral as well as material relief and its administration by "friendly visitors."

University settlements, now introduced in New York, Chicago, and Boston, promise to become influential centres of personal sacrifices and endeavors for the restoration and protection of the weak by the realization of their brotherhood with the strong.

The public and private agencies of benevolence already pointed out, with their manifold instrumentalities, are characterized by the self-sacrifice as well as the severity of sympathy seeking the highest relief. Their work is in full agreement with that enforced by the public conscience, which has been informed through such investigations as those by Mr. Brace, in his inquiries respecting "The Dangerous Classes of New York," and by Mr. Riis, in his "Studies Among the Tenements of New York," showing "How the Other Half Lives." Such new activities have, in this generation, arisen at different centres in the world. The "Rationalized Christianity" commended in Mr. Spencer's "Data of Ethics," as a popular equivalent for scientific altruism, does not account for the origin, however it may explain the movement, of such voluntary or spontaneous agencies. The awakening has been produced by Christianity, not in the abstract, but in the concrete, working in the hearts of men. Its practical pity for unhappy or unworthy men is the evolution of Christian experience, and is justified and inspired by the Christian scriptures ; and, as the writer believes, is informed by the providence and the person of Christ, who evidently works not through all who profess his name, but through those, confessing or non-confessing, who have been touched by his truth and Spirit.

With these general movements are others which were earlier in origin, though special, and on church and denominational lines. The various boards of home missions are doing much for the salvation of secular society. The City Mission and Tract Society and the City Mission Society, P. E., of New York, with their evangelistic labors, are working also on the same plane as Mr. Brace and Mr. Riis, and in similar lines—saving from pauperism as well as from other forms of vice and disease. May all churches, whose sincere members have the means in their own private resources, ultimately and speedily become convinced that it is their duty to call assistant ministers and consecrated laymen wholly set apart to "go out quickly into the streets and lanes of the city, and bring in hither the poor, and the maimed, and the halt, and the blind," and to "go out into the highways and hedges and compel them to come in." Philanthropists who are enlightened on these subjects appreciate the administration of the Roman Catholic Church and the Protestant Episcopal Church in their ministries to the socially and spiritually destitute and dependent classes.

The Jewish congregations in the United States are, in some respects, examples to distinctively Christian societies. Their ministers are frequently students of social science. The precepts which they put into practice have also their religious, as well as their scientific, credentials and authority. For they read the moral law of love as it is written, not only on the human heart, where it is so often illegible, or in pagan philosophy and in literature, or in the writings of the Christian covenant and dispensation, but also clearly and fully in their own sacred scriptures whose formula, "thou shalt love thy neighbor as thyself," is in these very terms adopted by Christ. The practice of these precepts by this ancient people respecting their poor, is unprecedented and unparalleled in its honor to the written word. If there are Jews in the poor-houses and almshouses of the counties and cities of the State, they are exceptions proving the rule. Perhaps they sometimes extend too liberal assistance to their dependent brethren, and demoralize by out-relief in even private dispensation ; but such cases are comparatively rare. The endeavor of ministers and members of their congregations is to relieve all classes of their indigent people, by helping them to help themselves through the personal agency of friendly visitors. The refugees from religious or political persecution in Europe, who have come under the protection and care of the Jews in America within the last few years, have been severe but successful tests of these principles for the prevention of pauperism.

In the united Jewish charities organized by the principal Jewish congregation, under their minister, Rev. Max Landsberg, Ph.D., in Rochester, N. Y., 106 new "cases," or families, of 262 persons, were received as Jewish immigrants from Russia, from October 1, 1891, to March 1, 1892. Nearly all of these cases came in a destitute and dependent condition, and thirty were men who had left their wives and children in Russia. One of these cases is given as a fair representation of them all, viz.: a family of 10 persons assisted as follows: October, $77.04 ; November, $17.75; December, $10; January, $12 ; February, $8 ; March, $5; besides three and one-half tons of coal, and aid in finding and doing work, with friendly counsel. This family is now self-supporting, though its head had been a fish-packer in Russia, and was obliged to learn a new trade here. Of the 106 cases, 19 were refused and 85 were assisted, of whom all are now earning their own maintenance without assistance except friendly advice.

Dr. Landsberg asserts that a large expense at first, in proper cases, may be true economy of means to the end of self-maintenance. Many other persons who deal with destitute classes gravitating toward dependence have arrived at this conclusion. The danger of out-relief, in such cases, arises, as we have seen, from the political nature of its public dispensation, but disappears on its private and organized administration by means of friendly visitors.

Indoor relief in county poor-houses and city almshouses, under proper laws, can be regulated and corrected by rules and checks, which cannot be applied to the conduct of political officials in matters of out-relief. There have been radical improvements in these houses during the past twenty-five years. The last beneficent

23

change in the State of New York was effected by Chapter 126 of the laws of 1890, known as the State Care Act. By this statute—excepting the Counties of New York, Kings, and Monroe, but providing that they may elect to waive such exception—it is enacted that the insane poor shall be transferred from county custody to care and treatment in State hospitals. Monroe County has already accepted both the benefits and burdens of this legislative act. It is to be regretted that the way is not made clear for the City and County of New York to pursue the same course, in accordance with the conclusions of the State Board of Charities, stated in several reports of its standing committee on the insane. The fact remains that the condition of the insane poor in the asylums of New York City, on Blackwell's, Ward's, and Hart's Islands, has been worse in some respects than in the rural and other interior counties of the State; and has been caused by crowding buildings, some of which are not tenantable, through the neglect of successive Boards of Estimate and Apportionment to make proper appropriations.

The Willard Asylum Act, passed in 1865, had provided for exclusive State care; but on account of deficient provisions in the State institutions, the State Board of Charities, in pursuance of its authority by law, exempted nineteen counties from its operation. The new departure under the State Care Act of 1890, has made such progress in the increase of accommodations at the State hospitals by means of inexpensive buildings, on detached or cottage plans, for the custody of the medically chronic classes of the insane, as to warrant the confident belief that, within one or two years, more or less, the transition from County to State care, except in the Counties of New York and Kings, will be happily completed.

The correction or prevention of pauperism is intimately related to the curative and humane treatment and care of the insane poor, for the reason that while, like many other classes of poor persons, they, with their families, may become dependent or demoralized through either neglect or unwise interference, they are neither necessarily nor presumptively paupers. The fact may be better stated by saying positively that an extremely small proportion of the indigent insane come from the classes tainted with pauperism. This conclusion, though contrary to popular apprehension, is sustained by the opinions of alienists and specialists. Insanity, when neglected, is the cause of pauperism, but pauperism is seldom the source of insanity. The workers in the poor-houses have been confined almost exclusively to the lunatics. The legislation in the great States of New York, Pennsylvania, Ohio, and Illinois, for exclusive State care, is absolutely justified on the ground of humanity, but may also be defended on the ground of economy. Opponents objected that the better care of the State would attract patients who, under the county system, would remain in their families. If the prediction shall be fulfilled, the results will not be deplored in the interest of society. The father, or mother, or bread-winner, of a family, when stricken with insanity, ceases to become a producer, and, at the same time, becomes an incumbrance upon not only the accumulations or earnings, but also the time, energy, and producing capacity of the other members of the family, thereby directly impoverishing the community, and perhaps further prejudicing it by the ultimate pauperization of the family. Here, as everywhere, the welfare of the State is consistent with humanity toward its citizens, and justice to its taxpayers is in harmony with mercy to its wards.

The *separation of the sexes*, which has been effected in the county houses, will, it is believed, be followed by better classification of the inmates. The obstacles now in the way are not so frequently the results of mal-administration, as they are the necessary effects of bad construction of old buildings. But all obstructions must give way to the obligation of respecting the worthy poor, who have become dependent from losses of friends, or health, or property, and of separating them from vagrant or vicious paupers. Such classification for indoor relief, with private charity properly organized outside, will remove the last excuse for the public dispensation of out-relief. The consummation will afford another illustration of the harmony between humanity, as a social and political duty, and public policy.

The *transference of children* from the demoralizing influences of poor-houses *to asylums* was effected by a law, recommended by the State Board of Charities, and enacted in the year 1875. Prior to this legislation, its subjects, many of whom on the death of their parents came from homes of relative industry and purity, and most of whom were presumptively innocent of the virus of pauperism though susceptible and in highly receptive states, were one and all detained in intimate association with the chronic cases of the disease, in the common wards of the county houses, until they could be placed by the county superintendents of the poor in private families. While the net results of the law have been good, the statistics gathered and compiled by the State Board of Charities show that its operation has been attended with incidental evils. The following figures are approximate, inasmuch as they relate to all institutions that reported such data in 1891, which are the majority of the whole number. Of 18,556 orphan and destitute children in such asylums, October 1, 1891, there were 3,671 orphans, 10,356 half orphans, 4,065 who had both parents living, and 465 whose social condition was not given; while there were supported by cities, counties, and towns, 11,061; by parents and friends, 1,717; by the institutions, 2,430; and not stated, 3,348; and there were committed, by magistrates and courts, 8,130; by commissioners of charities, 1,005; by superintendents of the poor, 1,823; by overseers of the poor, 938; by parents and friends, 4,422; and not stated, 2,238; and the duration of institution life had been 5,763 for less than one year; 5,757 for one year and less than three; 3,051 for three years and less than five; 2,782 for over five years; and not stated 303—though the total number of sick, infirm, crippled, deformed, or disabled was only about three per cent., and of feeble-minded, only one and two-tenths per cent., with thirteen cases of idiocy. *The indications from these statistics are that some asylums are taking on the character of permanent homes at public expense,* though they should be regarded as domiciliary for only transitional and provisional purposes, until their beneficiaries can be placed in good families. One evil is that while the institutions are thus enlarged and extended, they impose burdens on the taxpayers for maintenance of their wards, without commensurate benefits, but in many cases with positive injury. Children who are detained too long in asylums tend to become institutionized and unfitted to correspond with a free environment on their final discharge. The close corporations of private managers of these semi-public institutions sometimes lose their sense of responsibility to the people. Relief would be found in remedial legislation, providing among other things for county or city agents, or another paid secretary of the State Board, whose duty it should be to see that the asylums exercise due diligence in placing their wards, under proper conditions, in private families of good character and circumstances, in visiting them statedly, and in securing legal commitments to the institutions and proper indentures from them, thus protecting foster parents as well as their adopted children.

A high authority on these questions—Mrs. Charles Russell Lowell—in her report to the State Board of Charities, transmitted with its annual report to the Legislature in 1890, has given proofs of the evils in the present system or want of system, and proposed remedies. The report shows about $1,500,000 expended for the care and maintenance of about an average of 14,000 children for the preceding fiscal year, in the city of New York, with other facts, from which the inference is plain that many parents with their offspring are pauperized by removing them from the natural relations of life, with unwise kindness, if not inhumanity, to them, as well as injustice to the taxpayers.

In the *State Charities Record* for December, 1894, published by the State Charities Aid Association, the leading article, by Anna T. Wilson, formerly of Philadelphia, now of the Charity Organization

Society of New York, contrasts the care of dependent children in the two cities, and it is stated that, in the year 1890, the city of New York, with a population of 1,500,000, appropriated $1,647,295.10 for the support of 15,449 children in its private institutions, and $192,997.74 for the support of 909 children on Randall's Island, making $1,840,292.84 for an average of not less than 15,000 children ; while the city of Philadelphia, with a population of 1,000,000 appropriated $28,724.82 for the support of an average of less than 250 children in institutions. The system of boarding out children until they can be permanently placed by adoption in families, is in Philadelphia made the substitute for the system of asylums in New York ; and from all accounts appears to be working well, as also may be said of the new extension of the plan from dependent to destitute children, including those convicted of felonies, of which Homer Folks writes hopefully in the *Record* for November, 1894. It should, however, be borne in mind that the results have been partly due to fortunate combinations of circumstances, including the assistance of the Children's Aid Society of Pennsylvania ; and that data from large fields in other States and countries show that the boarding-out system has not always proved humane, even for dependent adults.*

There is now devolved by law upon the State Board of Charities of New York, the function of determining and certifying whether applications for the incorporation of institutions and societies having the care of children, shall be granted. This power is carefully exercised, and decisions are made under it only after full investigation.

Notwithstanding the safeguards and precautions vouchsafed by

---

* For juvenile dependents the system is reported from England as unsatisfactory (p. 171, appendix to the last edition of The Poor Law of England by T. W. Fowle ; Macmillan & Co.). The extended and successive reports of Hon. William P. Letchworth, on the asylums for orphan and destitute children in the State, transmitted and published with many of the annual reports of the State Board of Charities of New York, are here mentioned as of high authority and value, though they are but a small fraction of his labors and contributions in the general work of the board.

the Society for the Prevention of Cruelty to Children in New York and other cities, which are assumed to be all that are possible under existing laws, there is reason to believe that children are not infrequently committed to juvenile reformatories, including the House of Refuge on Randall's Island and the State Industrial School at Rochester, N. Y., on frivolous or false complaints of parents, in order to shift the burden of maintenance and education to the State, county, or city. The remedy should be found in new legislation, requiring corroboratory proofs on all complaints by parents or guardians or relations, and assessing, upon the persons responsible for the support of the children in the home, part of the cost of their maintenance in the institution.

The progress which has been made in some of these reformatories, during the last decade, furnishes great temptation for unwise if not fraudulent commitments to them. In the matter of technologic instruction alone, the State Industrial School of New York offers great inducements; as among the semi-public institutions of this sort in the same state the Catholic Protectory has, for the last decade, been in advance in the teaching of trades. That these juvenile institutions, and the reformatories for adults, do accomplish reformations in vastly greater proportions than could be effected in the same classes by the old time confinement and discipline in State prisons, county and city penitentiaries and jails, is a conclusion of fact from experience in the State of New York (whatever it may be in Massachusetts or elsewhere) respecting which there is no reasonable doubt among persons acquainted with the subject.

Recent discussions have appeared to throw doubts over some points that should be clear. If, in any county or state or institution, sentiment has been exchanged for sentimentalism, or ideas have been entertained without verification by facts, we may expect reactions swinging to the other extreme before there can be any stable equilibrium of opinion or feeling among the opposing parties on the questions in penology. That all progress in the

mental and social, as well as in the physical world, must be in
rhythm, is shown by Mr. Herbert Spencer, and illustrated by certain criticisms which lately have denied even the wise humanity
and practical righteousness of the recommendations of the great
prison reformer, Howard.

The sceptic who questions the superiority of remedial over retributive discipline of convicts, may resolve his doubts by visiting
the State Reformatory of New York. This institution, at Elmira,
is for men under thirty and over sixteen years of age, on first conviction of felony, and under sentence not to exceed the maximum
prison term, but otherwise indeterminate. The evidence shows
that about eighty per cent. of the criminals committed to it are reformed, in the sense that they are made over, not into perfected
saints, but into law-abiding citizens.

This is the end attained. What are the means employed?
They are measures not of conciliation, but of conversion. The culprit is conformed to the environment ; not the environment to him.
He is conformed to society, being formed, by pressure which is new,
to a standard which also is new to him, that is to say, he is reformed. The process is painful in proportion as it is needful. The
patient on reception is admitted to the middle grade, from which it
is possible for him to gain promotion to the highest grade, whence,
after due probation, he would be graduated to his home or other
proper place selected for him by the superintendent, but thus released on parole and trial until proved to be worthy of absolute discharge. The frequent experience, however, is of degradation to
the lowest grade, as the first actual step, seemingly backward, but
as the events prove, in most cases really forward. The subject
striving to regain his lost footing must use every exertion, physical,
mental, and moral, in continued effort and endeavor ; and before
success is apt to plunge into despair, to be lifted only by personal
intervention of the superintendent, inspiring in him a new will as
of grace. The writer once visited all the lowest grade men after
they were locked in their cells at night, and was pleased to hear

them ascribe their failures to themselves, and not to the system or
its administration ; while not a few, however, expressed their desire to be transferred to State-prison, in order to escape the discipline, and, as some of them illustrated their meaning, in order to
avoid the schools and study after the day's work, and to obtain tobacco and indulgence.

The process of such conversion, and the drill and discipline and
rehabilitation of the very nervous organism into a new character
and manhood, is necessarily painful. But to use this fact or the
natural laws accounting for it, to justify or excuse the old time discipline of prisons, where profane and obscene keepers cursed and
abused the convicts, and inflicted on them corporal punishments in
order to " get even with them," is no more sensible than it would be
for a surgeon or physician to subject his patient to pains of arbitrary cuttings and burnings and flagellations, in addition to the
necessary sufferings of curative processes.

The system of State-prisons of New York, as distinguished from
that of its reformatories, is vitiated by an inherited tendency to
political partisanship, contrary to the statute (Sub. 3, Sec. 50, of
Chapter 382 of the laws of 1889) ; and, with that of its county jails,
is thus to a great extent subsidized for the production of chronic
felons and paupers.

The work of reformatories must be inadequate, unless the preventive work of such associations as the Society for the Prevention
of Crime, and the restorative work of the Prison Association of
New York, shall sustain and supplement it.

The preventive measures respecting prisoners have an intimate
relation, with those regarding paupers. Any decrease in the number of recidivous criminals or misdemeanants diminishes the number of paupers manifoldly ; for habitual offenders, in their intervals
between prison terms, beget and educate races of variously demoralized and pauperized types of human beings, and criminals and
paupers succeed each other, as has been familiarly illustrated in
the annals of " The Jukes," in the State of New York, and in the

more recent history of the "Tribe of Ishmael," by Rev. Oscar McCulloch, the late President of the State Board of Charities of Indiana. The present practice under the laws is to sentence disturbers of the peace, on conviction of public drunkenness, debauchery, or disorder, to imprisonment for a term of ten days or upward, just sufficient to permit, not reformation of moral character, but recuperation of vitality and accumulation of physical energy for renewed dissipation and disturbance, with repetitions of transgression and punishment indefinitely prolonged, perhaps scores of times in one life.

Civil intervention, to be beneficent to such transgressors, or to society, whose laws they violate, should be prolonged and uninterrupted, until there is a reasonable evidence of reformation ; and in the absence of trustworthy evidence should be continued indefinitely, until death may release these cumberers of the ground.

This conclusion in favor of indeterminate sentences without maximum limits, applies to delinquent or depraved paupers, who now come and go to and from the public houses of counties and cities, with the primary effect of prolonging their own evil courses, and with the secondary consequence of continuing their kind by generation or succession. For, waiving the philosophical explanation of social environment on the one hand, and the theory of natural inheritance on the other, we know as matters of fact that often, in almost unbroken and indefinite lines, criminals and paupers succeed each other, under the intermittent treatment of civil governments, where, if either removed from society or left to nature, they would soon become extinct.

The *question of heredity* (though eliminated from the problem of the treatment of adult individuals belonging to the delinquent and dependent classes, the solution of which is on any hypothesis in their detention from their kind) is not so easily disposed of when we come to their offspring, to detain whom indefinitely in either prisons or asylums would be inhuman and unjust. The great work done by the Children's Aid Society of New York, in placing their wards in good homes in Western States, represents, on a grand scale of conception and execution, the proper treatment which is at once popular and philosophic. But the question has often returned to thoughtful minds. What has become of the taint or tendency in the blood of these children to evil, if any, when mixed in the veins of descendants in the Western States, where they have been adopted into pure families and developed under a pure atmosphere, and finally have intermarried with other stocks ?

The discussion of hereditary tendency came to the surface in some of the articles of the symposium entitled "Treatment of Juvenile Delinquents," in *The Independent* of March 3, 1892. The subject was there settled by overruling what were assumed to be the inductions or speculations of scientists, as opposed to the conclusions of practical workers in the field. The findings of fact from the experience, the observation, and the first sources of information of these philanthropic specialists, who deal directly with the matters involved in the inquiry, are worth more than hypotheses invented to account for general statements of phenomena in books.

In a recent letter Mr. C. Loring Brace, Secretary of the Children's Aid Society, said : "So far as we can judge, inheritance does not figure in the problem. It is want of care and judicious training in childhood which is responsible for whatever difficulties we have to cope with. This Society has placed 84,000 children in homes since it began this work forty years ago ; and it is our experience that no matter what the parents may be, if the child is taken away at an age so early that it has not yet understood the wickedness about it, if placed in a country home with kind and judicious adoptive parents, it is almost certain to do well. My father has always stated that not more than two per cent. turned out badly. But if the child is not transplanted early enough, then there are the bad examples, bad habits, and knowledge of evil ways to contend against. It is among these older children that we sometimes fail and of whom complaints are sometimes made, but inher-

itance is not responsible for this. It is early neglect and evil surroundings."

Happily, Mr. Brace is right, and there is no real contention
at the present time between science and the experience gained by
philanthropists. The last word of scientists is in accordance with
the words of these practical specialists. The theory of heredity
now held by Wallace, who shares with Darwin the credit of the hypothesis of natural selection, and by Weismann and the most eminent authorities, is that acquired characteristics of the parent do
not pass to the child by inheritance. The truth stated would seem
to admit a tendency of all traits of progenitors to pass, which in the
case of qualities that are the results of protracted accumulations
of experience, continued in long lines of successive generations,
will be transmitted, unless overcome by environment; but which
in the case of qualities that were acquired by the immediate ancestors, will not be propagated with any effectual or appreciable
force if opposed by outside influences. Hence, a foster parent
would assume less risk of blood in succoring the offspring of delinquent, diseased, or dependent parents whose remote lineage is
good, than in adopting the children whose father and mother are
both worthy in their own personal character, but one, if not both,
of whom come of general stock which was bad. These conclusions
make the matter so mixed as to remove it from practical consideration.

In this light we can appreciate the work done by the Children's
Aid Society of New York, not only in the magnitude of its proportions, but in the far-reaching effects of its beneficence. This society, during the last fiscal year, had charge of 36,363 children, of
whom it taught and partly clothed and fed 10,464 in its twenty-two
industrial schools and nine night schools, and sent 2,851 to homes,
mainly in the West. It is an approved agency for bringing to bear
the influences of environment and education upon character and
destiny at formative periods of growth.

And complementary to such work is that of the Societies for the

Prevention of Cruelty to Children, which interfere to protect children in their homes, become guardians of their persons, and take charge of them upon commitments, and thus by moral influence as well as actual intervention prevent not only untold suffering, but also the demoralizing effects upon the parent who inflicts as well as the child who suffers cruelty.

No presentation of the subject of liquor saloons is needed. The moral and religious people of the State know perfectly well that these saloons are the centres where political corruption finds its points of application, and whence flow unceasing currents creating most of the pauperism and public vice which infest the body politic. And the same respectable and dominant classes know as well that, without imposing prohibitory laws upon unwilling minorities, or unduly interfering with personal liberty, it is in their power to abate these public nuisances. A mighty crusade in this direction might be led by some agency such as the Church Temperance Society.

It may be hoped that remedies for many social evils, as well as reformations of abuses in public institutions of charity and correction, will, in the future, even more than in the past, be promoted by the State Charities Aid Association of the City of New York. This society was formed twenty years ago by Miss Louisa Lee Schuyler. While its work in some respects is subordinated to that of the State Board of Charities, as implied in its title and incorporation, its annual reports to the Board in printed book-form show that its labors extend on certain lines beyond those of the Board ; for being of voluntary character, its methods, including newspaper publications, are not constrained by official rules. It is not necessary to agree with all its conclusions in order to appreciate that they are of the highest authority, whether in conjunction or opposition to those of the State Board, or in extension of the same. The writer regards the society * as a social factor whose importance cannot be over-estimated.

* The great power of this association in advancing humanitarian movements is

The two general guides in the great works of reform and relief within the city of New York are, first, with primary and particular reference to public reforms, the State Charities Aid Association, No. 21 University Place, with its published journal, *The State Charities Record ;* and, second, with special regard to private relief, the Charity Organization Society at the same place, with its monthly periodical, *The Charities Review.* The last-named society, with the Association for Improving the Condition of the Poor, and the Children's Aid Society, is to have its home in the United Charities Building, Fourth Avenue, corner of Twenty-second Street, erected by Mr. John S. Kennedy.

Any review of laws, agencies, and labors for humanity and social economy should not lose sight of the vital relation between the primary work of protecting the producers in society from lapsing into indigence and the secondary work of preventing the poor from falling into pauperism. But the means of performing the paramount duty of protection to the workers come directly within the purview of this chapter upon the prevention of pauperism, only in the matter of the cost of private and public charity and relief. From the tables of statistics collected and compiled by the State Board of Charities, and appended as schedules in its annual reports to the Legislature of New York, the following comparative statement has been made, showing expenditures for charitable and reformatory purposes between the years 1880 and 1891, both inclusive, to wit :

Year.	Amount expended.	Year.	Amount expended.
1880	$8,482,648 71	1881	$9,260,147 77
1882	9,320,142 60	1883	9,938,037 05
1884	10,642,763 86	1885	11,538,739 86

due to the high character of its membership. Its officers are : Professor Charles F. Chandler, of Columbia College, President ; Mrs. William B. Rice, Vice-President ; Hon. Charles S. Fairchild, Treasurer ; Miss Abby Howland Woolsey, Librarian, and Mr. John H. Finley, Secretary. It will be difficult to fill the place of Mr. Finley, who has accepted the presidency of Knox College.

Year.	Amount expended.	Year.	Amount expended.
1886	12,027,990 01	1887	12,574,074 67
1888	13,315,698 97	1889	14,868,733 77
1890	16,349,842 43	1891	17,605,660 58

It thus appears that in this period of twelve years the expenditures have increased a little more than one hundred per cent. Though the population of the State increased only about nineteen per cent., as is shown on the basis of the Federal census, it also appears from the reports of the Comptroller of the State, that its wealth has increased about fifty per cent. during the same period. Of this increase in expenditures—$9,123,011.87—the sum of $1,222,-282.61 relates to institutions managed by the State; and the State Reformatory at Elmira, and the Soldiers' and Sailors' Home at Bath, two of the State institutions existing prior to 1880, did not appear in the statistics at the beginning of this period of twelve years. Again, of this increase the sum of $1,171,053.58 relates to institutions owned and controlled by counties and cities, leaving $6,729,675.68 increase in the institutions under the direction and control of incorporated benevolent associations. Thus it will be seen that more than two-thirds of the increase of the cost of public and private relief and charity is due to private charity, and that the fraction of less than one-sixth of such increase, owing to the State Institutions, is further reduced on account of two of them existing, but not reporting to the Board in 1880.

There is no reason to disbelieve or doubt that—excepting perhaps the Soldiers' and Sailors' Home, the existence of which is justified by patriotic sentiment—each and all the State institutions for relief or reform, including the eight State hospitals for the insane, the State Institution for Feeble-minded Children, at Syracuse, the Custodial Asylum for Feeble-minded Women, at Newark, the reformatories and the asylums for the blind and the deaf, do save to the people more than their cost in preventing pauperism, and therefore in protecting both the industrial and the indigent classes.

The conclusion of the whole matter is, that whatever protects the poor from pauperism, also protects the producer from poverty, and vice versa. Therefore the State, if justified in interfering for the good of any one of these three classes, may justly intervene at either end of the series.

The Factory Law, regulating the sanitary and moral conditions of labor, of adult as well as juvenile operatives congregated in masses, where the units have no separate control, and the principle of certain proposed legislation correcting the evils of what is known as the "sweating system," come within the legitimate scope of governmental authority. In the same sphere are many of the remedies proposed by reforms for improving the tenements of the working-classes in large cities, and for promoting the public health. To the objection that such civil laws interfere with the natural laws of trade, the answer is that, not only in society, but in all departments of nature, higher forces constantly intervene to regulate the action of lower forces, and so interfere, not in violation, but in pursuance, of the laws of the mental and the physical worlds. The advocates of extreme individualism, excluding the intervention of the State in matters of trade or industry, as also in matters of relief or charity, are inconsistent when they belong, as most of them do, to the class of thinkers who hold to the theory of society, not as an aggregation of individuals, but as an organism. The reasonable reconciliation of opposing theories seems to be that paternalism in the State shall govern, wherever the individual cannot properly control the conditions for his own protection, as in factory laws and charity laws ; but that in all other respects individualism should reign, leaving each person to work out his own salvation in the struggle for existence, as essential discipline for his own well being, as well as for the general welfare of society.

One objection, which is more specific and specious, opposes all interference by society in public relief or private charity, for the reason that the delinquent and dependent classes should as individuals be left to suffer, in order that the beneficent processes of nature, providing for the death and disappearance of the species, may not be defeated or delayed. This position is abhorrent to moral sentiment. It is also unsound in its philosophy, seeming to ignore that Mr. Darwin's law of "natural selection," as well as Mr. Spencer's law of "the survival of the fittest," which it cites, do in their full scope include society as symbolized under the figures of "the social organism" and "the body politic," in which is resident a moral force in correspondence with the environment of moral law. Humanity is superior to political economy or biology, and must leave the community which denies it to moral disintegration and dissolution, until, by reverse processes of selection, which sometimes occur in both the higher and the lower forms of life, it shall become unfit to survive.

The policy which has obtained of dispensing public charities as well as civil penalties so as to injure rather than benefit their objects and society, is an excuse though not a justification for such opposition to humanity.

The simple truth, as we have seen, is that the habitual and hardened pauper, as well as the congenital or confirmed criminal, should be restrained in his tendency to evil, and to the extent of his ability constrained to labor for the support of himself and his family, if any, dependent on him; and indefinitely continued in such discipline, with all needful instruction, recreation, and influence to recovery, under indeterminate sentence of confinement; and thus sequestered from society until he reforms or dies. This is the law for remedial, not retributive, and preventive, not punitive, relief; and is thus the law of kindness to the criminous or unworthy delinquents or dependants, and of safety to the virtuous workers and the honest poor, and therefore of justice. Such equity, rather than mere mercy, is the best expression of charity in public relations, and the true reconciliation of the scientific as well as the economical objections to the intervention of the State for the sake of humanity. Such relief would be within the practical reach, as well as the political right, of the State to-day, were the public conscience properly informed of the facts relating to the prevention of pauperism.

24

THE NEW YORK TENEMENT-HOUSE EVIL AND ITS CURE

By ERNEST FLAGG,

ARCHITECT OF ST. LUKE'S HOSPITAL, ETC., ETC.

CHIEF CAUSES OF THE PRESENT EVIL—RESTRICTIONS IMPOSED BY THE CONVEN-
TIONAL CITY LOT—TYPES OF TENEMENTS—DANGER FROM FIRE—NEED OF
RADICAL CHANGES—IGNORANCE IN REGARD TO ECONOMIC BUILDING—THE
ART OF COMMERCIAL PLANNING—THE PROBLEM IN OTHER CITIES—EXTRAVA-
GANCE OF PRESENT METHODS SHOWN—SUGGESTIONS FOR IMPROVEMENT—THE
QUESTION OF LIGHT—REFORM A MATTER OF BUSINESS ADVANTAGE.

THE greatest evil which ever befell New York City was the division of blocks into lots of 25 × 100 feet. So true is this,
that no other disaster can for a moment be compared with it.
Fires, pestilence, and financial troubles are as nothing in comparison ; for from this division has arisen the New York system of tenement-houses, the worst curse which ever afflicted any great community.

The object of this paper is to show that the evils of the system
lie almost entirely in the plàn ; that with another plan, light, air,
health, and comfort can be furnished at the same, if not at less, cost
than the great majority of the inhabitants of this town are now
forced to pay for dwellings not fit for the lower animals. Unfortunately, the same division of the land which led to the plan for
these houses is the chief obstacle in the way of reform.

The houses are built on lots 25 × 100 feet, and generally about
five stories high. A regulation of the Board of Health now limits
the depth to ninety feet, so that there is a space of ten feet by the

width of the lot at the rear for light. Of course, this is doubled
when similar houses are erected back to back. In addition there is
usually a narrow court, or well, at the sides, of about four feet wide,
when the houses are built side by side. That is to say, each owner
leaves a recess at the side of about two feet by forty odd, as shown in
Figures 1 (p. 373) and 4 (p. 384); each floor is arranged for two families in the better class of houses, but more generally four families
occupy one floor. Each family has a room facing the street or the
yard, and from two to three rooms lighted, or rather not lighted,
from the central slit or well. The front rooms measure about
twelve feet square. The others about seven by ten feet.

When the city was first laid out, the division of the blocks into
lots 25×100 feet was entirely unobjectionable. The people generally built houses of moderate dimensions, lighted at the front from
the street, and in the rear from the yard. If a larger dwelling was
required more land was taken, and the house was made wider; but
as the city grew the land increased so greatly in value that an effort
was made to occupy more of the 25×100 feet lot than was consistent
with the proper lighting of the interior.

As every one knows, the fashionable quarter of the town, first at
the Battery, has removed steadily and rapidly to the north. As the
richer people vacated their houses to go farther uptown, they were
turned over to the poor. Houses built for one family were occupied
by twice as many families as the building had floors. The city
grew at such a rate that it soon became necessary to erect new
houses as tenements. The builders having been in the habit of
building houses on lots of 25×100 feet, saw no better way than to
continue the practice, and this new style of building took a form
which the shape of the lot suggested.

This arbitrary division of the city into lots of twenty-five feet, more
or less, in width by one hundred feet deep, and the custom of dealing in and building on plots of that size, has worked most disas-
trous results for the tenement-house population. The system of
houses which has resulted is a monstrous evil, which can scarcely be

over-estimated. The modern tenement is not only detrimental to the health, morals, and comfort of the people, but also a severe tax upon their earnings. In no place do the poor pay such high rents as in this city, and in no place are the accommodations so bad in proportion to the prices paid. These results are due to two causes :

First. The excessive value of the land, caused by the shape and situation of the city.

Second. To the extravagant type of house which has resulted from the shape and size of the lot.

Of the two evils the latter is the greater, for it affects the health and welfare of the people, besides being a tax upon their earnings, but, fortunately, it is the one which can be remedied.

All the tenement-houses of New York, except corner houses, certain old buildings, constructed originally for other purposes, and a few model tenements, belong to one of two classes, or types.

1. Those having two buildings to the lot, one being in the rear and known as the rear tenement, and which together cover about ninety per cent. of its area.

2. Those of one building to the lot, which usually covers about eighty per cent. of its area ; in both cases the lot being twenty-five feet or a little more or less in width and one hundred feet deep.

The erection of houses of the former type is now prohibited, and those in existence are all old. The building on that part of the lot nearest the street formerly served as a dwelling for one family, and the rear building owed its existence to the greed of the owner, who begrudged the liberal space left vacant at the rear of these old houses for light and air. As no more of these rear tenements can be built, we may dismiss this class from consideration, with the devout hope that speedy legislation will soon work their complete destruction. They are the most vicious tenements which we have, so far as the rear building is concerned.

Of the second class there are several varieties, all having a strong family resemblance. They are all long and narrow, and may be classified as follows :

1. Houses with windows only at the front and rear, all the central rooms being dark. A regulation of the Board of Health also prevents the erection of more of this kind. Those now in existence, like the rear tenements, should be destroyed.

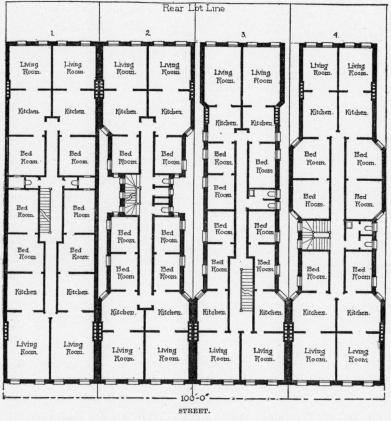

Figure 1.

2. Houses having enclosed courts or wells at the sides.

3. Houses having spaces at the sides which are open at the rear.

4. Houses having the characteristics of both of the two former varieties.

Figure 1 shows an upper-floor plan of four houses belonging to these varieties. Thousands upon thousands of such buildings have been built during the last few years, hundreds are now in the course of erection, and others of the same kind, at an ever-increasing rate, will be built in the future unless something is done to prevent it.

A glance at Figure 1 will show how objectionable this type of house is. The slit at the side is from four to five feet wide ; all interior rooms open upon it, consequently each bedroom window has another bedroom window belonging to the next house directly opposite to it, and only four or five feet distant ; privacy is not to be thought of under such circumstances. In summer these windows must be left open, and all the noise, odors, dust, and heat circulate from one house to the other ; these conditions are, of course, greatly aggravated when the slit is enclosed on all four sides as in the second and fourth varieties, in which case it becomes a veritable nuisance, not only dangerous to the health and morals of the occupants, but also to their lives by reason of fire, as it forms a flue which could scarcely be better contrived for the quick spreading of flames from one floor to another on both sides of it. Indeed the danger from fire is greatly increased in all these so-called improved varieties (those having slits at the sides), for no fire walls are provided such as existed in houses of the old type, and a fire once started, there is no barrier to it except the Fire Department. It may sweep through the entire block, for the narrow slit forms no obstacle to the spread of the flames, which can leap across it and spread to the adjoining houses, and so on through the entire row.

It would seem as if the increased danger from fire alone would serve to prevent the erection of such buildings, instead of which it simply serves to increase the insurance rate, which eventually falls on the tenant, as the landlord must reimburse himself by charging more rent than he otherwise would. Thus the tenant, besides having to risk his life by fire, must pay a higher rent for the privilege.

If a method of building can be devised whereby the cost of erection and the danger from fire will be lessened, such an achievement will be a very great boon, not so much to the landlord as to the working population of the city. For as every tax on property is eventually laid on the tenant, so every saving will, in time, work to his advantage. Now, if it can also be shown that much more light and air can be given, and a better and more liberal arrangement of the rooms can be devised, a great good will have been accomplished.

In order to work such a reform we must first convince the public, or the powers that be, of a fact which seems to be too apparent to need stating, viz.: *No satisfactory tenement, from both the commercial and sanitary stand-point, can be erected, under the conditions which prevail in New York, upon a lot of 25 × 100 feet, or one of about these dimensions, for if a sufficient space be left vacant to properly light the interior, the building cannot be profitable, owing to the high price of the land, and if enough land is covered to make the building profitable as an investment, the interior cannot be properly lighted and ventilated.*

One would think that the truth of this had been too thoroughly demonstrated to need insisting upon. Have we not before our eyes ten thousand object-lessons which demonstrate it? Has not every conceivable combination of plan for a twenty-five by one hundred feet lot been tried over and over again? Yet where is the satisfactory tenement-house on such a lot—that is to say, the house which is satisfactory from both the commercial and sanitary stand-point? To meet both these requirements is incompatible with lots of this size and shape in view of the high cost of land. If the present plan is retained, one of two considerations must give way; less profit must be made, or else the health, safety, and comfort of the tenant must be sacrificed. It does not require much knowledge of human nature to guess which of these interests will prevail.

If our tenements are to be improved, half-way measures will not do. During the last fifteen or twenty years the Board of Health has made feeble efforts at reform, and we now have houses of an improved type, that is to say, buildings of the kind described above.

It is unnecessary to comment farther on this style of house. Very little imagination is required to picture to one's self the wretched condition of people forced to live under such circumstances, and the great danger arising therefrom to the health and morals of the community. By far the greater number of the inhabitants of this city live in such houses : from sixteen to twenty families to a single lot.

From the time of its first introduction there has been no radical change in the plan of these houses. Acres upon acres have been covered by them, all constructed on the same general plan, based upon the shape of the lot 25 × 100 feet. Strange to say, they are not usually built singly. In most cases they are put up in blocks of from two, three, and four, up to twenty or more, yet no attempt is ever made to depart from the stereotyped plan. If an owner has a plot one hundred feet square, instead of building one house he builds four houses. It never seems to have occurred to anyone that this is an extremely extravagant and wasteful way of building ; yet such is the case, for the system involves the erection of an unnecessary amount of wall, partitions, and corridor, also an unnecessary amount of entrances, halls, etc., and a consequent loss of room. So great is the loss from these causes that it is possible to plan buildings of a different type which, while having the same amount of rentable space in rooms, shall cover so much less of the lot as to leave an abundant space free for light and air. Covering a smaller area they will cost less to erect, so that properly lighted and well-ventilated apartments can be supplied at less than it costs to build the dreadful affairs which we now have.

The difficulty has arisen, and persistently flourishes, because we are ignorant of the art of economical planning. For who would waste money in erecting unnecessary walls, halls, etc., if he knew how to obtain the same amount of rentable space much better lighted without them? By the present system the ground is encumbered, the light obstructed, and the building rendered unhealthy and unfit to live in ; all of which is accomplished at an increased expense over what the same rentable space, well lighted, might be obtained for. Great sums of money are yearly squandered upon making the buildings unfit to live in. Then other great sums are contributed by charitable people to relieve the resulting distress. Hospitals are kept full, children die, misery, disease, and crime flourish, because the people are huddled together without sufficient light and air.

The art of commercial or economical planning is an exact science very little understood anywhere, and least of all here. It is a curious fact that, although thousands of books have been written upon architecture, there are practically none on planning, which is unquestionably the most important part of architecture.

One of the two chief difficulties in economical planning lies in the admission of light to the interior. If the building is to be erected on valuable land, that architect shows the greatest skill who so arranges the plan that the interior shall receive a sufficient amount of light with the least expenditure of open space. If courts enclosed on all sides are used, the best results can be obtained from those which are about square, for we can imagine the court drawn out into the form of an oblong parallelogram, always of the same superficial area, but finally becoming a slit too narrow for the transmission of light. The shape of the lots upon which our tenements are built forces the designer to choose the most uneconomical form of court. Thus he gets the least amount of light from the space left vacant.

The second great difficulty in economical planning is to obtain the best results as regards the strength of the building and the convenient disposition of the rooms with the least expenditure of building materials and the least waste of floor in corridors, passages, etc.; economy of materials, means a double saving, for not only is the cost of such materials saved, but also the space which they occupy. The shape of our tenement-houses forces the designer to choose the most uneconomical construction; as the houses must be long and narrow they require the maximum of wall and also the maximum of passages or corridors, for to reach all parts of a long narrow building there must be long passage-ways, while if the building is compact and square such corridors can be reduced to a minimum.

In short, no worse type of plan could well be devised. There is absolutely nothing to recommend it either as regards economy or healthfulness. It seems as if the builders had gone out of the way to produce the worst possible results. With the greatest expenditure of materials they obtain the least amount of rentable space in proportion to the area covered, and what area is not covered is so arranged as to afford almost the least proportional light to the interior.

In planning houses for the poor economy of space is of the most vital importance, for any waste in the arrangement lays an added burden on people least able to bear it. Our tenement-house system is the result of accident. No intelligent thought has been bestowed on the problem, or at least all such thought has been wasted upon the 25 × 100 feet plan, where the conditions are such as to preclude the possibility of a successful solution.

In the great cities of Europe nothing of the kind is found. In London the houses for the poor, if on narrow lots, are low and shallow, having rooms opening to the front and rear, a type of house only compatible with low-priced land. In Paris, within the fortifications, where land is dear, what do we find? The houses are almost all built upon plots of land of from seventy-five to one hundred feet in width. To those who have not the requisite knowledge or skill to solve the problem for themselves, this fact should be of great significance, for the French are universally admitted to be the most logical and economical of builders, and certainly in no country is the education of the architect so thorough and the skill displayed in planning so great. If, then, the French do not build upon narrow strips of land, it is because such a method is not economical and is inconsistent with the best results.

The first law of economical planning is this: The more nearly one can keep to the square the more economical the house, a truth so evident that anyone but a New York builder ought to grasp it without difficulty, and one which needs no other demonstration than to picture to one's self a square house, then to imagine it drawn out into an oblong, always occupying the same area; as it increases in length it diminishes in breadth. One can imagine the house drawn out until it becomes all walls. Every foot of length which is added at the expense of breadth adds to the amount of walls required and deducts just as much from the area enclosed, besides rendering corridors necessary, which might otherwise be dispensed with.

The fact that so much of the land is held in narrow oblong parcels is our misfortune; but the obstacle is not insuperable, as shown by our office buildings. The land down-town was held under the same conditions, but when it became apparent that it was not economical to erect office buildings on lots of the standard size, the difficulty was gradually overcome, and such buildings are now almost always built on lots of greater dimensions. The tenement-house evil is staring us in the face, and the community is daily becoming more and more alive to the imperative necessity for reform. A desperate disease needs a desperate remedy. It should be made unprofitable to erect the kind of tenement we now have. If it is clearly shown that the present evils can be overcome by the adoption of a different type of building, erected on larger lots, certain restrictions established by law would in time bring about the desired change.

In order to show how extravagant the present type of plan is, let us take a hypothetical case. Suppose that it is desired to build a small habitation in an open space. Here we can say definitely that the most economical rectangular plan is an exact square, for every deviation from it involves the erection of more wall to enclose a given area in rooms.

Let Figure 2 (p. 380) be the plan of such a building, of the dimensions shown, which we will call the first type. The number of running feet of wall necessary to inclose it is roughly $4 \times 20 = 80$ feet. The area inclosed is $20 \times 20 = 400$ square feet. Now, any deviation from this plan will be found to be more extravagant, as shown in Figure 3, which we will call the second type. In this case we have a quad-

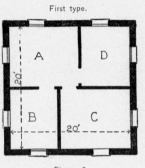

First type.

Figure 2.

rilateral inclosing the same area, measuring 10 × 40 feet. The number of running feet of wall necessary to inclose this is 2 × 40 + 2 × 10 = 100 feet. Area inclosed is 10 × 40 = 400 square feet as before. Thus there is a saving of twenty per cent. in wall by the former method. Moreover, no corridor is required by the first plan. The corridor is of no use to the tenant, except as a passage, and it costs as much to build as a like area in rooms. In the dwelling of the first type, divided as shown in Figure 2, let A be the living-room, B, C, and D the bedrooms. Any of these rooms can be reached directly from A. Also in the dwelling of the second type, as shown in Figure 3, let A be the living-room, and B, C, and D bedrooms. To reach any of these rooms from A, without going through other rooms, requires a corridor of 3 feet × 20 feet, or 60 square feet. There is thus a saving of space on this score, between the two plans, of fifteen per cent. There is also a saving of fifteen per cent. in the number of running feet of interior partitions required to separate the various rooms.

As a more complete demonstration of the importance of this principle let us suppose these two figures to be the plans of one-story structures with interior dimensions as given, and having exterior walls of brick one foot thick ; and that the cost to erect the one shown in Figure 3 would be twelve cents per cubic foot. The contents of the building, supposing it to be twelve feet high, would be 6,048 cubic feet, and the cost

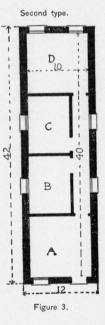

Second type.

Figure 3.

to erect $725. Now, let us suppose that the cost of the other would be at the same rate, less the saving effected in the amount of wall required to inclose it. Its contents would be 5,808 cubic feet, which, at twelve cents per cubic foot, equals $697 ; from which deduct the cost of 20 running feet of wall 12 feet high ; estimating the cost of the brick-work at $12 per thousand brick laid, this would amount to $60, making the net cost $637. Now, by the first type we have 380 square feet of available floor-space in the rooms after deducting space occupied by partitions, etc., and in the second type only 317 square feet of such space. By the first type each square foot of rentable floor-space in rooms would cost, to erect, $16.76, while by the second type each square foot of such space would cost $22.87. Therefore there is a saving in the first type over the second type of more than twenty-six per cent., to say nothing of the fact that it covers less ground, an item of great importance in cities.

The comparison might be pushed further, and an additional saving calculated on the partitions necessary to separate the rooms, cost of foundations, and other matters, all in favor of the first type ; but enough has been shown to demonstrate the principle involved ; and one may say here, by way of parenthesis, that, if the art of commercial or economical planning were understood by our architects, enough money might be saved in a few years on buildings erected in this city to endow all the charitable institutions which we have. The Building Department records show that the value of tenements, flats, etc., erected in this city during the last fourteen years, amounts to three hundred and twenty-five million dollars ; of this amount at least fifteen per cent. might have been saved, or nearly fifty million dollars, on this one class of buildings. The money has been worse than thrown away, because the vast amount of useless masonry which these millions represent has served no other purpose than to obstruct the light and render the buildings unhealthy and expensive.

While it is possible to build dwellings exactly according to the first type in the country, where the cost of land is not a consideration, and there may be an open space on all sides, it is not practi-

cable to so arrange them in the city, where the same conditions do
not prevail. But, as will be shown, in order to arrive at the best
results we must conform to this law as nearly as circumstances will
admit. The more nearly we can approach to the first type the more
economical will be the plan.

Now, the plan of our tenements, of necessity, owing to the shape
of the lot, are based upon the second type. The plans which are
submitted in Figures 5, 6, and 7 (pp. 385, 388, 389), are based upon
the first type. It will be shown that the actual saving by these
plans over those in common use, while not so great as between the
hypothetical plans shown in Figures 2 and 3, is still very considerable. In the present tenement there is no proper provision for
light and air. In the plans submitted there is such provision, yet,
owing to the saving effected by the method of planning, the cost
per square foot of available space by these plans would be much
less than by the present vicious method.

The law provides that in buildings of this class a certain percentage of the area of the land shall be left vacant for light and air.
Again, a certain percentage of the area of the lots must be occupied
by supports; that is, the constructional parts, such as walls and
partitions; there must also be staircases and means of communication, that is to say, parts occupied in public. What is left after
these deductions have been made is the kernel of the nut, so to
speak. It forms the net rentable area or space in rooms. Now,
that plan is the most economical which gives the greatest amount
of such rentable space with the least expenditure of building material and the least waste of space in the parts to be used in public,
always provided that the necessary strength is secured. But the
value of the rentable space depends largely upon the way it is
lighted and upon the convenient arrangement of the rooms.

In comparing the relative value of two plans, therefore, we must
take into consideration:

1. The proportion which the net available rentable area bears
to the whole gross area of the building.

2. The way this rentable portion is lighted, and how the rooms are arranged with reference to the convenience of those who are to occupy them.

The absurdity of building tenements of the ordinary kind can be understood by the following comparison between the plans shown in Figures 4 and 5. Figure 4 shows the plan of four tenements occupying a plot one hundred feet square; Figure 5 shows one tenement planned as nearly as possible upon the system illustrated by Figure 2 and designed for a plot also one hundred feet square.

We will call Figure 4 plan A, and Figure 5 plan B; both have been carefully drawn to the same scale and the following calculation accurately made. For convenience walls are taken at one foot and partitions at six inches thick. The walls between the houses in plan A are supposed to be party walls.

PLAN A.

Plan A represents four houses of the ordinary type.

Net rentable area on each floor, exclusive of walls, partitions, stairs, corridors, and other public parts, 5,550 square feet.

Left vacant for light and air, 2,060 square feet.

Space occupied by constructive parts : walls, partitions, etc., 1,400 square feet.

Space occupied by stairs, corridors, and other public parts, 990 square feet.

Has no fire-walls, but a fire starting in one house can leap across the narrow courts and sweep through the block.

PLAN B.

Plan B represents one house designed for four lots.

Net rentable area on each floor, exclusive of walls, partitions, stairs, corridors, and other public parts, 5,500 square feet.

Left vacant for light and air, 3,000 square feet. In favor of this plan, thirty per cent.

Space occupied by constructive parts : walls, partitions, etc., 1,100 square feet. In favor of this plan twenty-one per cent.

Space occupied by stairs, corridors, and other public parts, 433 square feet. In favor of this plan, fifty-six per cent.

Has four unpierced fire-walls from top to bottom, affording protection against the spread of fire. The courts at the side are so wide that the flames could not under ordinary circumstances spread from one building to another.

Plan A.

Has no brick walls around the staircases, which are thus unprotected against fire.

Five-sevenths of the rooms open on

Plan B.

Has brick walls around area enclosing each staircase, so that it can be made fireproof.

No rooms have windows opening on

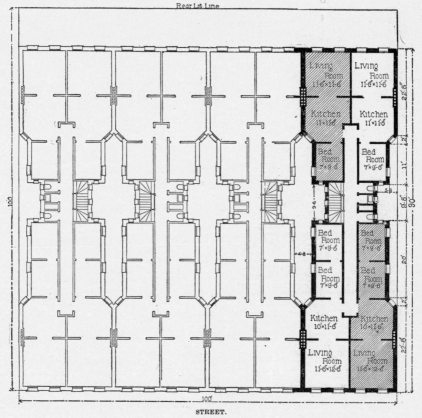

STREET.

Figure 4—Plan A.

narrow shafts four feet eight inches wide, which cannot provide sufficient light for the lower floors, but which act as an excellent conductor of noise, odors, etc., at ordinary times, and as a flue for spread of flames in case of fire.

There is only one water-closet to

a court less than eighteen feet wide. The central court measures thirty feet square, so that every room would be abundantly lighted directly from the outer air.

Each apartment has its own water-

PLAN A.

PLAN B.

each two apartments, and as these water-closets open directly from the public hall, they are apt to be a nuisance.

No lift is provided.

closet, opening directly upon the outer air, from which it is reached by means of a balcony.

There is one lift to each three apartments.

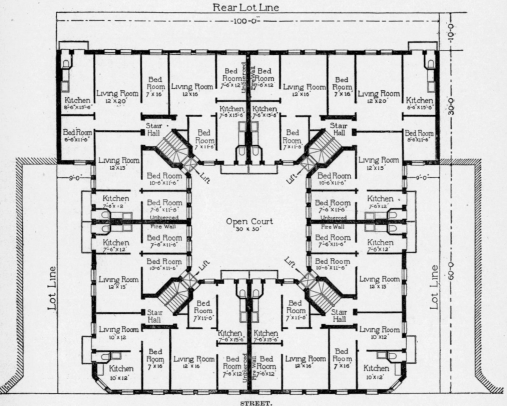

Figure 5—Plan B.

One-half the apartments only are front apartments.

Five-sixths of the apartments are front apartments, either facing the street or courts recessed from the street.

There is only one sink for four apartments.

Each apartment has its own sink.

Many of the bedrooms can only be

Every bedroom can be entered di-

25

PLAN A.

entered by passing through other bed-rooms or the public corridor.

The stairs are poorly lighted from a court about eleven feet square, and the passages are not so well lighted as the stairs.

PLAN B.

rectly from the living-room or kitchen, without passing through any other bedroom.

The stairs and landings are abundantly lighted from a court thirty feet square, and there are no corridors.

It will be seen that in the case of the two plans above compared the net rentable area is the same for both, but that the four houses of the ordinary type require twenty-one per cent. more building material with which to erect them than would be required in the other case, and that the space allotted to parts used in common or by the public is fifty-six per cent. greater. Of the total area of the lot, 10,000 square feet, 2,390 square feet, or nearly twenty-four per cent. of the whole, is required on each floor for these purposes, while with plan B only a little over fifteen per cent. of the area is thus used ; the saving being effected in the economy of the planning.

It will also be noticed that although the space left vacant for light and air is almost one-half more, or nearly one thousand square feet greater, in plan B than in plan A, yet the amount of rentable space in rooms is the same in both ; but even this increased area does not adequately represent the relative advantage of the former plan over the latter in this respect, for the light is concentrated in plan B in large bodies. The lighting of a building does not depend so much upon the area of the unoccupied space as upon how that space is managed. Thus the central court in plan B is smaller than the united area of the light wells in plan A; but the rooms opening upon the wells will receive an insufficient amount of light, while those opening upon the court shown in plan B, where the least dimension is thirty feet, will be well lighted. Indeed, every room upon this latter plan would receive an abundance of light, for none of them have windows opening upon a space less than eighteen feet wide, while the windows of most of the rooms of the other plan open upon a space only about four feet wide ; nor do these widths, either, represent the relative amount of light, as up to a certain point the light increases in a greater proportion than the increase in the width of the court. Also, a court, unless very large, which is open on one side is of very much more service than one of the same dimensions closed on all sides. The difference, then, in the lighting of the two plans is out of all proportion to the increased light area.

A building constructed in accordance with plan B would be properly lighted; tenements of the ordinary type are only properly lighted at the two ends. The available rentable space cannot be compared, for one is fit for human habitation and the other is not.

It is not fair to compare the relative economy of plans of such different characters, still plan B can well bear such comparison. Plan A has no fire-walls or walls around staircases, yet to erect the four buildings shown would require more than one hundred running feet of wall over what would be needed in the erection of one building of the kind shown in plan B. The cubical contents of this building, estimating its height at 60 feet, would be 420,000 cubic feet; assuming the cost at fifteen cents per cubic foot, the total cost of building would be $63,000. The cubical contents of the four buildings shown in plan A, assuming that the height was the same, would be 476,400 cubic feet, and the cost to erect at fifteen cents per cubic foot, $71,460.

From the above it will be seen that the building shown by plan B, although infinitely better lighted, and containing the same amount of rentable floor area, would cost less to build than the other, even if both were calculated at the same rate per cubic foot; but this would not be the case, for while 850 running feet of wall is required by plan A, only 750 running feet of such wall is required by plan B, nor is the increased amount of wall required by plan A any advantage for fire or otherwise, but rather the contrary. For it will be seen that, while there are four divisions which might be called separate buildings in both cases, yet in plan B the dividing walls are true fire-walls, unpierced, extending from top to bottom, while in the case of plan A, the dividing walls are pierced by windows, only about four feet distant from those in the next house, so that these walls offer no security against fire.

In addition to the saving of 100 running feet of brick wall ex-

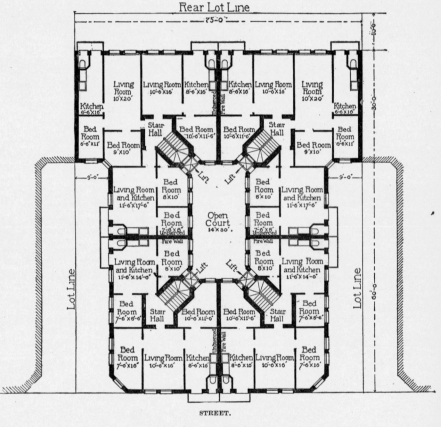

Figure 6—Plan C.

tending from foundation to roof, there is another saving of 330 running feet of partition, plastered on both sides, on each floor; the cost of these two items would amount to over $5,000, which should be deducted from the estimated cost by plan B. Now we have:

	PLAN A.	PLAN B.
Net cost of building.............	$71,460	$58,000
Add cost of land, say $8,000 per lot, or $32,000 in both cases....	32,000	32,000
	$103,460	$90,000

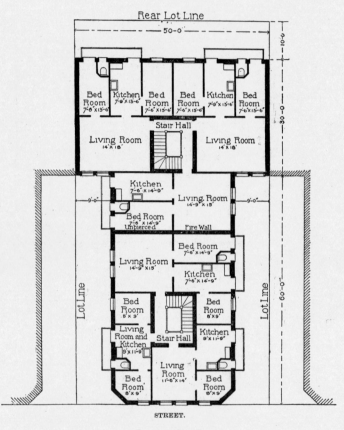

Figure 7—Plan D.

Thus the well-lighted space shown on plan B could be rented for about thirteen per cent. less than the improperly lighted quarters shown on plan A, and the owner would still receive the same rate of interest on the investment; or the owner of a house planned

according to plan B could give his tenants thirteen per cent. more
room for the same rent than the owner of a building planned according to plan A, and still receive the same rate of interest on the
investment.

The above comparisons have been made between four ordinary
houses, and one building designed for a lot 100 feet square; but
the same principles which govern plan B are applicable to a certain extent to buildings intended for lots of smaller dimensions, as
shown in plans C and D. Plan C is for a lot 75 × 100 feet, and plan
D for one 50 × 100 feet. While the best results are obtained the
more nearly we can approach to the square, yet fairly economical
plans can be made for buildings on lots not less than 50 feet
wide.

There are two methods of lighting a building: one may be called
the independent method, and the other the dependent method. In
the first case the owner depends entirely upon his own property for
light, in the other case he counts more or less upon his neighbor's
land.

The first is the French method. Buildings in France are generally provided with a central court of sufficient size to properly
light the house. The latter method is that in vogue in this city;
we depend for light partly upon the area of unoccupied space on
our own land, and partly upon what we hope our neighbors will
leave unoccupied. The latter method is the more economical, provided one is sure that the adjoining property-holder will kindly
adapt his structure to the needs of our building. Unfortunately, it
is seldom one can depend upon such consideration.

If tenement-houses are to receive a part of their light from the
outside, then restrictions should be placed upon the adjoining land
which will insure this light.

It will be noticed that in plans B, C, and D a space 9 feet wide is
left at the side of the house, extending from the street to a line
about 30 feet from the rear of the lot; a similar space should be
required to be left unoccupied at the side of all tenement-houses,

or buildings which adjoin tenement-houses; such a regulation would amount to a prohibition in the case of lots only 25 feet wide, which ought to be the case.

If houses are to be built of the present type, there is only one possible way to make them habitable—that is, to reduce the depth of the buildings to such an extent as will make them unprofitable for tenement purposes. Something more must be required than a mere percentage of unoccupied space. As shown in plans B, C, and D, about seventy per cent. of the lot may be covered and the building thoroughly lighted in every part, but to insure such a result the lot must measure at least 50 feet in width.

The power to make the necessary restriction is already in the hands of the Board of Health, and needs only to be enforced. A simple regulation requiring space to be left vacant at the side of the building, like that now enforced for such space at the rear, would quickly bring about a change of plan. Such a restriction would result in the adoption of buildings of the type shown in plans B, C, and D, and the New York tenement-house problem would be solved so far as new buildings are concerned. Many years would be required to bring about a complete change, but the buildings already constructed are of such a flimsy character that they cannot last forever; moreover, when it is once realized what a great economy there is in this type of planning over the one in ordinary use, many owners will be inclined to rebuild.

In plan B there are three apartments for each lot occupied, or twelve in all, while in plan A, there are sixteen. In other words, the apartments of plan B have about twenty-five per cent. more floor space than those of plan A. The rooms are, upon an average, twenty-five per cent. larger, which ought to be the case. To crowd four families on each floor of a twenty-five foot house is not right or decent; nor is it right to provide bedrooms 7 × 9 feet which never receive a ray of sunlight, and which must often be occupied by several people continuously. The rooms shown on plan B are small enough in all conscience, but what an improvement over those of the ordinary kind. Not only are they one-quarter larger and well lighted, but also more conveniently arranged.

Notwithstanding their twenty-five per cent. larger size, proper light and ventilation, greater security against fire and better arrangement, these apartments could doubtless be rented for the same price as those of the kind we now have, owing to the greater economy of the plan, and to the fact that there would be fewer vacancies than is usually the case, and loss of rent from unoccupied apartments would count less as a factor in estimating the returns from the property.

The philanthropic method of reform can accomplish but little. What if a hundred or five hundred landlords erect model tenements and rent them at a low rate? Such relief would only be a drop in the bucket, so long as the vast majority of owners continue the erection of houses of the kind we now have.

Reform can only be brought about through the pockets of the landlords. Show them how they can build good houses for less than it now costs them to build bad ones. Show them how they can get the same amount of desirable properly lighted floor space at less cost than they have heretofore paid for undesirable, improperly lighted floor space. This is to strike at the root of the evil. Then let the Board of Health do its part to bring about the change. For twenty years this body has been temporizing with the subject, and with the best intentions has accomplished little. It is now high time to call a halt and to root out the evil, making use of the powers which years ago were vested in it for this very purpose.

INDEX

SOCIALISM IN HYDE PARK, LONDON.

[A meeting on Sunday afternoon, near the Marble Arch.]

own days, are of the former class; passages in Carlyle, "Alton Locke," and of late years Besant's "All Sorts and Conditions of Men," are in the latter. All of them dealt with the suffering and the problems of a single city; and all but the last named in each list dealt with conditions altogether different from the present. Each was an appeal to an unawakened audience, and each had a condition complicated by centuries to show in colors that could not be too dark, without any remedial experiments to discuss—for none worth the name had been tried; and without any comparisons of its facts with others—for none had been made.

The conditions are quite different now. Awakening is not needed. Every thinking man has thoughts upon this matter. And along with this realization has come practical experiment, in many places and on an immense scale, toward a solution. Americans especially are to be congratulated on the fact that they receive the question, at the moment when the conditions of their large cities begin to make it vital to them, with much of the light of older experience upon it, and (even with the peculiar difficulties with which unrestricted immigration complicates it) in by no means its most hopeless form. It is at our doors; but not in a shape, if we recognize fully its difficulties and take hold of it in earnest, where we may not hope to prevent its dominating us in any sense. We have Mulberry Street tenements and "Hell's Kitchens," sporadic and the growth of a generation or two; it is largely our own affair whether we shall some time have Tom-All-Alones as a permanent institution, or the century-old sediment of Whitechapel.

What we need to know is what is doing, here and elsewhere, in the general and efficient activity that has been the growth of the last few years; and especially, what are the facts with which our own efforts are to deal, and how facts elsewhere compare with them. It is believed that the present volume tells this with a new vividness and force—the vividness derived from actual experience among and keen sympathy with the poor, and the force from a strong conviction of the fitness of this moment for intelligent and

INTRODUCTION

THE papers composing this book were contributed to *Scribner's Magazine* during the years 1891–1893 by authors whose work embodied personal experience and close and sympathetic study, and by artists whose drawings were made among the life they represent. They form perhaps the most important group of essays thus far printed upon one of the most vital and (what is by no means the same thing) one of the most widely discussed subjects of the time. It is, indeed, the central subject of all social questions; for all of these, under whatever name, deal with the means of improving the conditions of life and with the relief of suffering as the necessary forerunners of all other reforms; and whatever may be the difficulties of those conditions, or the amount of that suffering in rural communities or among special classes away from towns, it is only in the centres of population that they present their great general problems to the observation of all people alike, and compel an answer to the question of their remedy.

Any series of papers on the Poor in Great Cities will have had many predecessors—has indeed in England a whole literature behind it, of whose masterpieces some show their practical results to-day in different individual directions, and some have become, so to speak, the literary classics of their subject. The famous series in the London *Morning Chronicle* in 1848, on "London Labor and the London Poor" (perhaps the first to attract wide attention), the "Parson Lot" papers of Charles Kingsley, the publications of the group of men of whom Frederick Maurice was the centre, and a long succession down to the "Bitter Cry of Outcast London" in our

CONTENTS

vigorous effort. The contributors of the articles—varying in literary experience from Mr. Besant to those who here wrote for the first time publicly upon the subject—have had that qualification and conviction in common.

If a word need be said as to the illustration of the book, it may best be an assurance of its accuracy, since its other qualities, it is hoped, may be made to be their own commendation. The artists who co-operated in the series of papers made their studies the places and among the life described, by sketches and by drawings after photographs made under their own supervision or the author's.

Copyright, 1895, by

CHARLES SCRIBNER'S SONS

TROW DIRECTORY
PRINTING AND BOOKBINDING COMPANY
NEW YORK

THE POOR IN GREAT CITIES

THEIR PROBLEMS AND WHAT IS DOING TO SOLVE THEM

BY

ROBERT A. WOODS
W. T. ELSING
JACOB A. RIIS
WILLARD PARSONS
EVERT J. WENDELL
ERNEST FLAGG

WILLIAM JEWETT TUCKER
JOSEPH KIRKLAND
SIR WALTER BESANT
EDMUND R. SPEARMAN
JESSIE WHITE MARIO
OSCAR CRAIG

ILLUSTRATED BY

HUGH THOMSON, OTTO H. BACHER, C. BROUGHTON, V. PÉRARD,
IRVING R. WILES, HERBERT DENMAN, V. GRIBAYÉDOFF,
ELLA P. MORILL, H. T. SCHLADERMUND, ETTORE TITO

NEW YORK
CHARLES SCRIBNER'S SONS
1895